TALES
OF A
HIPPY KID

STORIES BY
JON KROLL
ART BY
DAVE BOHN

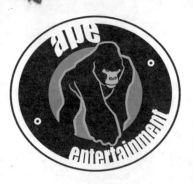

APE ENTERTAINMENT

Brent E. Erwin
Co-Publisher | General Partner
BErwin@Ape-Entertainment.com

David Hedgecock
Co-Publisher | General Partner
DHedgecock@Ape-Entertainment.com

Jason Burns
Editor-in-Chief
JBurns@Ape-Entertainment.com

Troy Dye
Submissions Editor
TDye@Ape-Entertainment.com

Kevin Freeman
Managing Editor
KFreeman@Ape-Entertainment.com

Jay Carvajai
on-line Marketing Manager
JCarvajai@Ape-Entertainment.com

Company Information:
Ape Entertainment
P.O. Box 7100
San Diego, CA 92167

APE WEBSITE
Apecomics.com

APE DIGITAL COMIC SITE:
Apecmx.com

TWITTER:
Twitter.com/ApeComics

FACEBOOK:
Facebook.com/ape.comics

MYSPACE:
MySpace.com/ApeEntertainment

WANNA DO SOME YOGA?
NAH, I'M GOO

Popsicle Pictures, Inc.
P.O. Box 57224, Sherman Oaks, CA 91403

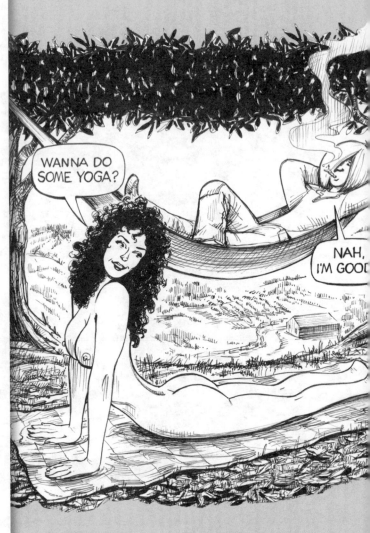

First Edition: July 2010

Stories by Jon Kroll
Art by Dave Bohn
Pre-Press and Layouts by Diana Davis
Color and Layouts by Karen Kroll

www.talesofahippykid.com

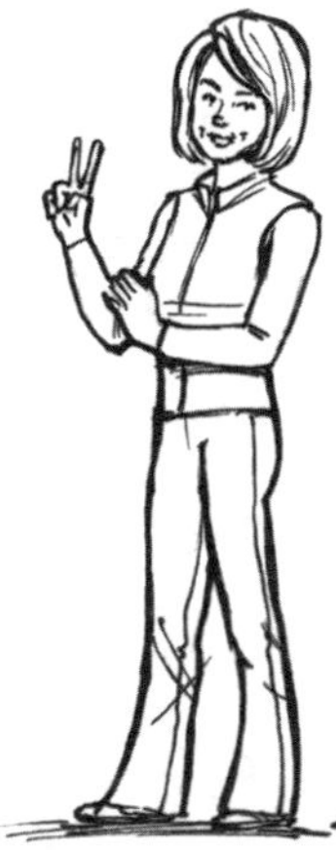

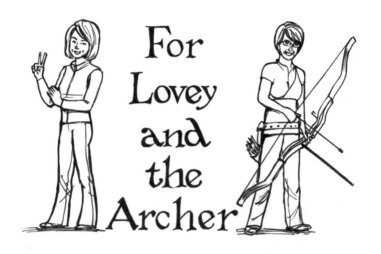

For
Lovey
and
the
Archer

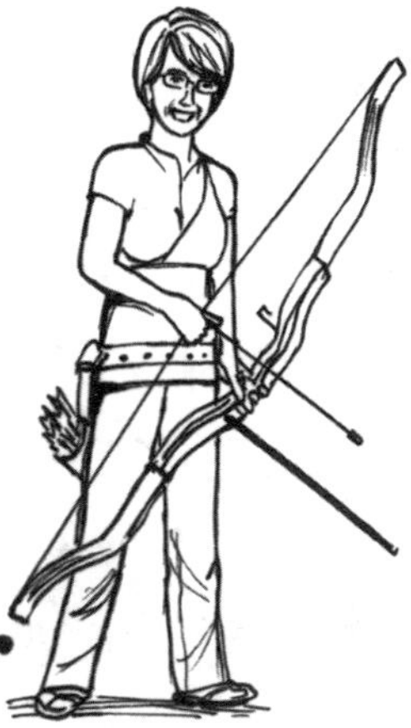

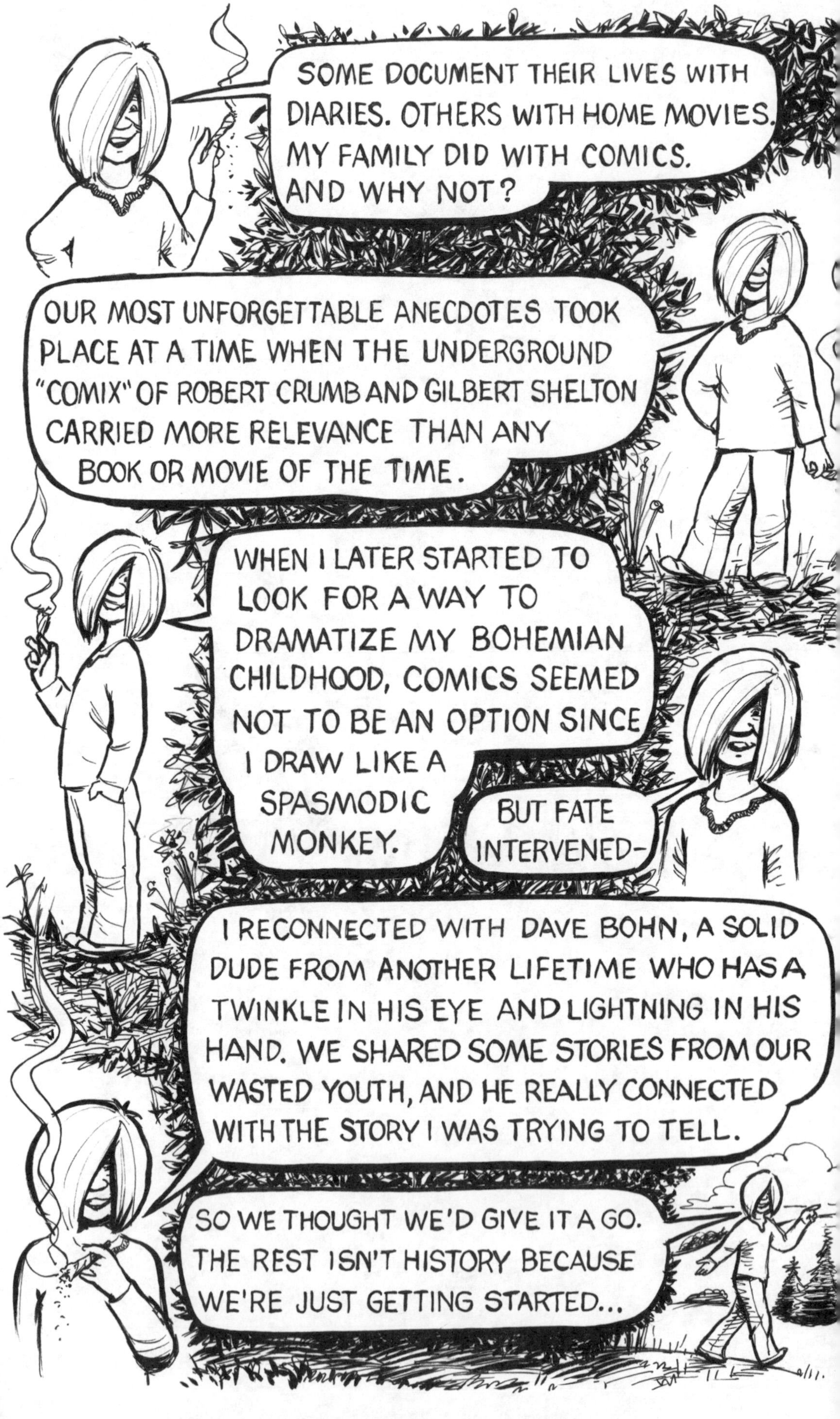

SOME DOCUMENT THEIR LIVES WITH DIARIES. OTHERS WITH HOME MOVIES. MY FAMILY DID WITH COMICS. AND WHY NOT?
OUR MOST UNFORGETTABLE ANECDOTES TOOK PLACE AT A TIME WHEN THE UNDERGROUND "COMIX" OF ROBERT CRUMB AND GILBERT SHELTON CARRIED MORE RELEVANCE THAN ANY BOOK OR MOVIE OF THE TIME.
WHEN I LATER STARTED TO LOOK FOR A WAY TO DRAMATIZE MY BOHEMIAN CHILDHOOD, COMICS SEEMED NOT TO BE AN OPTION SINCE I DRAW LIKE A SPASMODIC MONKEY.
BUT FATE INTERVENED-
I RECONNECTED WITH DAVE BOHN, A SOLID DUDE FROM ANOTHER LIFETIME WHO HAS A TWINKLE IN HIS EYE AND LIGHTNING IN HIS HAND. WE SHARED SOME STORIES FROM OUR WASTED YOUTH, AND HE REALLY CONNECTED WITH THE STORY I WAS TRYING TO TELL.
SO WE THOUGHT WE'D GIVE IT A GO. THE REST ISN'T HISTORY BECAUSE WE'RE JUST GETTING STARTED...

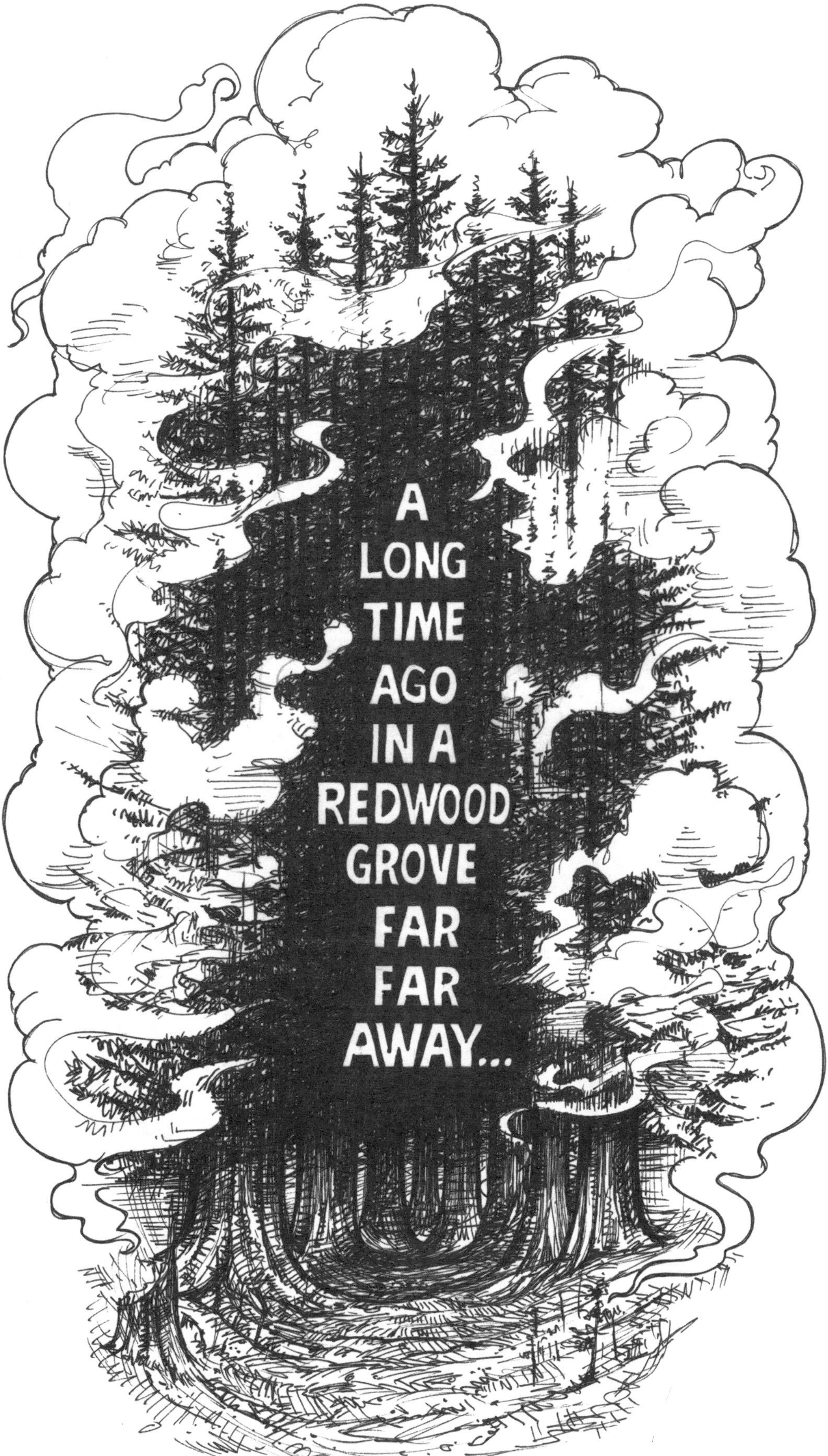
A LONG TIME AGO IN A REDWOOD GROVE FAR FAR AWAY...

CHUGA-CHUGA-CHUGA-CHUGA-CHUGA-CHUGA-CHUGA-CHUG

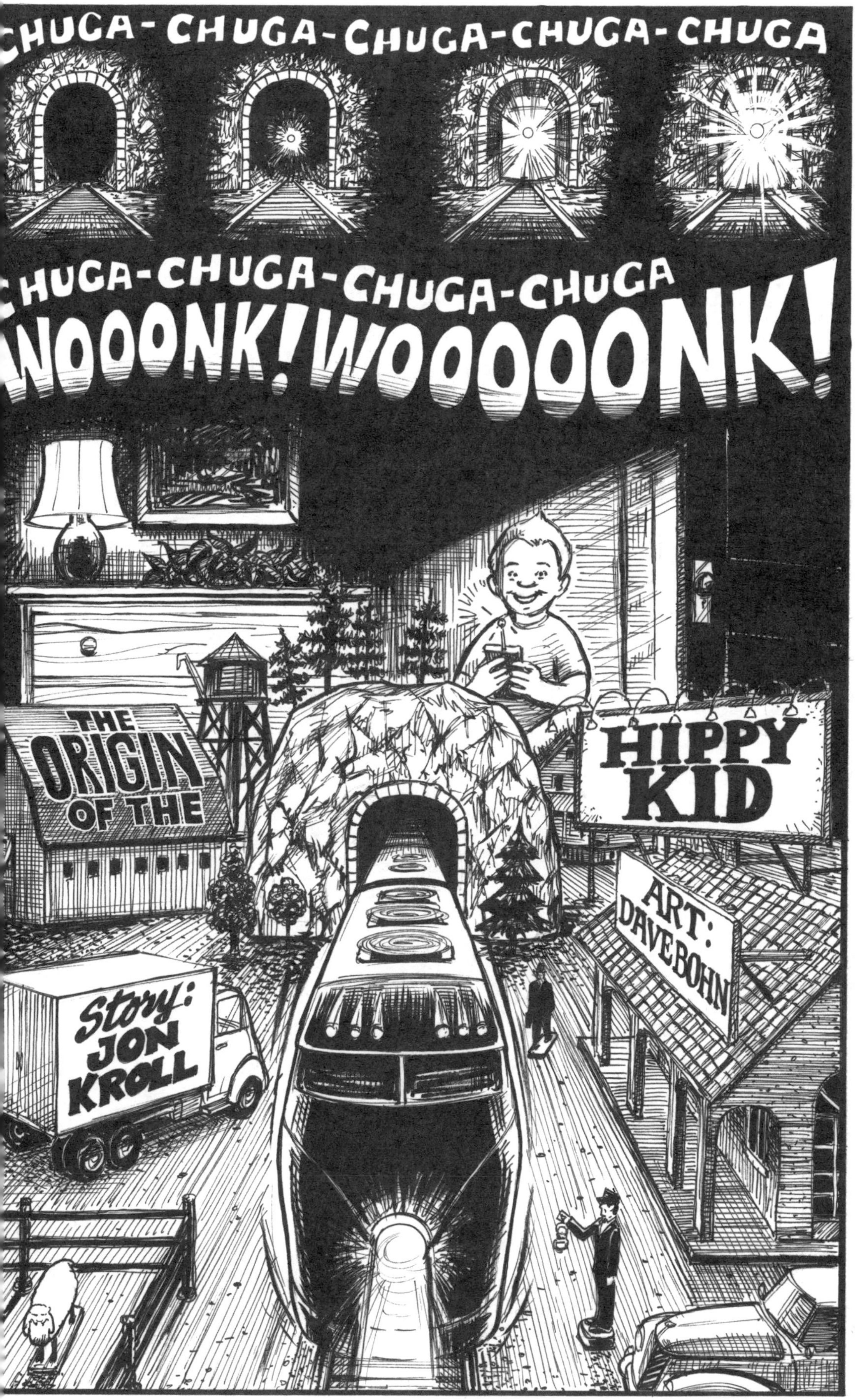

CHUGA-CHUGA-CHUGA-CHUGA-CHUGA
CHUGA-CHUGA-CHUGA-CHUGA
WOOONK! WOOOOONK!
THE ORIGIN OF THE
HIPPY KID
ART: DAVE BOHN
Story: JON KROLL

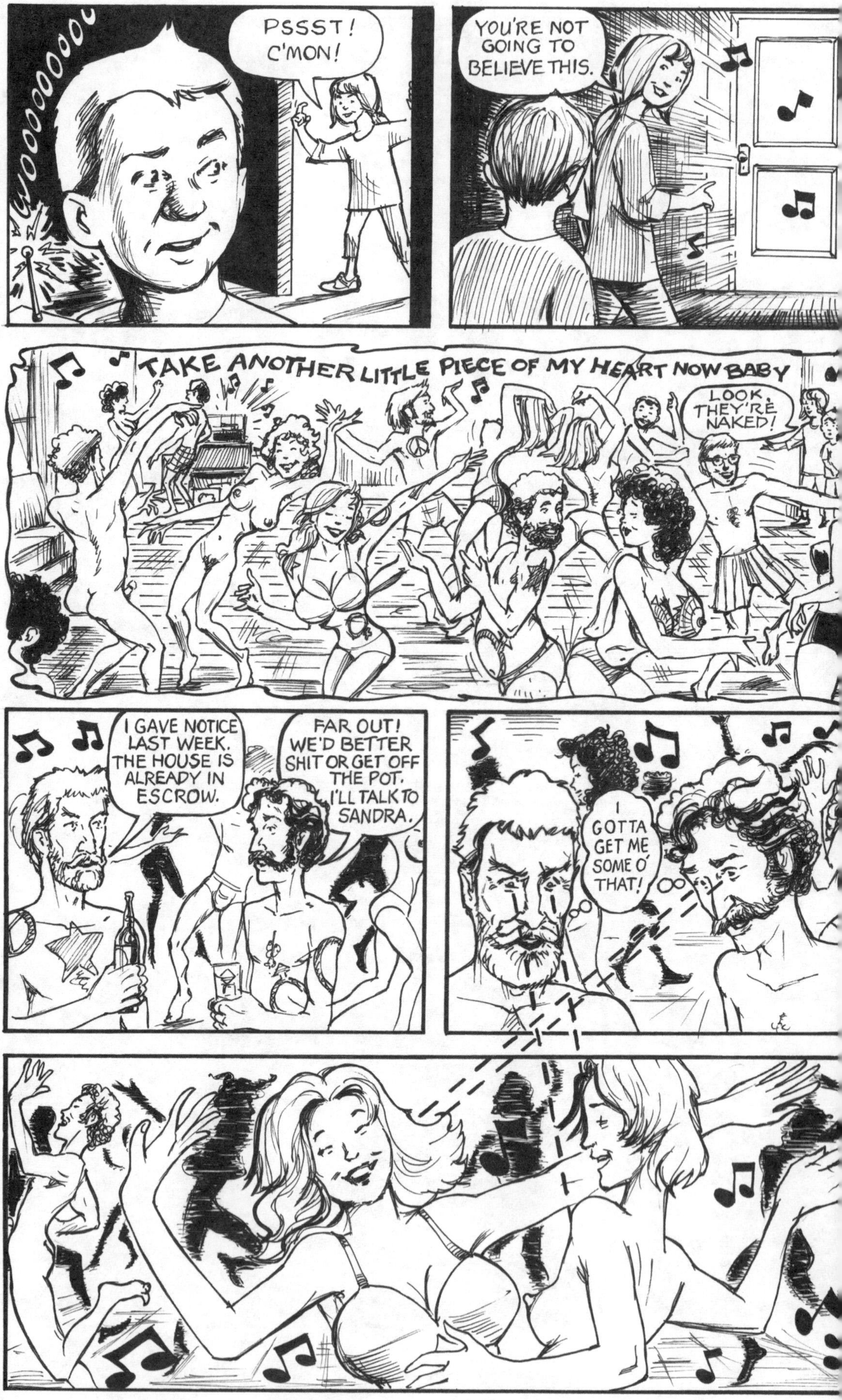
WOOOOOOOO
PSSST! C'MON!
YOU'RE NOT GOING TO BELIEVE THIS.
TAKE ANOTHER LITTLE PIECE OF MY HEART NOW BABY
LOOK. THEY'RE NAKED!
I GAVE NOTICE LAST WEEK. THE HOUSE IS ALREADY IN ESCROW.
FAR OUT! WE'D BETTER SHIT OR GET OFF THE POT. I'LL TALK TO SANDRA.
I GOTTA GET ME SOME O' THAT!

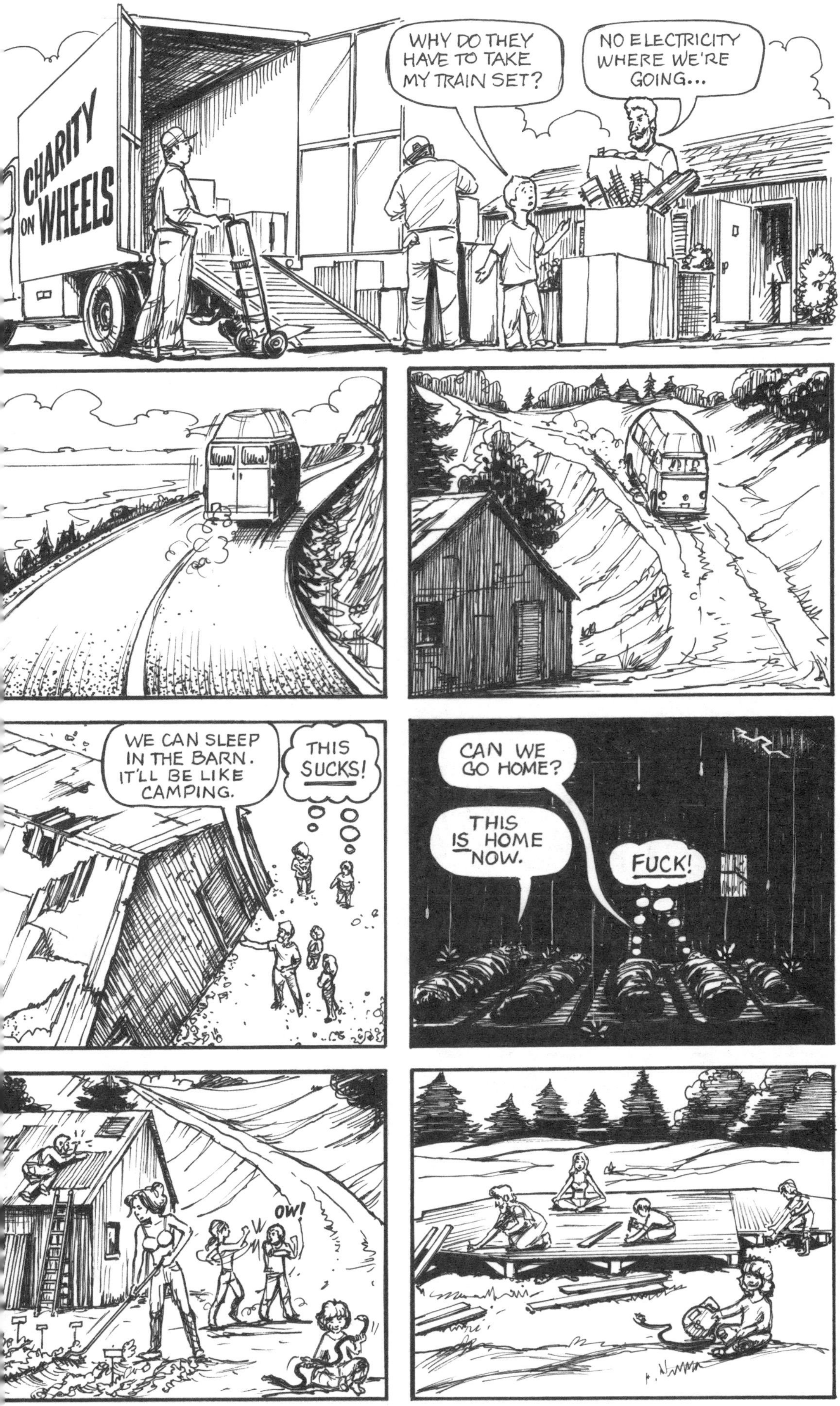
CHARITY ON WHEELS
WHY DO THEY HAVE TO TAKE MY TRAIN SET?
NO ELECTRICITY WHERE WE'RE GOING...
WE CAN SLEEP IN THE BARN. IT'LL BE LIKE CAMPING.
THIS SUCKS!
CAN WE GO HOME?
THIS IS HOME NOW.
FUCK!
OW!

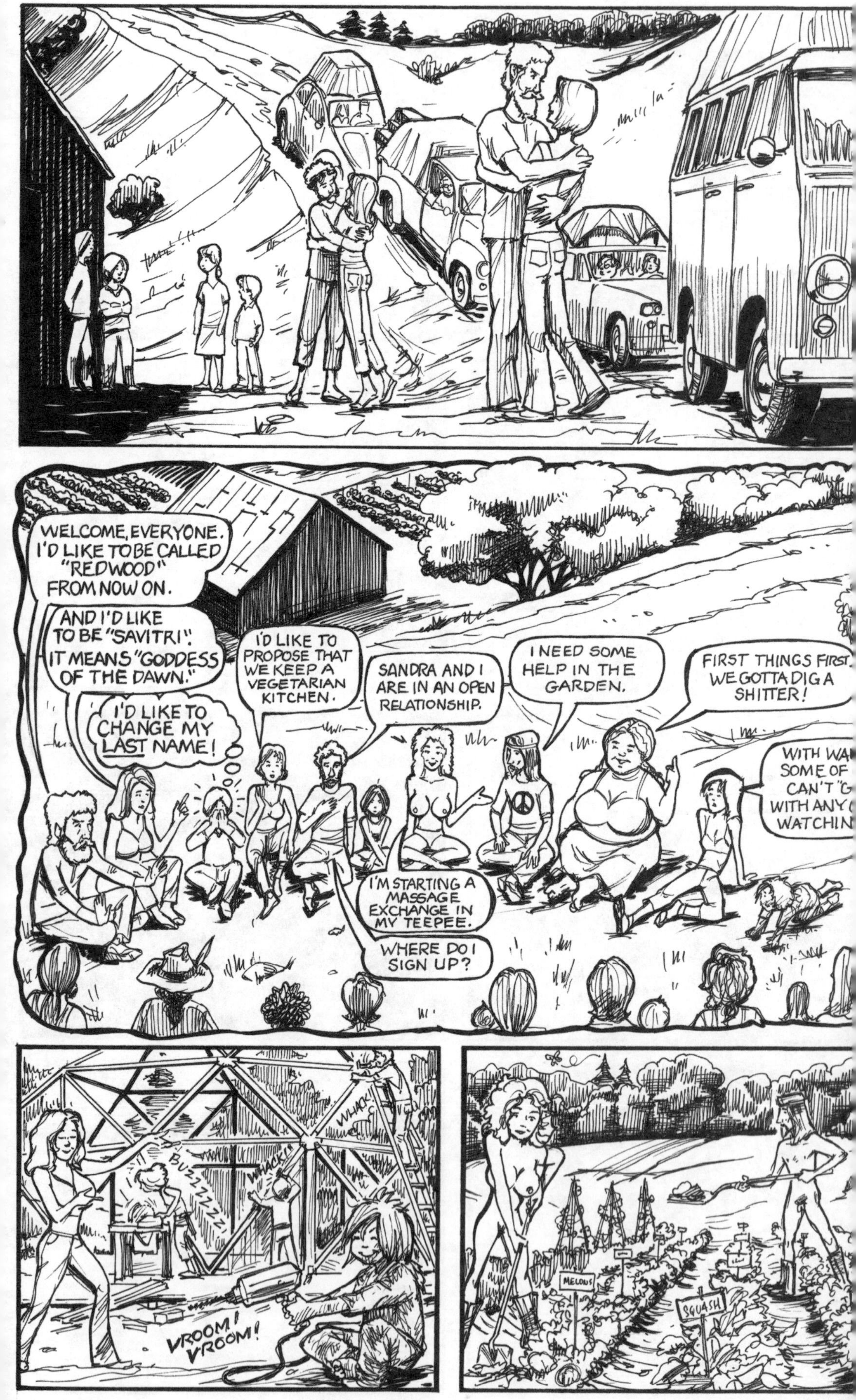
WELCOME, EVERYONE. I'D LIKE TO BE CALLED "REDWOOD" FROM NOW ON.
AND I'D LIKE TO BE "SAVITRI". IT MEANS "GODDESS OF THE DAWN."
I'D LIKE TO CHANGE MY LAST NAME!
I'D LIKE TO PROPOSE THAT WE KEEP A VEGETARIAN KITCHEN.
SANDRA AND I ARE IN AN OPEN RELATIONSHIP.
I'M STARTING A MASSAGE EXCHANGE IN MY TEEPEE.
WHERE DO I SIGN UP?
I NEED SOME HELP IN THE GARDEN.
FIRST THINGS FIRST, WE GOTTA DIG A SHITTER!
WITH WA SOME OF CAN'T "G WITH ANY WATCHIN
BUZZZZZZ
WHACK!
WHACK!
VROOM! VROOM!
MELONS
SQUASH

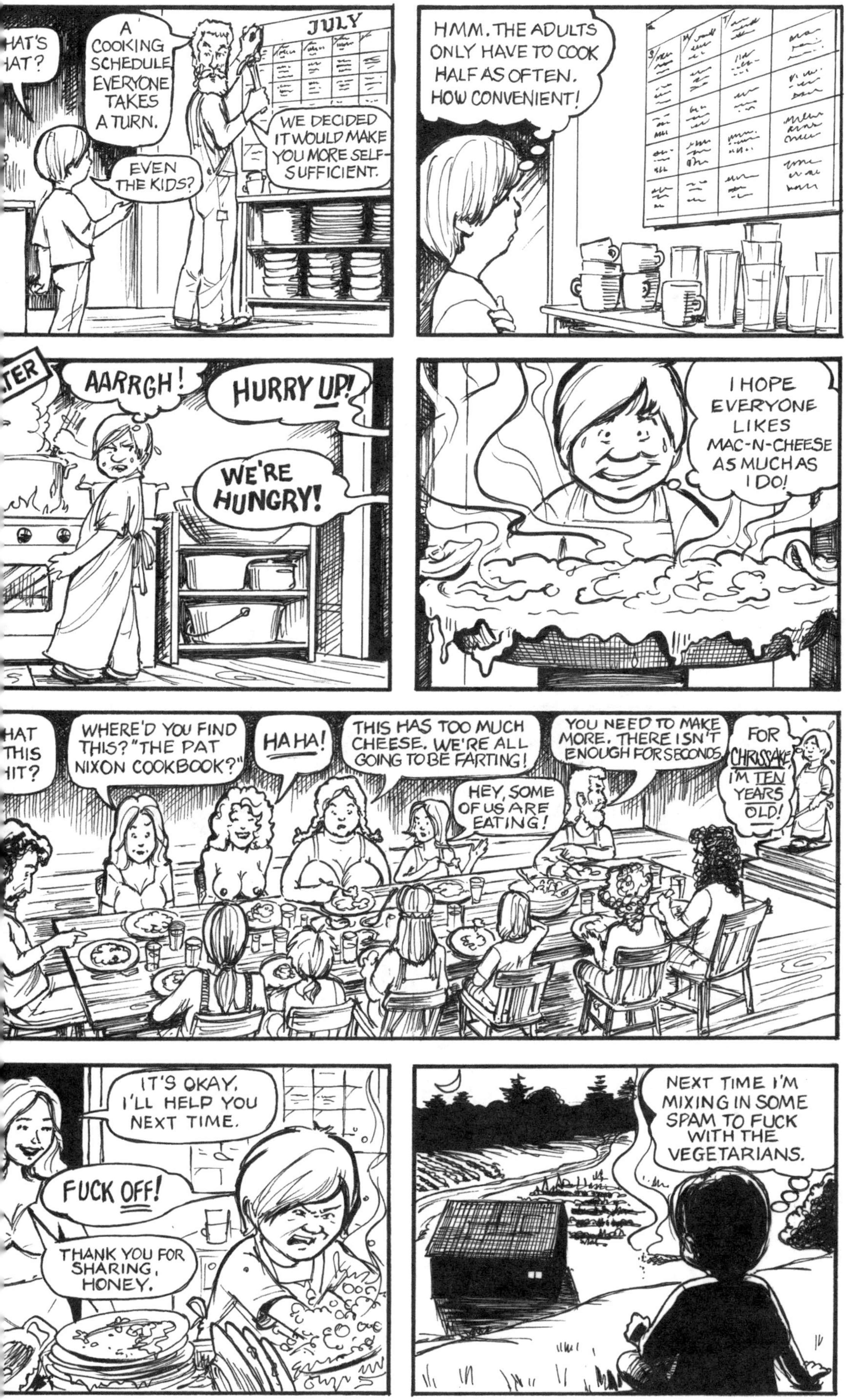
HAT'S
HAT?
A COOKING SCHEDULE. EVERYONE TAKES A TURN.
EVEN THE KIDS?
WE DECIDED IT WOULD MAKE YOU MORE SELF-SUFFICIENT.
JULY
HMM. THE ADULTS ONLY HAVE TO COOK HALF AS OFTEN. HOW CONVENIENT!
TER
AARRGH!
HURRY UP!
WE'RE HUNGRY!
I HOPE EVERYONE LIKES MAC-N-CHEESE AS MUCH AS I DO!
HAT THIS HIT?
WHERE'D YOU FIND THIS? "THE PAT NIXON COOKBOOK?"
HA HA!
THIS HAS TOO MUCH CHEESE. WE'RE ALL GOING TO BE FARTING!
YOU NEED TO MAKE MORE. THERE ISN'T ENOUGH FOR SECONDS.
FOR CHRISSAKE! I'M TEN YEARS OLD!
HEY, SOME OF US ARE EATING!
IT'S OKAY. I'LL HELP YOU NEXT TIME.
FUCK OFF!
THANK YOU FOR SHARING, HONEY.
NEXT TIME I'M MIXING IN SOME SPAM TO FUCK WITH THE VEGETARIANS.

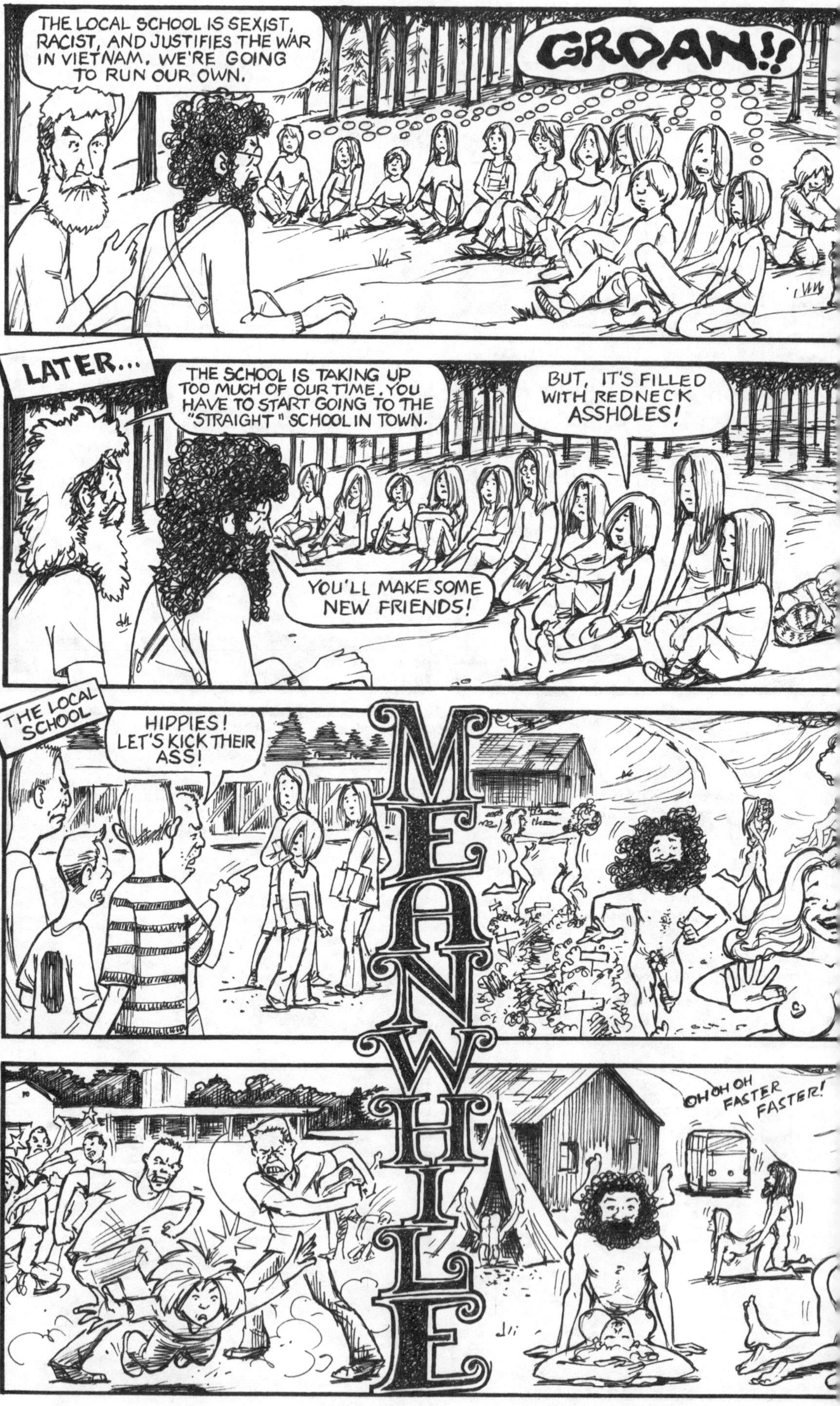
THE LOCAL SCHOOL IS SEXIST, RACIST, AND JUSTIFIES THE WAR IN VIETNAM. WE'RE GOING TO RUN OUR OWN.
GROAN!!
LATER...
THE SCHOOL IS TAKING UP TOO MUCH OF OUR TIME. YOU HAVE TO START GOING TO THE "STRAIGHT" SCHOOL IN TOWN.
BUT, IT'S FILLED WITH REDNECK ASSHOLES!
YOU'LL MAKE SOME NEW FRIENDS!
THE LOCAL SCHOOL
HIPPIES! LET'S KICK THEIR ASS!
MEANWHILE
OH OH OH FASTER FASTER!

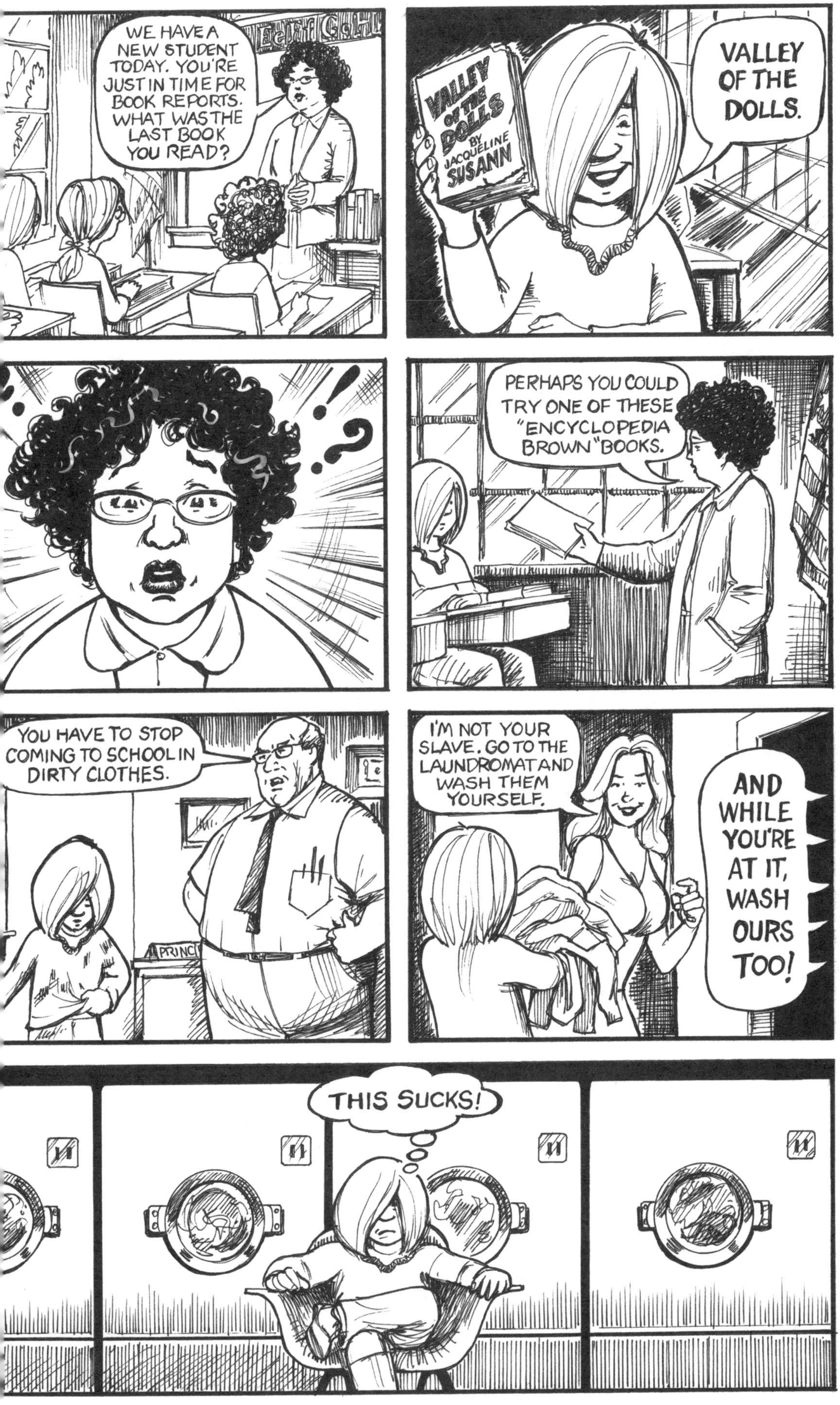

WE HAVE A NEW STUDENT TODAY. YOU'RE JUST IN TIME FOR BOOK REPORTS. WHAT WAS THE LAST BOOK YOU READ?
VALLEY OF THE DOLLS BY JACQUELINE SUSANN
VALLEY OF THE DOLLS.
PERHAPS YOU COULD TRY ONE OF THESE "ENCYCLOPEDIA BROWN" BOOKS.
YOU HAVE TO STOP COMING TO SCHOOL IN DIRTY CLOTHES.
PRINC
I'M NOT YOUR SLAVE. GO TO THE LAUNDROMAT AND WASH THEM YOURSELF.
AND WHILE YOU'RE AT IT, WASH OURS TOO!
THIS SUCKS!

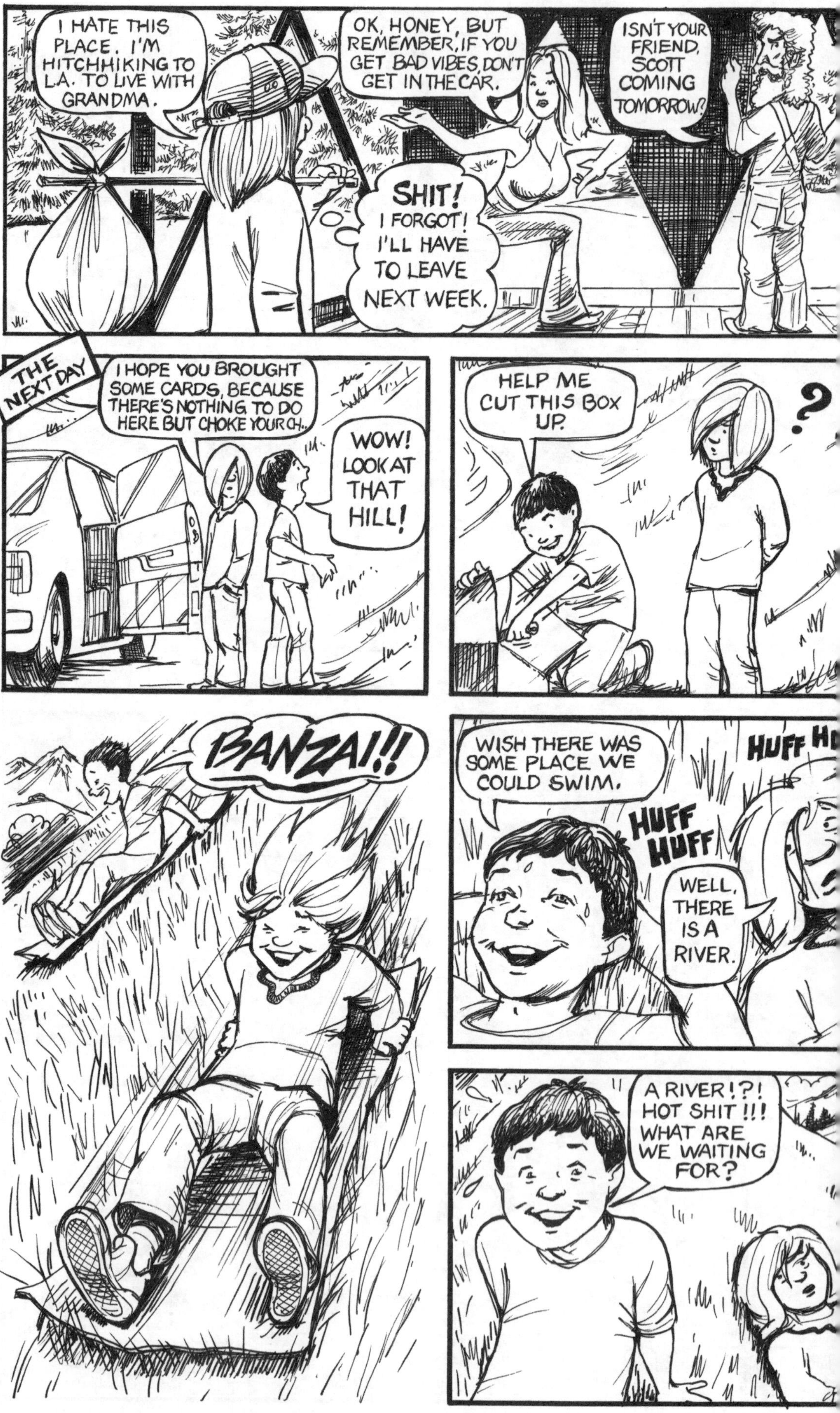
I HATE THIS PLACE. I'M HITCHHIKING TO L.A. TO LIVE WITH GRANDMA.
OK, HONEY, BUT REMEMBER, IF YOU GET BAD VIBES, DON'T GET IN THE CAR.
ISN'T YOUR FRIEND, SCOTT COMING TOMORROW?
SHIT! I FORGOT! I'LL HAVE TO LEAVE NEXT WEEK.
THE NEXT DAY
I HOPE YOU BROUGHT SOME CARDS, BECAUSE THERE'S NOTHING TO DO HERE BUT CHOKE YOUR CH..
WOW! LOOK AT THAT HILL!
HELP ME CUT THIS BOX UP.
?
BANZAI!!
WISH THERE WAS SOME PLACE WE COULD SWIM.
HUFF HUFF
HUFF HUFF
WELL, THERE IS A RIVER.
A RIVER!?! HOT SHIT!!! WHAT ARE WE WAITING FOR?

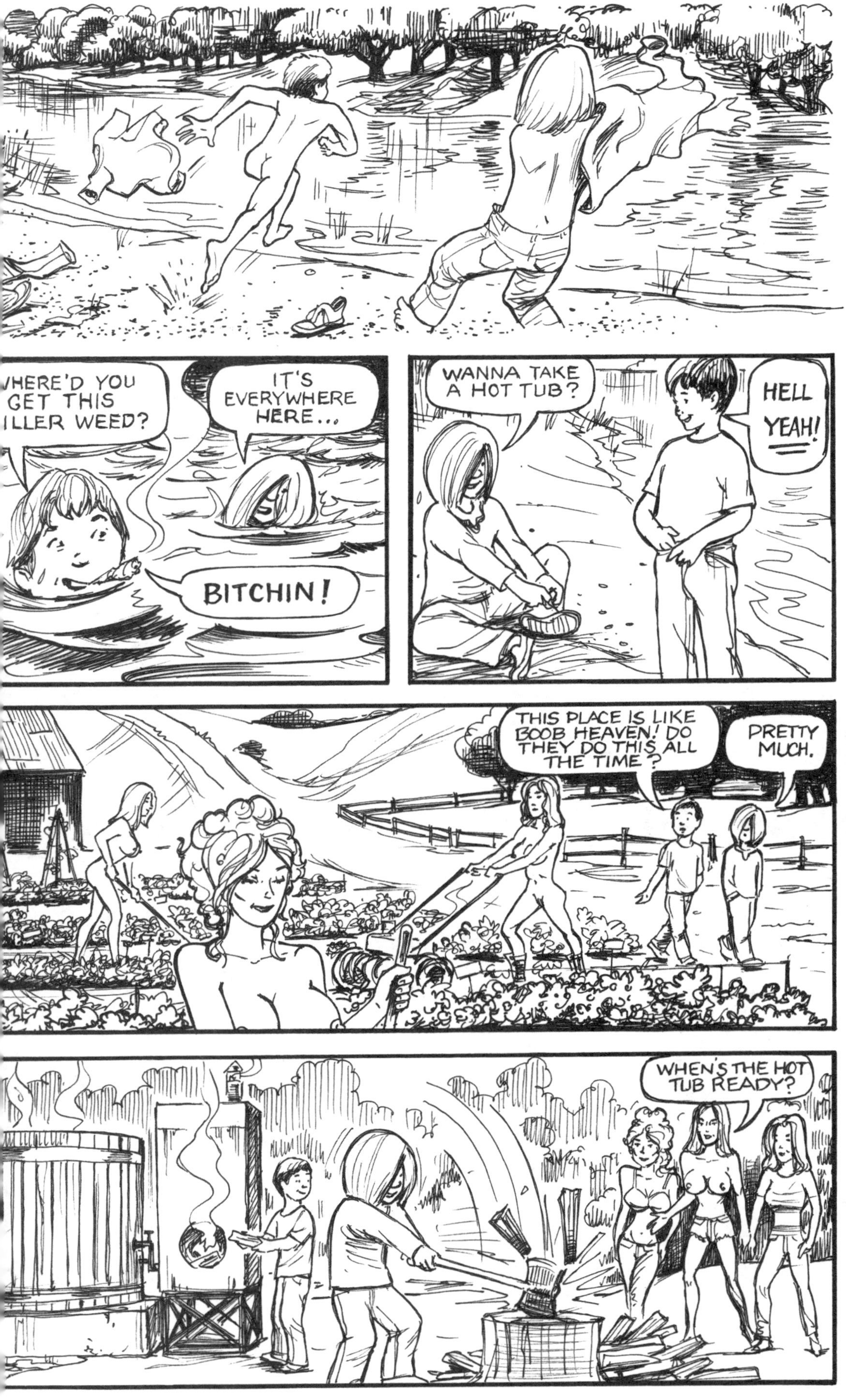
HERE'D YOU GET THIS ILLER WEED?
IT'S EVERYWHERE HERE...
BITCHIN!
WANNA TAKE A HOT TUB?
HELL YEAH!
THIS PLACE IS LIKE BOOB HEAVEN! DO THEY DO THIS ALL THE TIME?
PRETTY MUCH.
WHEN'S THE HOT TUB READY?

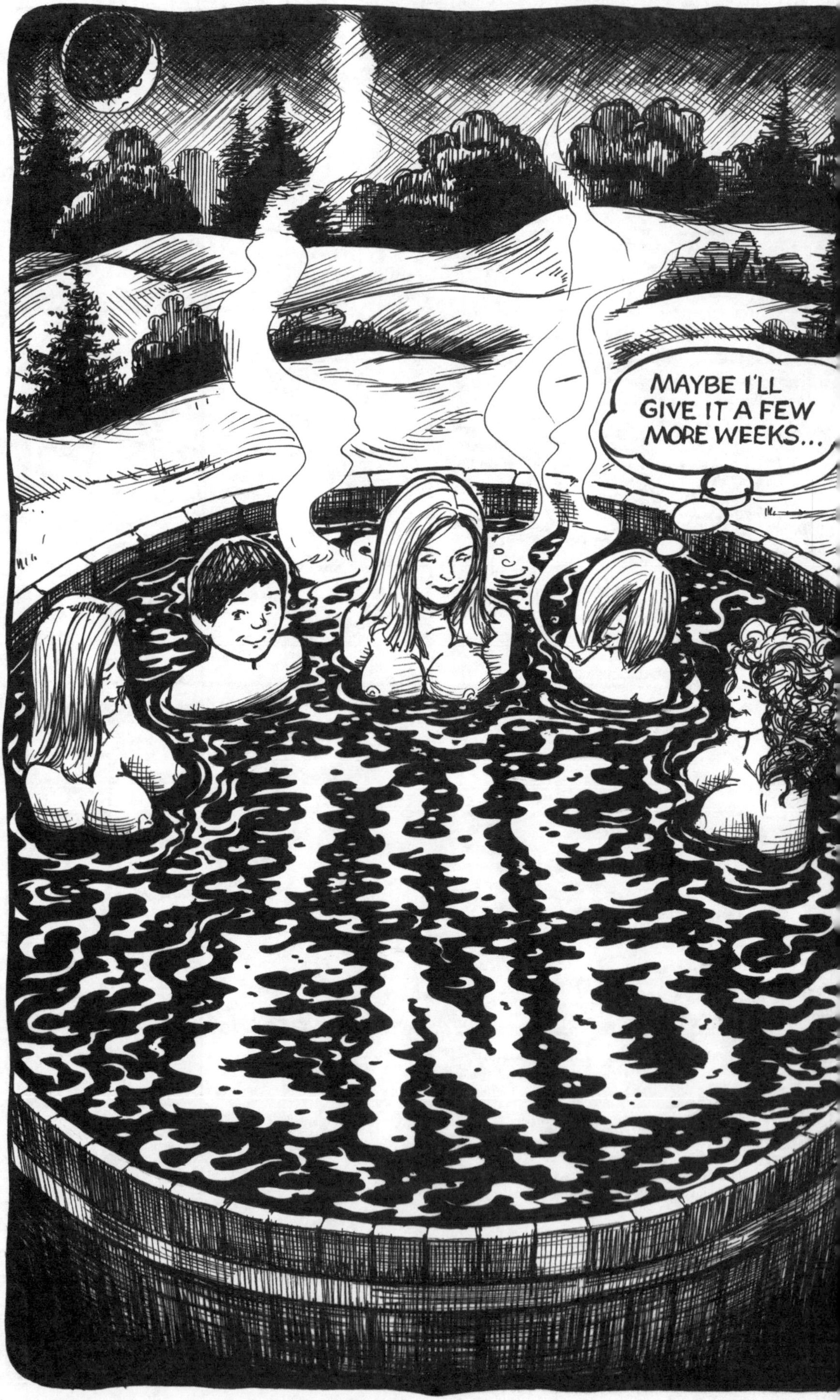
MAYBE I'LL GIVE IT A FEW MORE WEEKS...

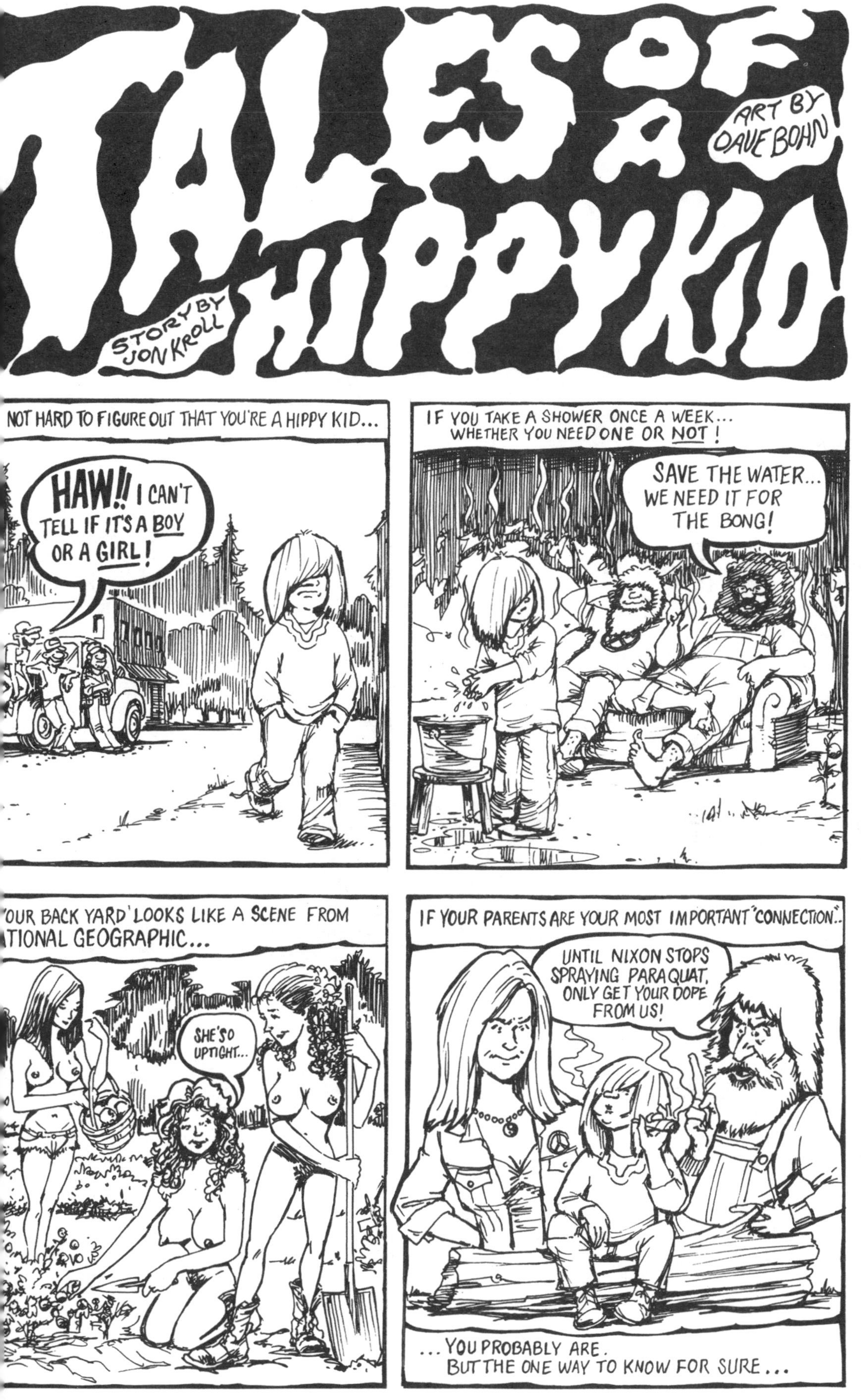
TALES OF A HIPPY KID
STORY BY JON KROLL
ART BY DAVE BOHN
NOT HARD TO FIGURE OUT THAT YOU'RE A HIPPY KID...
HAW!! I CAN'T TELL IF IT'S A BOY OR A GIRL!
IF YOU TAKE A SHOWER ONCE A WEEK... WHETHER YOU NEED ONE OR NOT!
SAVE THE WATER... WE NEED IT FOR THE BONG!
OUR BACK YARD LOOKS LIKE A SCENE FROM
TIONAL GEOGRAPHIC...
SHE'S SO UPTIGHT...
IF YOUR PARENTS ARE YOUR MOST IMPORTANT "CONNECTION"...
UNTIL NIXON STOPS SPRAYING PARAQUAT, ONLY GET YOUR DOPE FROM US!
...YOU PROBABLY ARE.
BUT THE ONE WAY TO KNOW FOR SURE...

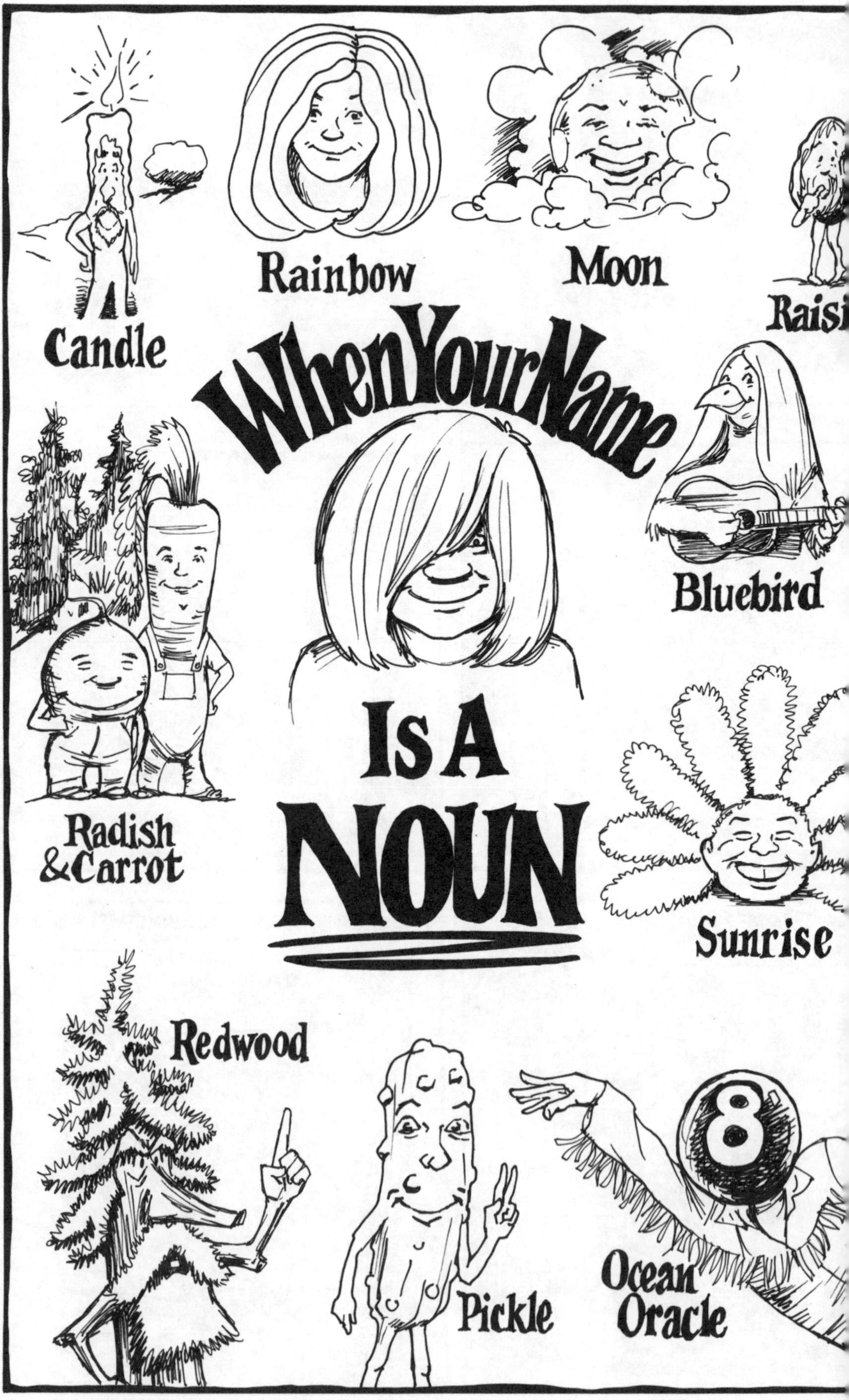

Candle
Rainbow
Moon
Raisi
When Your Name
Bluebird
Is A
NOUN
Radish
&Carrot
Sunrise
Redwood
8
Pickle
Ocean
Oracle

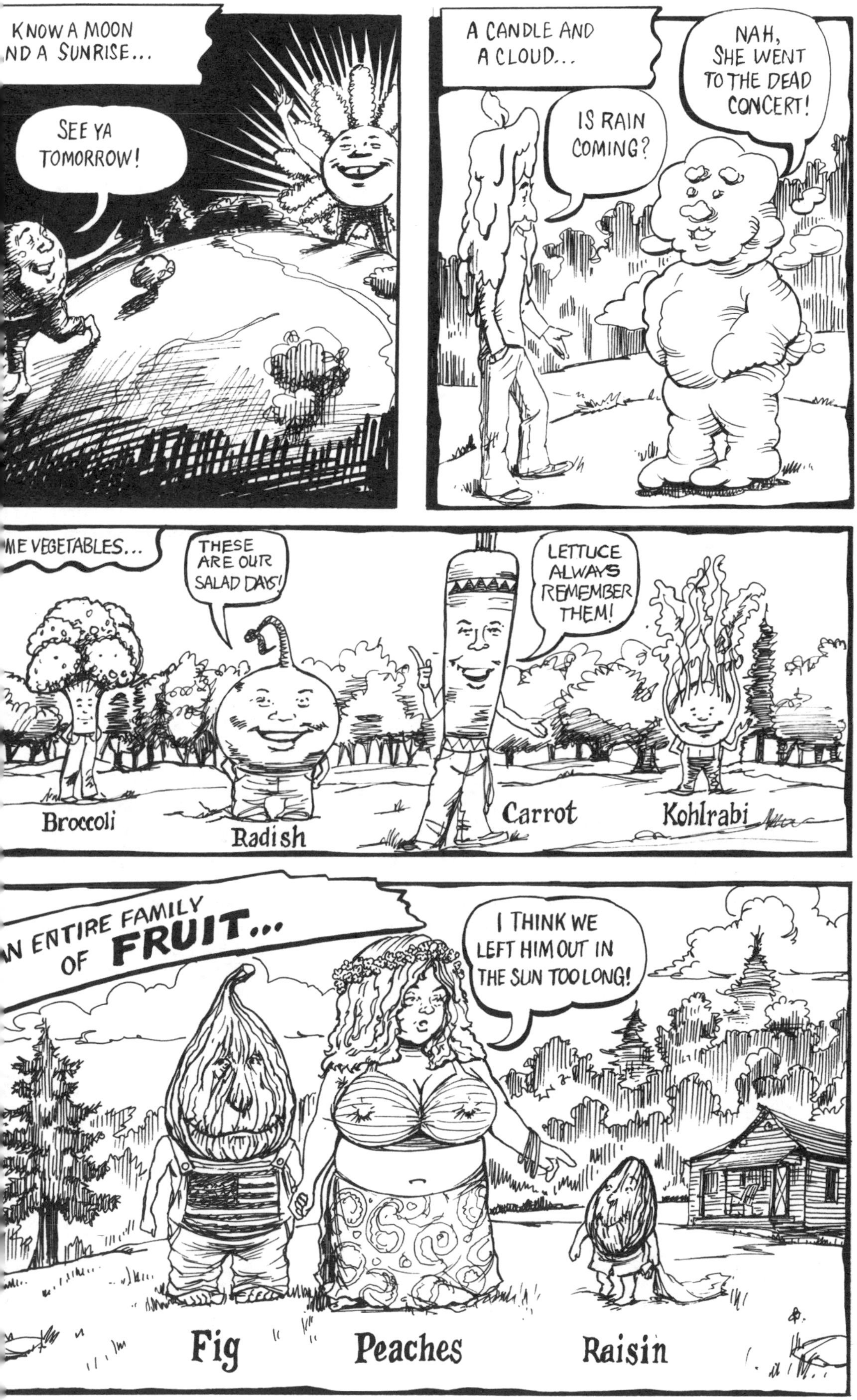
KNOW A MOON
ND A SUNRISE...
SEE YA TOMORROW!
A CANDLE AND A CLOUD...
IS RAIN COMING?
NAH, SHE WENT TO THE DEAD CONCERT!
ME VEGETABLES...
THESE ARE OUR SALAD DAYS!
LETTUCE ALWAYS REMEMBER THEM!
Broccoli
Radish
Carrot
Kohlrabi
N ENTIRE FAMILY OF FRUIT...
I THINK WE LEFT HIM OUT IN THE SUN TOO LONG!
Fig
Peaches
Raisin

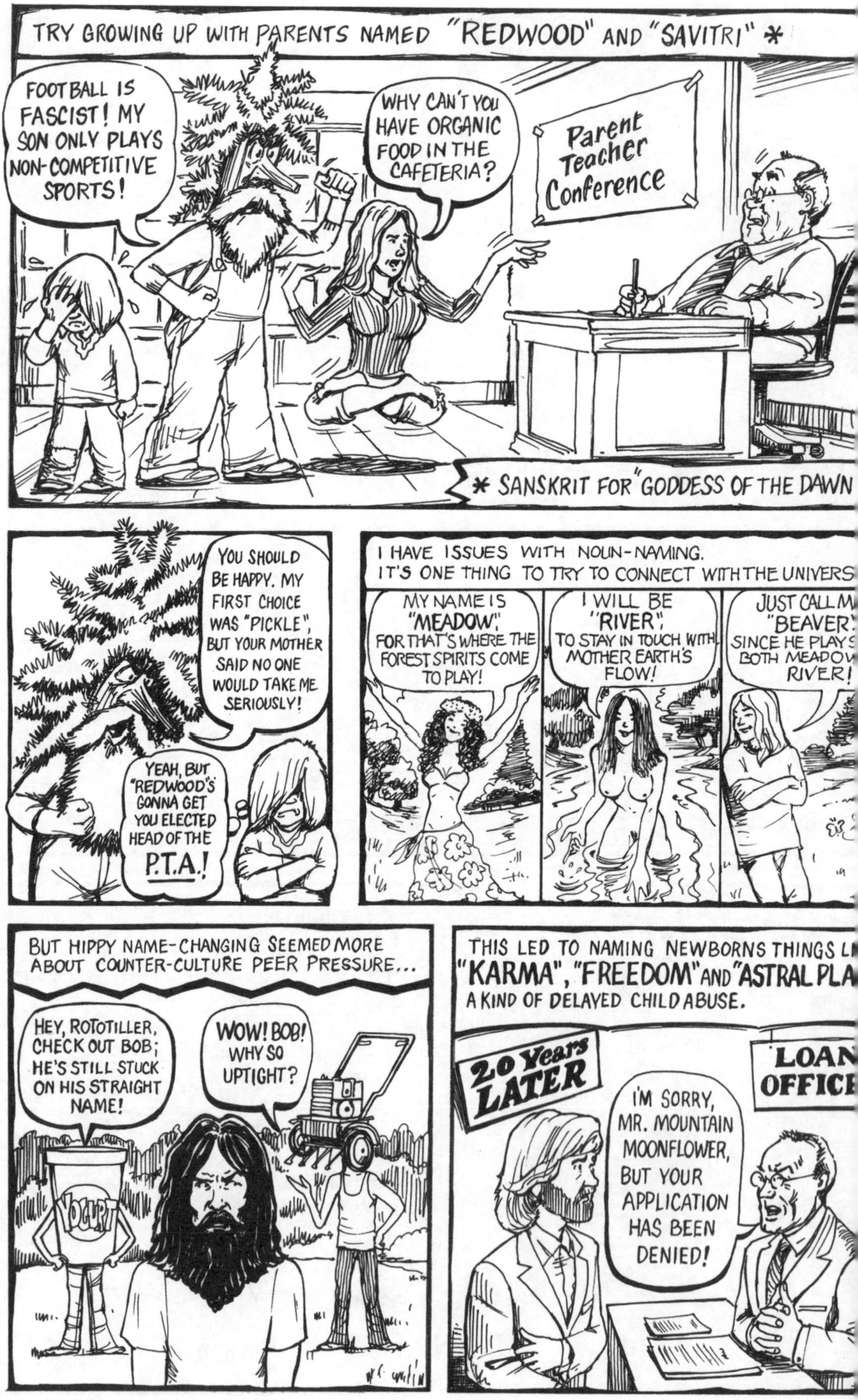

TRY GROWING UP WITH PARENTS NAMED "REDWOOD" AND "SAVITRI" *
FOOTBALL IS FASCIST! MY SON ONLY PLAYS NON-COMPETITIVE SPORTS!
WHY CAN'T YOU HAVE ORGANIC FOOD IN THE CAFETERIA?
Parent Teacher Conference
* SANSKRIT FOR "GODDESS OF THE DAWN
YOU SHOULD BE HAPPY. MY FIRST CHOICE WAS "PICKLE", BUT YOUR MOTHER SAID NO ONE WOULD TAKE ME SERIOUSLY!
YEAH, BUT "REDWOOD'S" GONNA GET YOU ELECTED HEAD OF THE P.T.A.!
I HAVE ISSUES WITH NOUN-NAMING.
IT'S ONE THING TO TRY TO CONNECT WITH THE UNIVERS
MY NAME IS "MEADOW", FOR THAT'S WHERE THE FOREST SPIRITS COME TO PLAY!
I WILL BE "RIVER", TO STAY IN TOUCH WITH MOTHER EARTH'S FLOW!
JUST CALL M "BEAVER" SINCE HE PLAYS BOTH MEADOV RIVER!
BUT HIPPY NAME-CHANGING SEEMED MORE ABOUT COUNTER-CULTURE PEER PRESSURE...
HEY, ROTOTILLER, CHECK OUT BOB; HE'S STILL STUCK ON HIS STRAIGHT NAME!
WOW! BOB! WHY SO UPTIGHT?
YOGURT
THIS LED TO NAMING NEWBORNS THINGS LI
"KARMA", "FREEDOM" AND "ASTRAL PLA
A KIND OF DELAYED CHILD ABUSE.
20 Years LATER
LOAN OFFIC
I'M SORRY, MR. MOUNTAIN MOONFLOWER, BUT YOUR APPLICATION HAS BEEN DENIED!

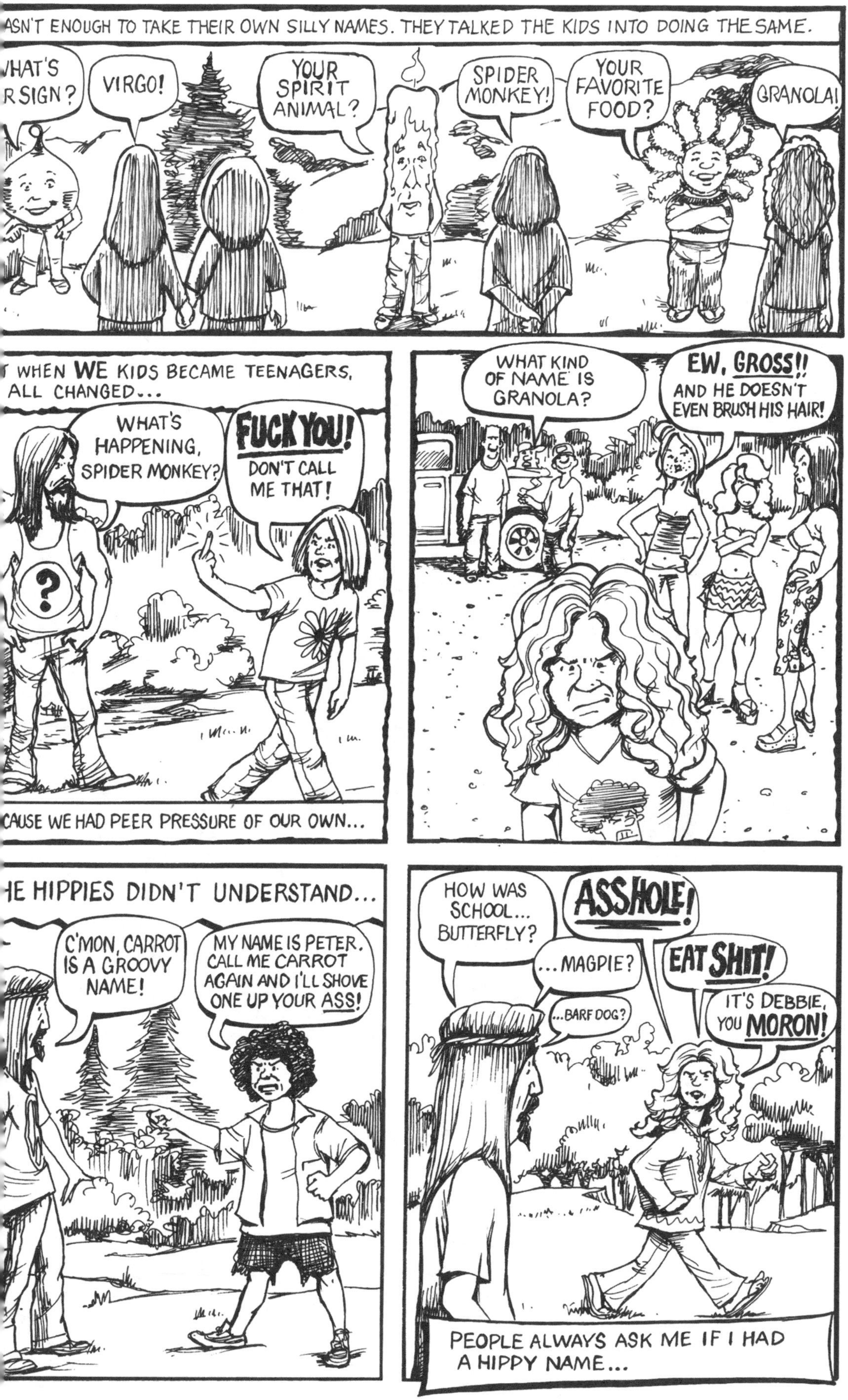

ASN'T ENOUGH TO TAKE THEIR OWN SILLY NAMES. THEY TALKED THE KIDS INTO DOING THE SAME.
HAT'S R SIGN?
VIRGO!
YOUR SPIRIT ANIMAL?
SPIDER MONKEY!
YOUR FAVORITE FOOD?
GRANOLA!
T WHEN WE KIDS BECAME TEENAGERS, ALL CHANGED...
WHAT'S HAPPENING, SPIDER MONKEY?
FUCK YOU! DON'T CALL ME THAT!
CAUSE WE HAD PEER PRESSURE OF OUR OWN...
WHAT KIND OF NAME IS GRANOLA?
EW, GROSS!! AND HE DOESN'T EVEN BRUSH HIS HAIR!
HE HIPPIES DIDN'T UNDERSTAND...
C'MON, CARROT IS A GROOVY NAME!
MY NAME IS PETER. CALL ME CARROT AGAIN AND I'LL SHOVE ONE UP YOUR ASS!
HOW WAS SCHOOL... BUTTERFLY?
ASSHOLE!
...MAGPIE?
EAT SHIT!
...BARF DOG?
IT'S DEBBIE, YOU MORON!
PEOPLE ALWAYS ASK ME IF I HAD A HIPPY NAME...

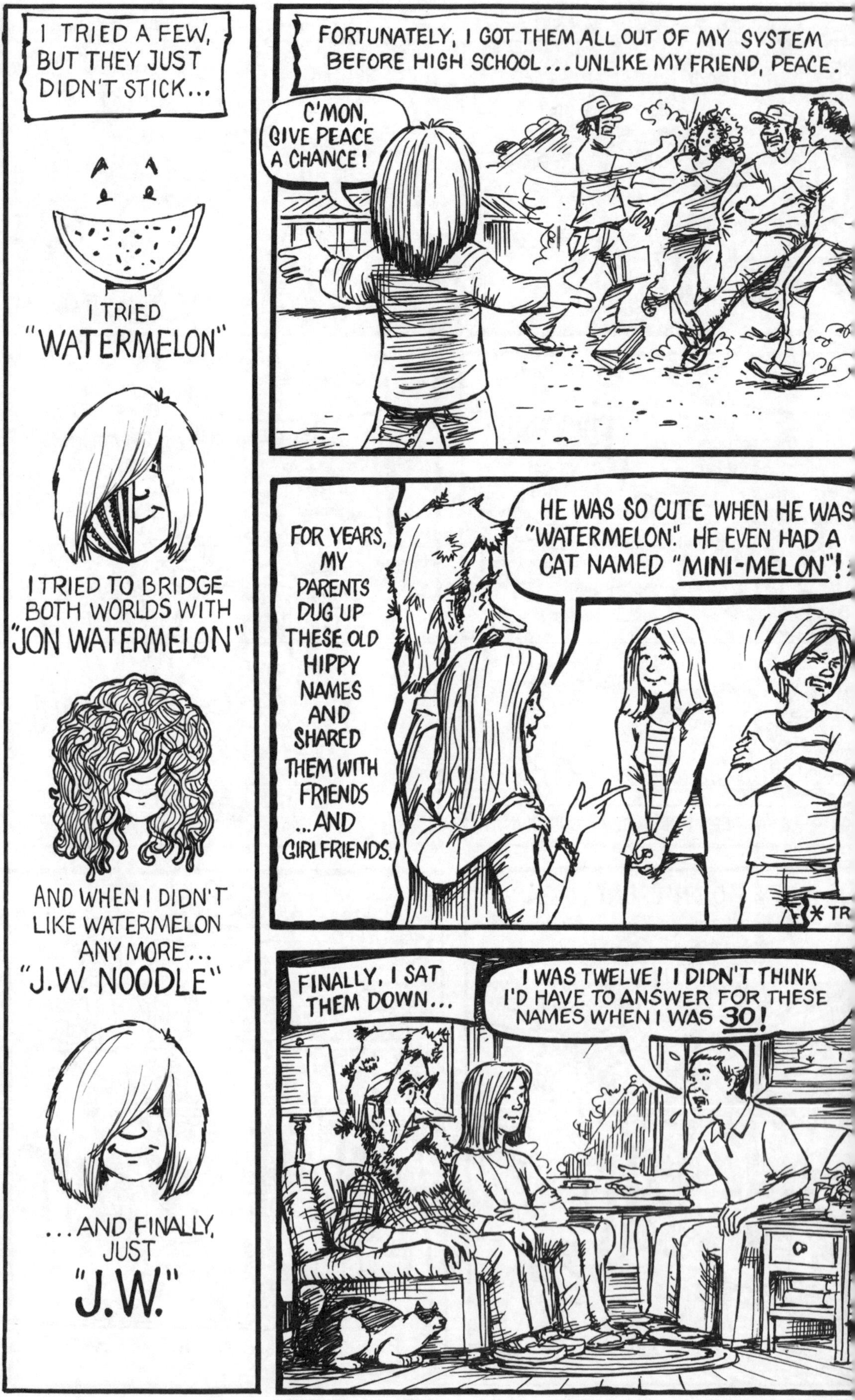
I TRIED A FEW, BUT THEY JUST DIDN'T STICK...
I TRIED "WATERMELON"
I TRIED TO BRIDGE BOTH WORLDS WITH "JON WATERMELON"
AND WHEN I DIDN'T LIKE WATERMELON ANY MORE... "J.W. NOODLE"
...AND FINALLY, JUST "J.W."
FORTUNATELY, I GOT THEM ALL OUT OF MY SYSTEM BEFORE HIGH SCHOOL... UNLIKE MY FRIEND, PEACE.
C'MON, GIVE PEACE A CHANCE!
FOR YEARS, MY PARENTS DUG UP THESE OLD HIPPY NAMES AND SHARED THEM WITH FRIENDS ...AND GIRLFRIENDS.
HE WAS SO CUTE WHEN HE WAS "WATERMELON." HE EVEN HAD A CAT NAMED "MINI-MELON"!
FINALLY, I SAT THEM DOWN...
I WAS TWELVE! I DIDN'T THINK I'D HAVE TO ANSWER FOR THESE NAMES WHEN I WAS 30!

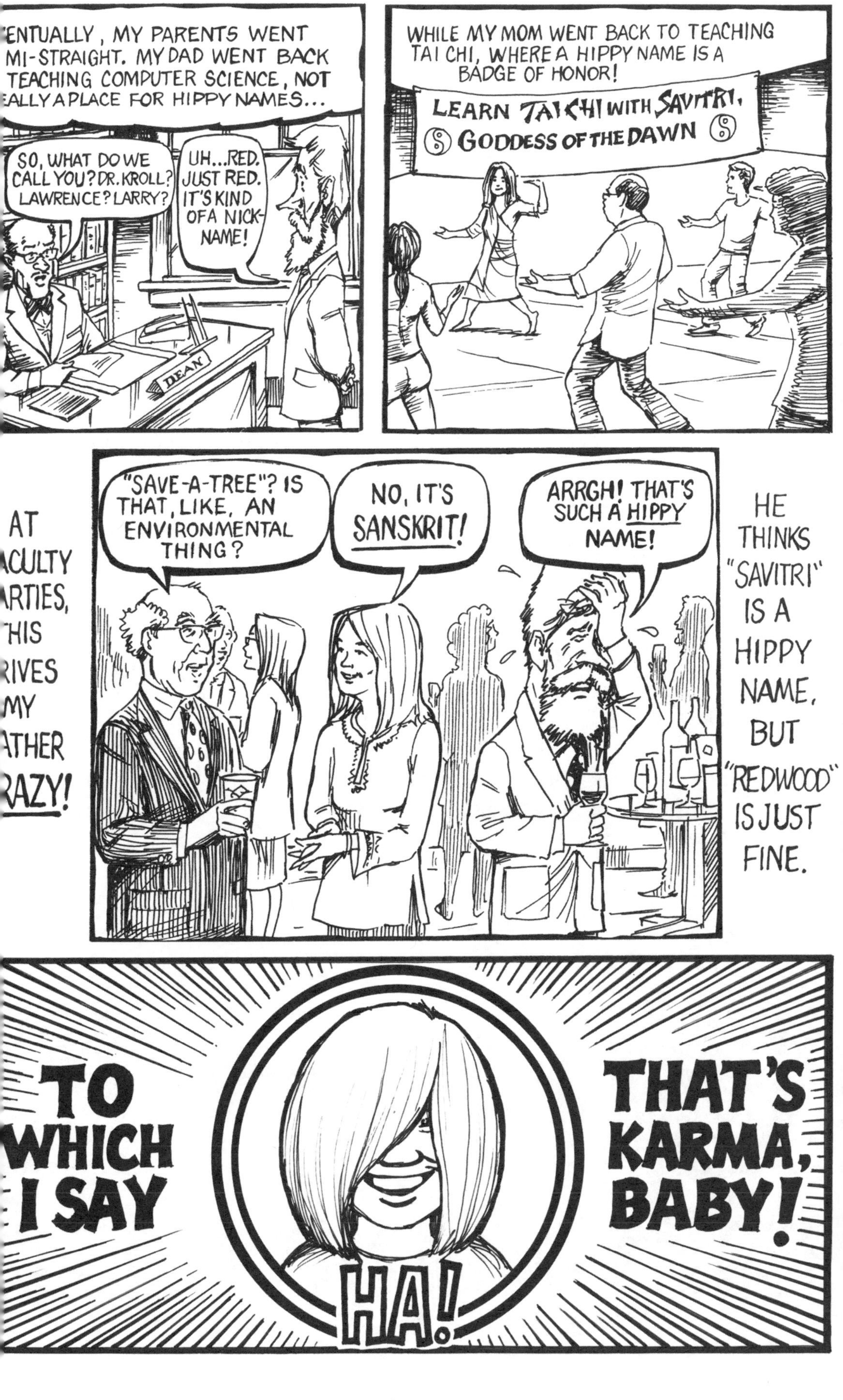
ENTUALLY, MY PARENTS WENT MI-STRAIGHT. MY DAD WENT BACK TEACHING COMPUTER SCIENCE, NOT ALLY A PLACE FOR HIPPY NAMES...
SO, WHAT DO WE CALL YOU? DR. KROLL? LAWRENCE? LARRY?
UH... RED. JUST RED. IT'S KIND OF A NICK-NAME!
DEAN
WHILE MY MOM WENT BACK TO TEACHING TAI CHI, WHERE A HIPPY NAME IS A BADGE OF HONOR!
LEARN TAI CHI WITH SAVITRI, GODDESS OF THE DAWN
AT ACULTY ARTIES, HIS RIVES MY ATHER RAZY!
"SAVE-A-TREE"? IS THAT, LIKE, AN ENVIRONMENTAL THING?
NO, IT'S SANSKRIT!
ARRGH! THAT'S SUCH A HIPPY NAME!
HE THINKS "SAVITRI" IS A HIPPY NAME, BUT "REDWOOD" IS JUST FINE.
TO WHICH I SAY
HA!
THAT'S KARMA, BABY!

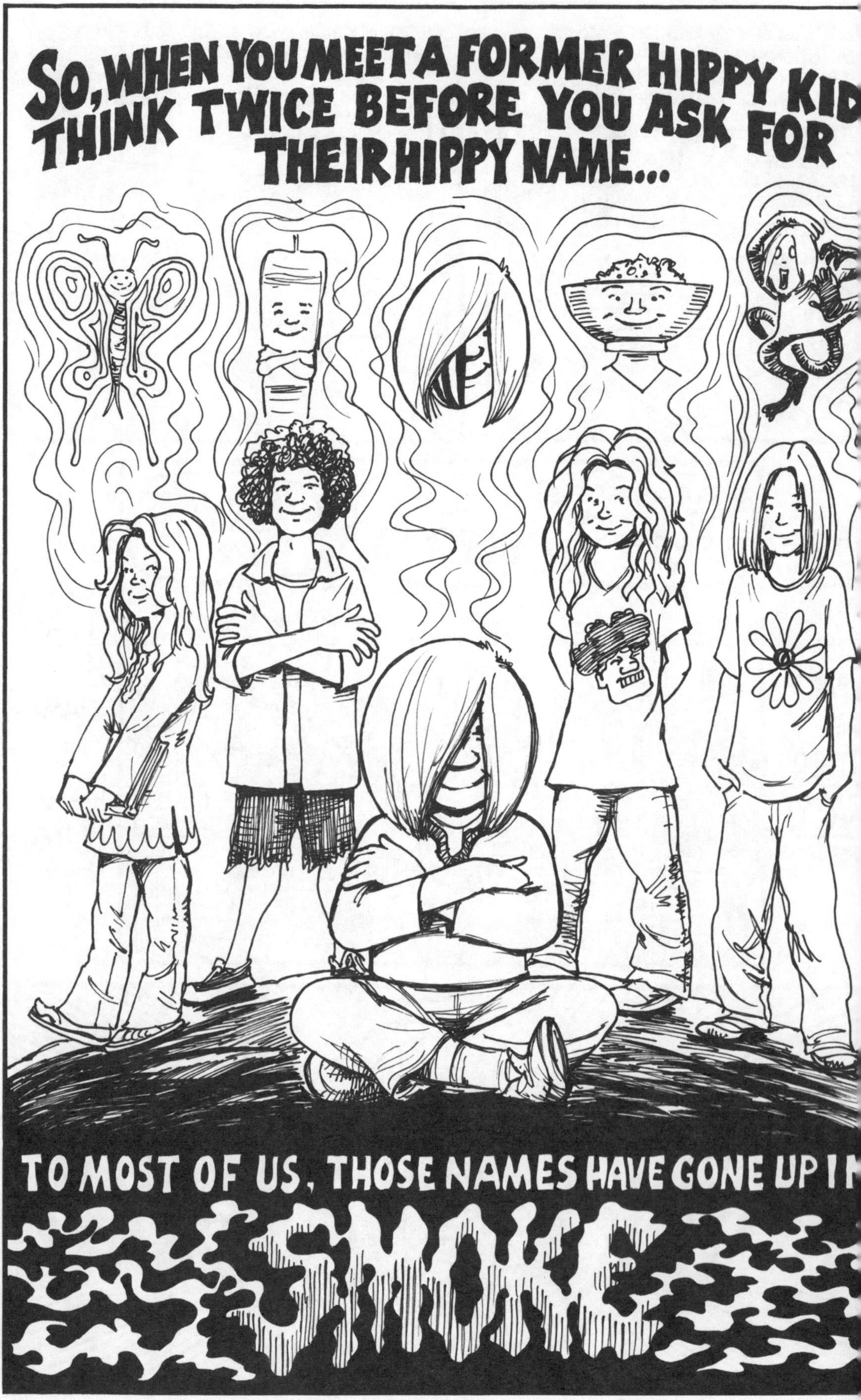
SO, WHEN YOU MEET A FORMER HIPPY KID
THINK TWICE BEFORE YOU ASK FOR
THEIR HIPPY NAME...
TO MOST OF US, THOSE NAMES HAVE GONE UP I
SMOKE

The Parents' Guide

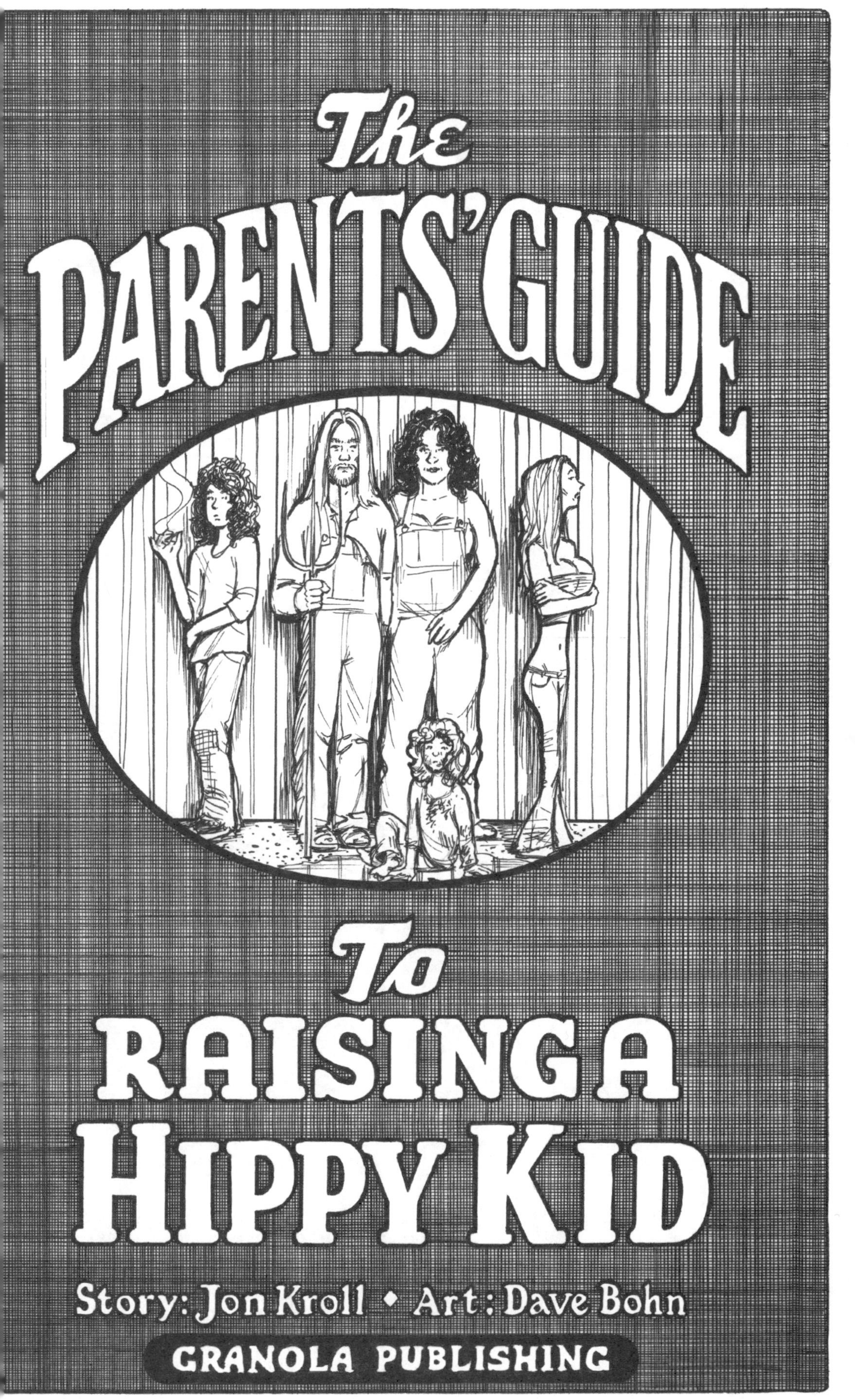

To Raising a Hippy Kid

Story: Jon Kroll • Art: Dave Bohn

GRANOLA PUBLISHING

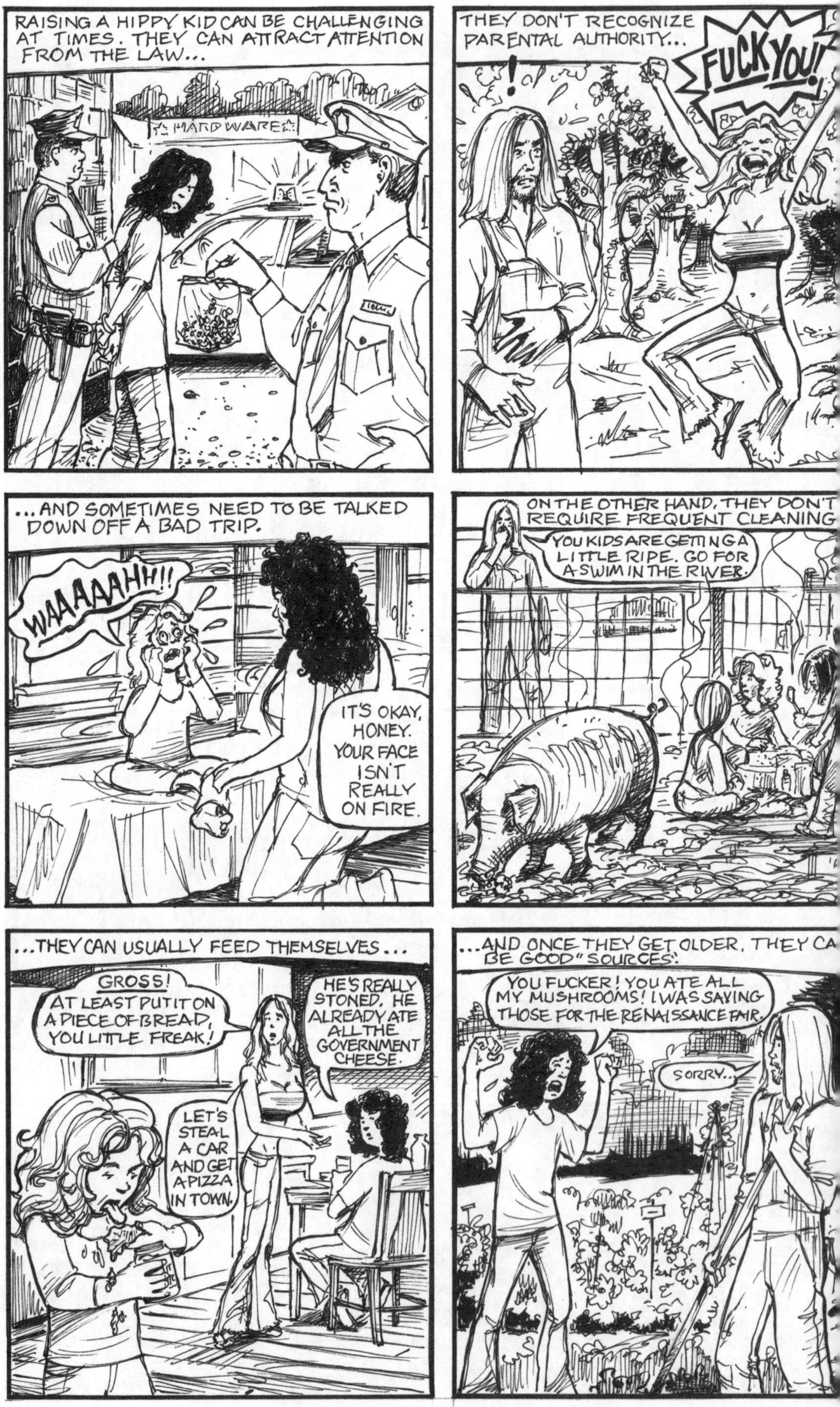
RAISING A HIPPY KID CAN BE CHALLENGING AT TIMES. THEY CAN ATTRACT ATTENTION FROM THE LAW...
HARDWARE
THEY DON'T RECOGNIZE PARENTAL AUTHORITY...
FUCK YOU!
...AND SOMETIMES NEED TO BE TALKED DOWN OFF A BAD TRIP.
WAAAAAHH!!
IT'S OKAY, HONEY. YOUR FACE ISN'T REALLY ON FIRE.
ON THE OTHER HAND, THEY DON'T REQUIRE FREQUENT CLEANING
YOU KIDS ARE GETTING A LITTLE RIPE. GO FOR A SWIM IN THE RIVER.
...THEY CAN USUALLY FEED THEMSELVES...
GROSS! AT LEAST PUT IT ON A PIECE OF BREAD, YOU LITTLE FREAK!
HE'S REALLY STONED. HE ALREADY ATE ALL THE GOVERNMENT CHEESE.
LET'S STEAL A CAR AND GET A PIZZA IN TOWN.
...AND ONCE THEY GET OLDER, THEY CA BE GOOD "SOURCES".
YOU FUCKER! YOU ATE ALL MY MUSHROOMS! I WAS SAVING THOSE FOR THE RENAISSANCE FAIR.
SORRY...

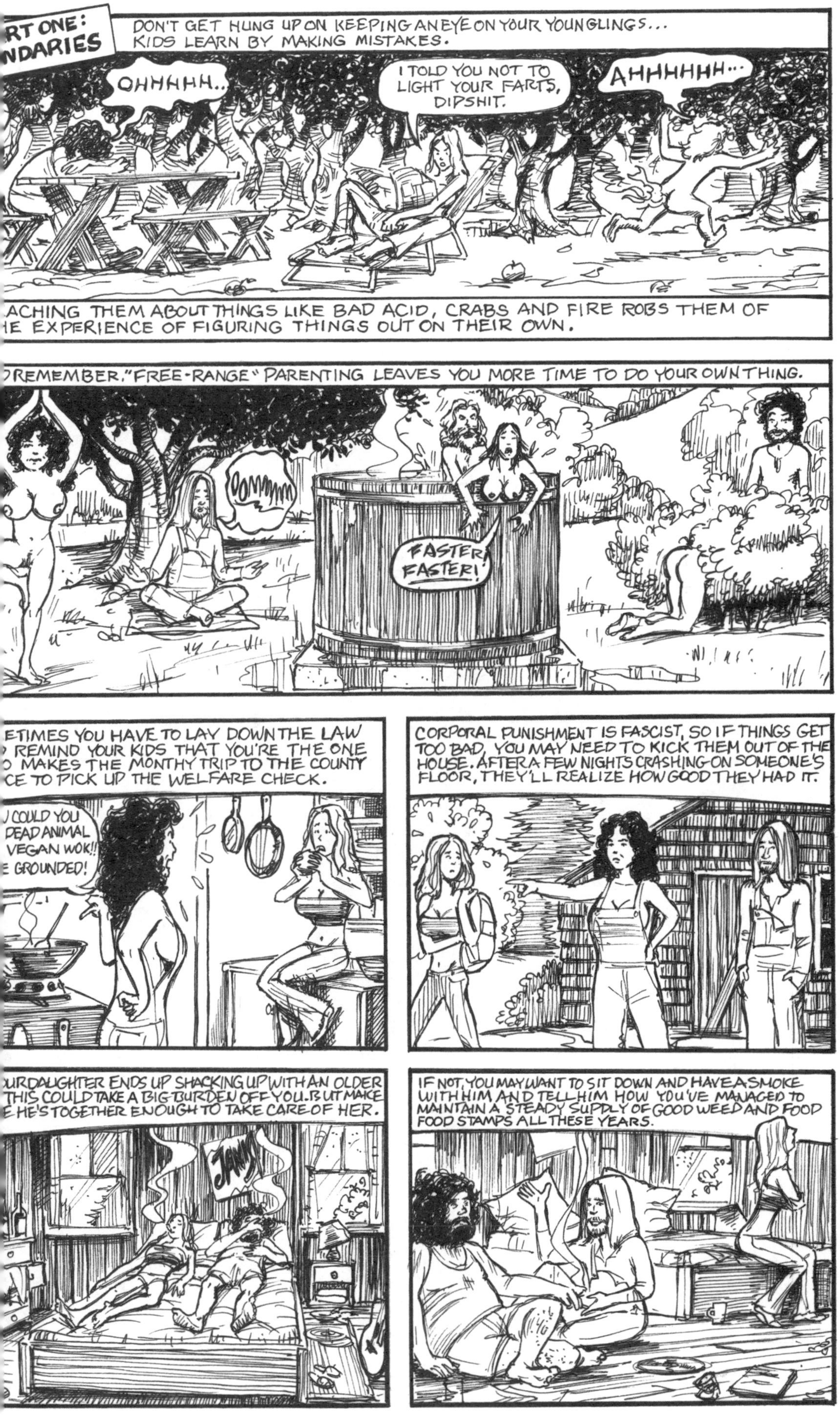
RT ONE:
NDARIES
DON'T GET HUNG UP ON KEEPING AN EYE ON YOUR YOUNGLINGS... KIDS LEARN BY MAKING MISTAKES.
OHHHHH..
I TOLD YOU NOT TO LIGHT YOUR FARTS, DIPSHIT.
AHHHHHH...
ACHING THEM ABOUT THINGS LIKE BAD ACID, CRABS AND FIRE ROBS THEM OF
IE EXPERIENCE OF FIGURING THINGS OUT ON THEIR OWN.
REMEMBER, "FREE-RANGE" PARENTING LEAVES YOU MORE TIME TO DO YOUR OWN THING.
OOMMMM
FASTER! FASTER!
ETIMES YOU HAVE TO LAY DOWN THE LAW
REMIND YOUR KIDS THAT YOU'RE THE ONE
O MAKES THE MONTHY TRIP TO THE COUNTY
CE TO PICK UP THE WELFARE CHECK.
U COULD YOU
DEAD ANIMAL
VEGAN WOK!!
E GROUNDED!
CORPORAL PUNISHMENT IS FASCIST, SO IF THINGS GET TOO BAD, YOU MAY NEED TO KICK THEM OUT OF THE HOUSE. AFTER A FEW NIGHTS CRASHING ON SOMEONE'S FLOOR, THEY'LL REALIZE HOW GOOD THEY HAD IT.
OUR DAUGHTER ENDS UP SHACKING UP WITH AN OLDER
THIS COULD TAKE A BIG BURDEN OFF YOU. BUT MAKE
E HE'S TOGETHER ENOUGH TO TAKE CARE OF HER.
IF NOT, YOU MAY WANT TO SIT DOWN AND HAVE A SMOKE WITH HIM AND TELL HIM HOW YOU'VE MANAGED TO MAINTAIN A STEADY SUPPLY OF GOOD WEED AND FOOD
FOOD STAMPS ALL THESE YEARS.

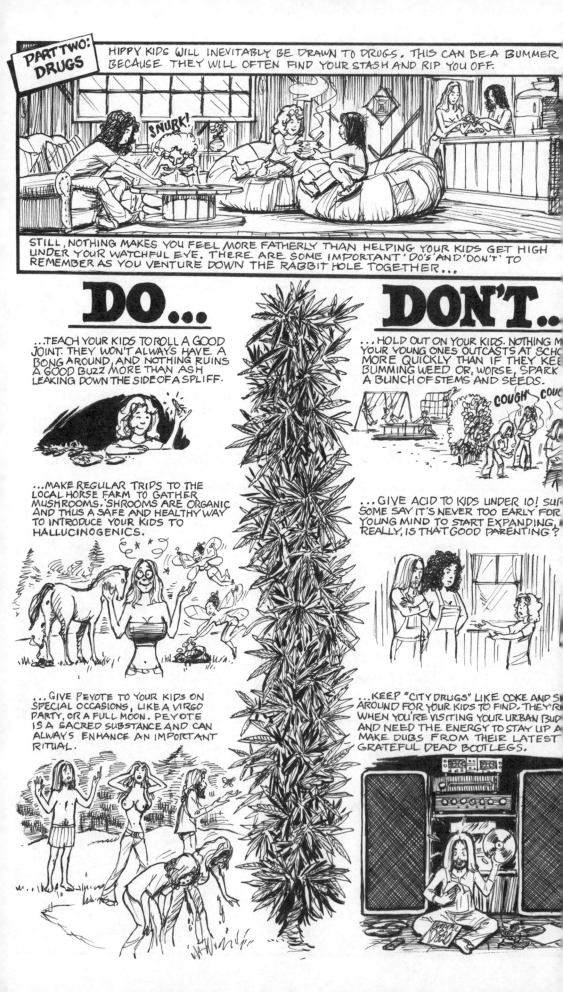

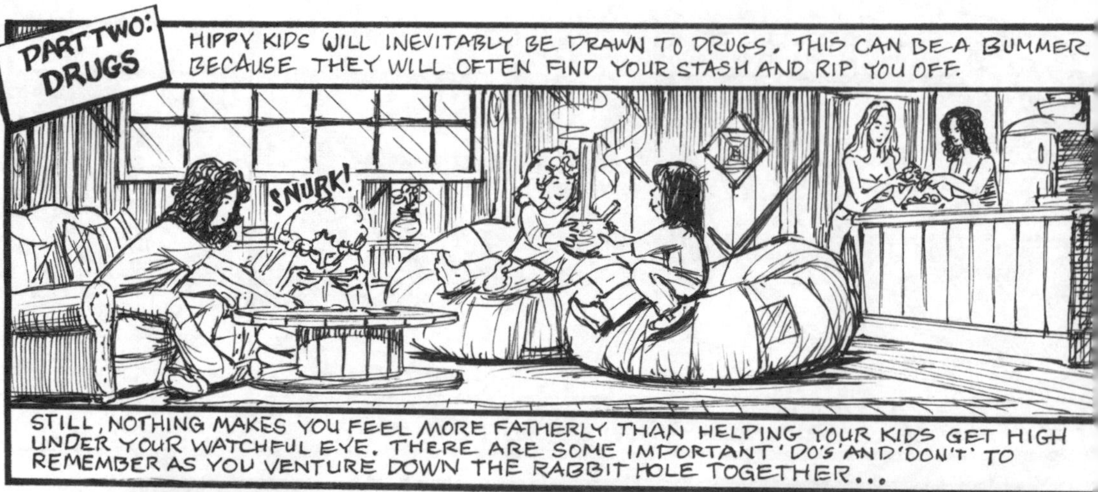
PART TWO: DRUGS
HIPPY KIDS WILL INEVITABLY BE DRAWN TO DRUGS. THIS CAN BE A BUMMER BECAUSE THEY WILL OFTEN FIND YOUR STASH AND RIP YOU OFF.
SNURK!
STILL, NOTHING MAKES YOU FEEL MORE FATHERLY THAN HELPING YOUR KIDS GET HIGH UNDER YOUR WATCHFUL EYE. THERE ARE SOME IMPORTANT 'DO'S' AND 'DON'T' TO REMEMBER AS YOU VENTURE DOWN THE RABBIT HOLE TOGETHER...

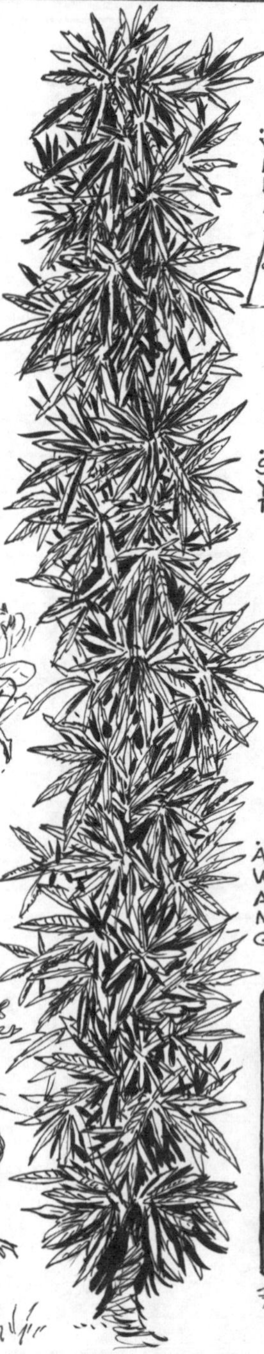

DO...

...TEACH YOUR KIDS TO ROLL A GOOD JOINT. THEY WON'T ALWAYS HAVE A BONG AROUND, AND NOTHING RUINS A GOOD BUZZ MORE THAN ASH LEAKING DOWN THE SIDE OF A SPLIFF.

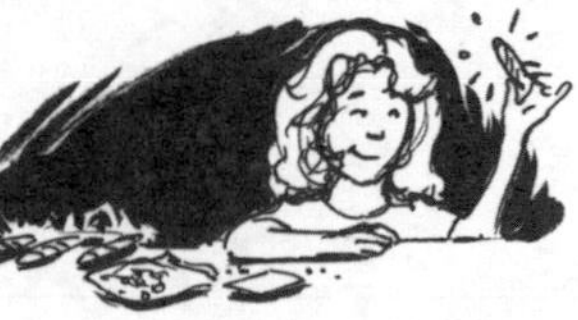

...MAKE REGULAR TRIPS TO THE LOCAL HORSE FARM TO GATHER MUSHROOMS. 'SHROOMS ARE ORGANIC AND THUS A SAFE AND HEALTHY WAY TO INTRODUCE YOUR KIDS TO HALLUCINOGENICS.

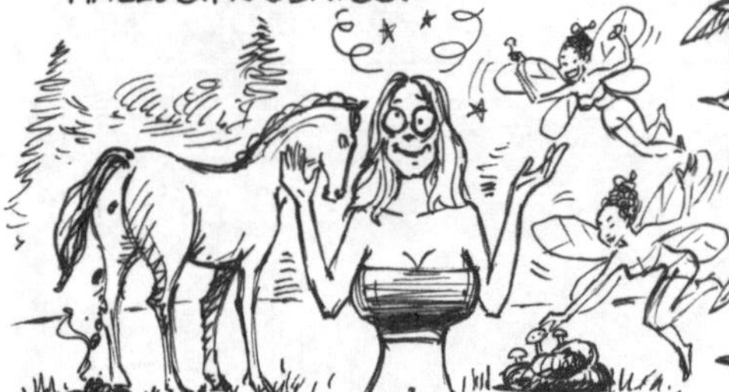

...GIVE PEYOTE TO YOUR KIDS ON SPECIAL OCCASIONS, LIKE A VIRGO PARTY, OR A FULL MOON. PEYOTE IS A SACRED SUBSTANCE AND CAN ALWAYS ENHANCE AN IMPORTANT RITUAL.

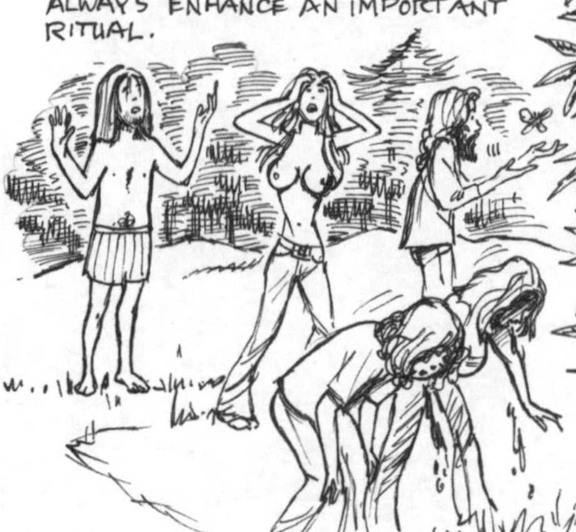

DON'T..

...HOLD OUT ON YOUR KIDS. NOTHING M YOUR YOUNG ONES OUTCASTS AT SCHO MORE QUICKLY THAN IF THEY KEE BUMMING WEED OR, WORSE, SPARK A BUNCH OF STEMS AND SEEDS.

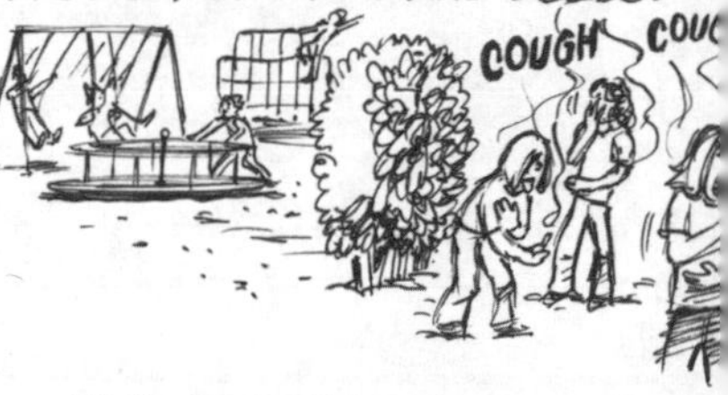
COUGH
COUG

...GIVE ACID TO KIDS UNDER 10! SU SOME SAY IT'S NEVER TOO EARLY FOR YOUNG MIND TO START EXPANDING, REALLY, IS THAT GOOD PARENTING?

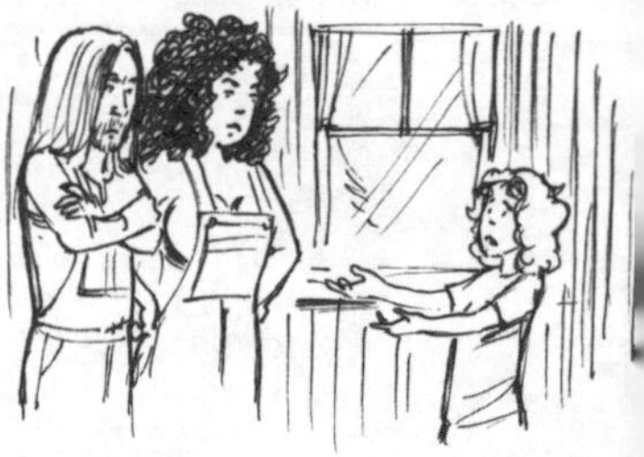

...KEEP "CITY DRUGS" LIKE COKE AND S AROUND FOR YOUR KIDS TO FIND. THEY'R WHEN YOU'RE VISITING YOUR URBAN BUD AND NEED THE ENERGY TO STAY UP A MAKE DUBS FROM THEIR LATEST GRATEFUL DEAD BOOTLEGS.

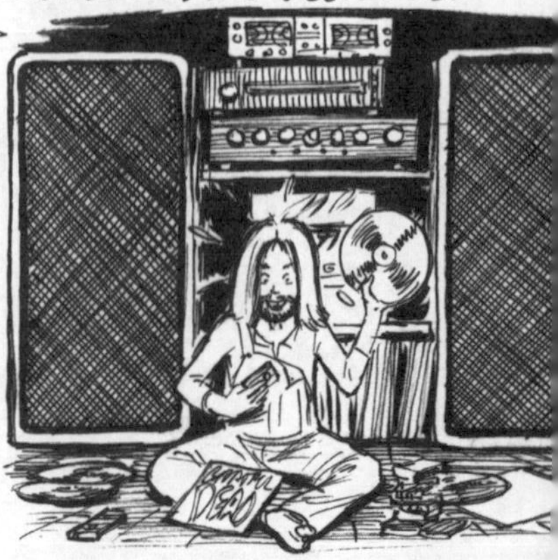

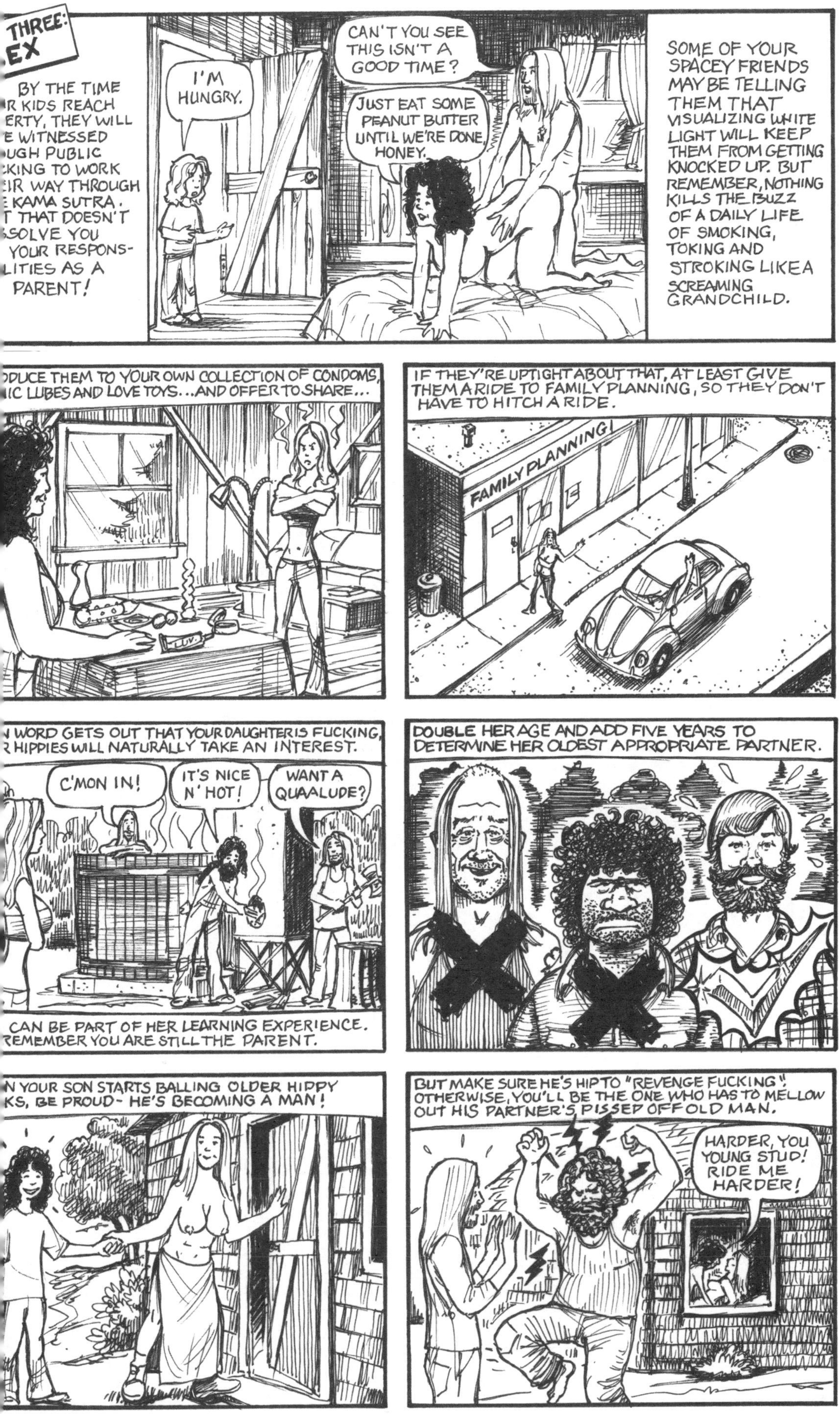
THREE:
EX
BY THE TIME
R KIDS REACH
ERTY, THEY WILL
E WITNESSED
UGH PUBLIC
CKING TO WORK
EIR WAY THROUGH
E KAMA SUTRA.
T THAT DOESN'T
SOLVE YOU
YOUR RESPONS-
LITIES AS A
PARENT!
I'M HUNGRY.
CAN'T YOU SEE THIS ISN'T A GOOD TIME?
JUST EAT SOME PEANUT BUTTER UNTIL WE'RE DONE, HONEY.
SOME OF YOUR SPACEY FRIENDS MAY BE TELLING THEM THAT VISUALIZING WHITE LIGHT WILL KEEP THEM FROM GETTING KNOCKED UP. BUT REMEMBER, NOTHING KILLS THE BUZZ OF A DAILY LIFE OF SMOKING, TOKING AND STROKING LIKE A SCREAMING GRANDCHILD.
ODUCE THEM TO YOUR OWN COLLECTION OF CONDOMS,
IC LUBES AND LOVE TOYS...AND OFFER TO SHARE...
LUV.
IF THEY'RE UPTIGHT ABOUT THAT, AT LEAST GIVE THEM A RIDE TO FAMILY PLANNING, SO THEY DON'T HAVE TO HITCH A RIDE.
FAMILY PLANNING
FAMILY PLANNING
N WORD GETS OUT THAT YOUR DAUGHTER IS FUCKING,
R HIPPIES WILL NATURALLY TAKE AN INTEREST.
C'MON IN!
IT'S NICE N' HOT!
WANT A QUAALUDE?
CAN BE PART OF HER LEARNING EXPERIENCE.
REMEMBER YOU ARE STILL THE PARENT.
DOUBLE HER AGE AND ADD FIVE YEARS TO DETERMINE HER OLDEST APPROPRIATE PARTNER.
N YOUR SON STARTS BALLING OLDER HIPPY
KS, BE PROUD- HE'S BECOMING A MAN!
BUT MAKE SURE HE'S HIP TO "REVENGE FUCKING"! OTHERWISE, YOU'LL BE THE ONE WHO HAS TO MELLOW OUT HIS PARTNER'S PISSED OFF OLD MAN.
HARDER, YOU YOUNG STUD! RIDE ME HARDER!

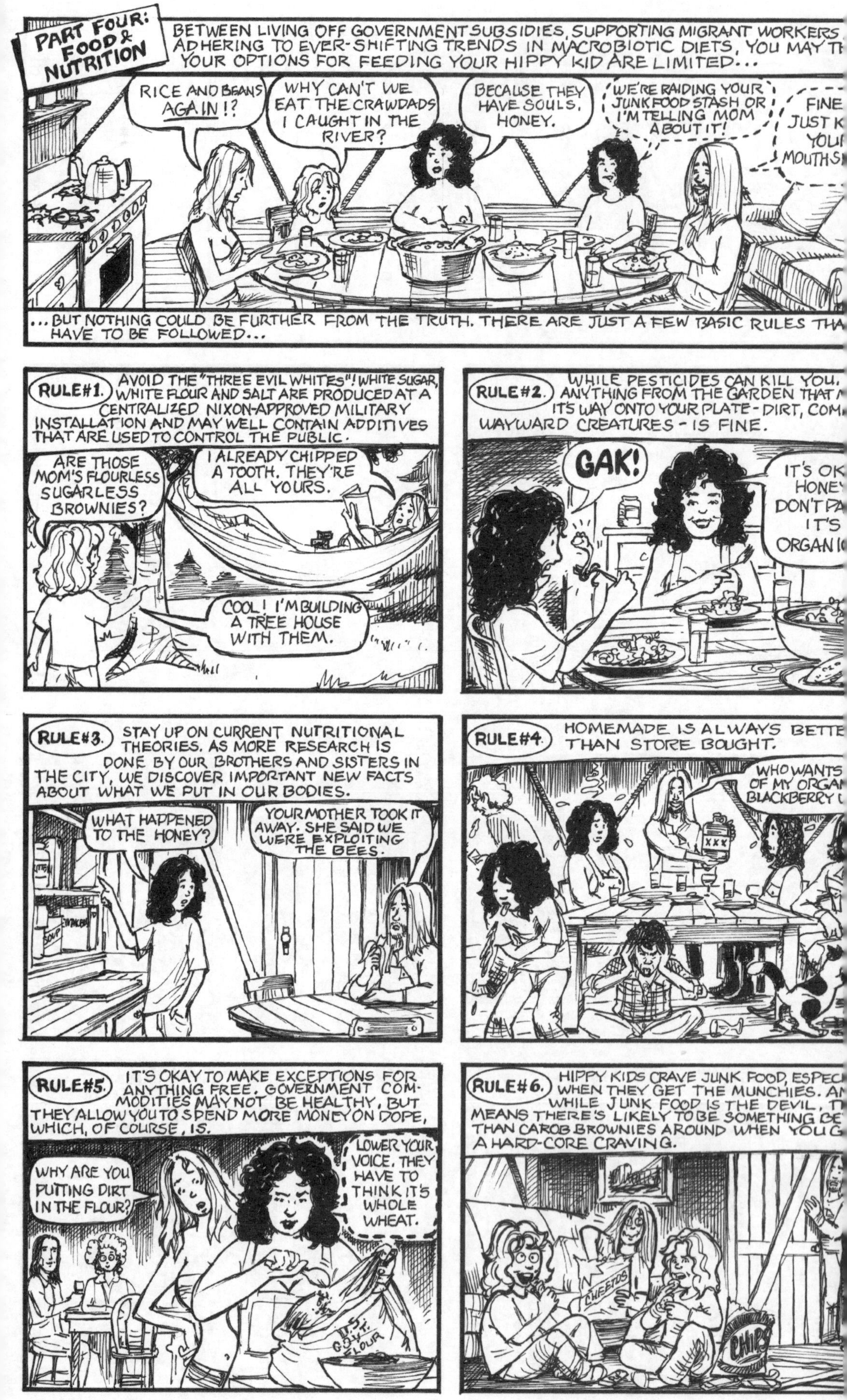
PART FOUR: FOOD & NUTRITION
BETWEEN LIVING OFF GOVERNMENT SUBSIDIES, SUPPORTING MIGRANT WORKERS ADHERING TO EVER-SHIFTING TRENDS IN MACROBIOTIC DIETS, YOU MAY TH YOUR OPTIONS FOR FEEDING YOUR HIPPY KID ARE LIMITED...
RICE AND BEANS AGAIN!?
WHY CAN'T WE EAT THE CRAWDADS I CAUGHT IN THE RIVER?
BECAUSE THEY HAVE SOULS, HONEY.
WE'RE RAIDING YOUR JUNK FOOD STASH OR I'M TELLING MOM ABOUT IT!
FINE JUST K YOUR MOUTH S
...BUT NOTHING COULD BE FURTHER FROM THE TRUTH. THERE ARE JUST A FEW BASIC RULES THA HAVE TO BE FOLLOWED...
RULE #1. AVOID THE "THREE EVIL WHITES"! WHITE SUGAR, WHITE FLOUR AND SALT ARE PRODUCED AT A CENTRALIZED NIXON-APPROVED MILITARY INSTALLATION AND MAY WELL CONTAIN ADDITIVES THAT ARE USED TO CONTROL THE PUBLIC.
ARE THOSE MOM'S FLOURLESS SUGARLESS BROWNIES?
I ALREADY CHIPPED A TOOTH. THEY'RE ALL YOURS.
COOL! I'M BUILDING A TREE HOUSE WITH THEM.
RULE #2. WHILE PESTICIDES CAN KILL YOU, ANYTHING FROM THE GARDEN THAT IT'S WAY ONTO YOUR PLATE - DIRT, COM WAYWARD CREATURES - IS FINE.
GAK!
IT'S OK HONEY DON'T PA IT'S ORGANI
RULE #3. STAY UP ON CURRENT NUTRITIONAL THEORIES. AS MORE RESEARCH IS DONE BY OUR BROTHERS AND SISTERS IN THE CITY, WE DISCOVER IMPORTANT NEW FACTS ABOUT WHAT WE PUT IN OUR BODIES.
WHAT HAPPENED TO THE HONEY?
YOUR MOTHER TOOK IT AWAY. SHE SAID WE WERE EXPLOITING THE BEES.
SOUP
RULE #4. HOMEMADE IS ALWAYS BETTE THAN STORE BOUGHT.
WHO WANTS OF MY ORGAN BLACKBERRY
XXX
RULE #5. IT'S OKAY TO MAKE EXCEPTIONS FOR ANYTHING FREE. GOVERNMENT COMMODITIES MAY NOT BE HEALTHY, BUT THEY ALLOW YOU TO SPEND MORE MONEY ON DOPE, WHICH, OF COURSE, IS.
WHY ARE YOU PUTTING DIRT IN THE FLOUR?
LOWER YOUR VOICE. THEY HAVE TO THINK IT'S WHOLE WHEAT.
U.S. GOV'T. FLOUR
RULE #6. HIPPY KIDS CRAVE JUNK FOOD, ESPEC WHEN THEY GET THE MUNCHIES. AN WHILE JUNK FOOD IS THE DEVIL, T MEANS THERE'S LIKELY TO BE SOMETHING BE THAN CAROB BROWNIES AROUND WHEN YOU G A HARD-CORE CRAVING.
CHEETOS
CHIPS

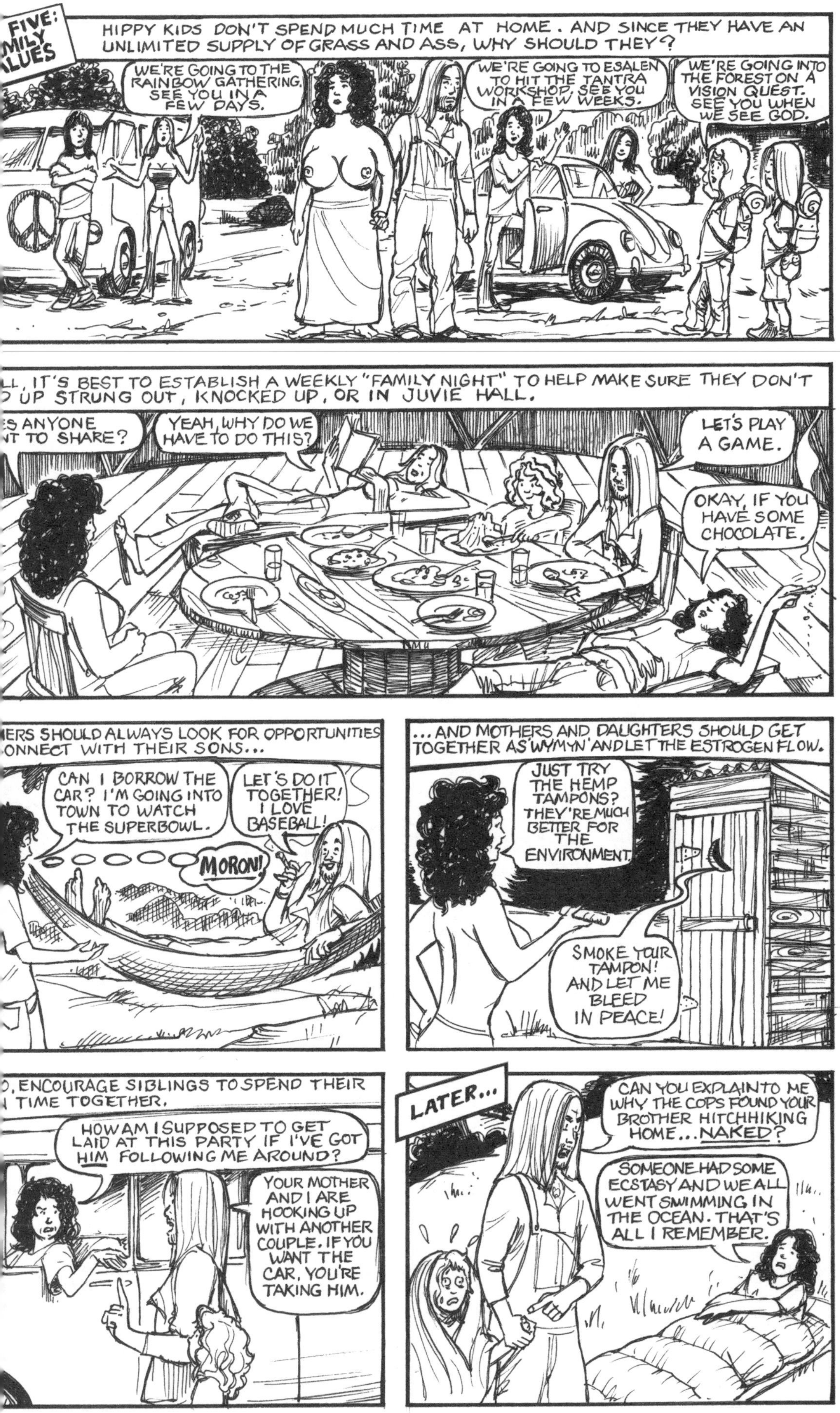
FIVE: MILY ALUES
HIPPY KIDS DON'T SPEND MUCH TIME AT HOME. AND SINCE THEY HAVE AN UNLIMITED SUPPLY OF GRASS AND ASS, WHY SHOULD THEY?
WE'RE GOING TO THE RAINBOW GATHERING. SEE YOU IN A FEW DAYS.
WE'RE GOING TO ESALEN TO HIT THE TANTRA WORKSHOP. SEE YOU IN A FEW WEEKS.
WE'RE GOING INTO THE FOREST ON A VISION QUEST. SEE YOU WHEN WE SEE GOD.
LL, IT'S BEST TO ESTABLISH A WEEKLY "FAMILY NIGHT" TO HELP MAKE SURE THEY DON'T D UP STRUNG OUT, KNOCKED UP, OR IN JUVIE HALL.
ES ANYONE NT TO SHARE?
YEAH, WHY DO WE HAVE TO DO THIS?
LET'S PLAY A GAME.
OKAY, IF YOU HAVE SOME CHOCOLATE.
HERS SHOULD ALWAYS LOOK FOR OPPORTUNITIES ONNECT WITH THEIR SONS...
CAN I BORROW THE CAR? I'M GOING INTO TOWN TO WATCH THE SUPERBOWL.
LET'S DO IT TOGETHER! I LOVE BASEBALL!
MORON!
...AND MOTHERS AND DAUGHTERS SHOULD GET TOGETHER AS 'WYMYN' AND LET THE ESTROGEN FLOW.
JUST TRY THE HEMP TAMPONS? THEY'RE MUCH BETTER FOR THE ENVIRONMENT.
SMOKE YOUR TAMPON! AND LET ME BLEED IN PEACE!
O, ENCOURAGE SIBLINGS TO SPEND THEIR TIME TOGETHER.
HOW AM I SUPPOSED TO GET LAID AT THIS PARTY IF I'VE GOT HIM FOLLOWING ME AROUND?
YOUR MOTHER AND I ARE HOOKING UP WITH ANOTHER COUPLE. IF YOU WANT THE CAR, YOU'RE TAKING HIM.
LATER...
CAN YOU EXPLAIN TO ME WHY THE COPS FOUND YOUR BROTHER HITCHHIKING HOME... NAKED?
SOMEONE HAD SOME ECSTASY AND WE ALL WENT SWIMMING IN THE OCEAN. THAT'S ALL I REMEMBER.

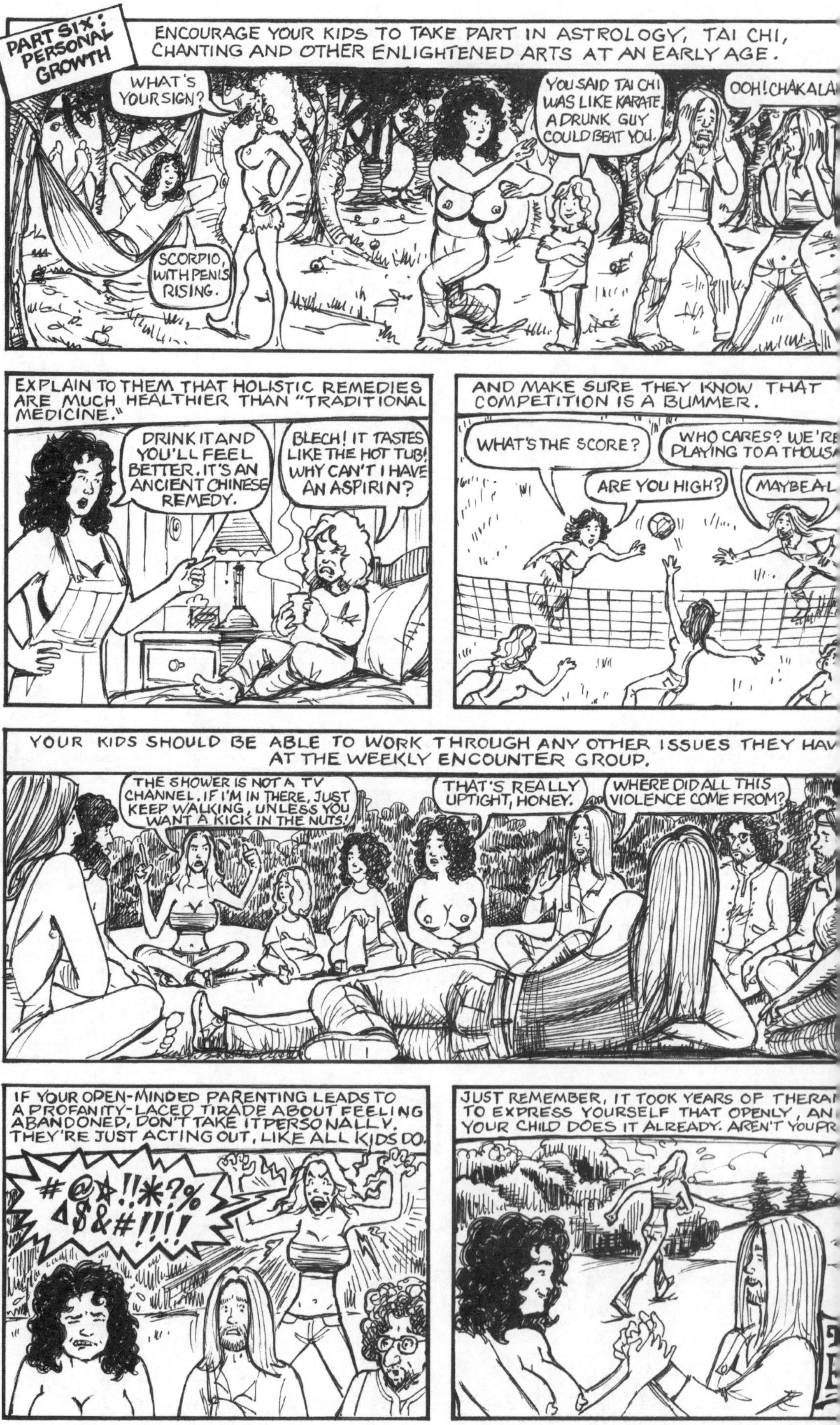
PART SIX: PERSONAL GROWTH
ENCOURAGE YOUR KIDS TO TAKE PART IN ASTROLOGY, TAI CHI, CHANTING AND OTHER ENLIGHTENED ARTS AT AN EARLY AGE.
WHAT'S YOUR SIGN?
SCORPIO, WITH PENIS RISING.
YOU SAID TAI CHI WAS LIKE KARATE. A DRUNK GUY COULD BEAT YOU.
OOH! CHAKALA
OOH! CHAKALA
EXPLAIN TO THEM THAT HOLISTIC REMEDIES ARE MUCH HEALTHIER THAN "TRADITIONAL MEDICINE."
DRINK IT AND YOU'LL FEEL BETTER. IT'S AN ANCIENT CHINESE REMEDY.
BLECH! IT TASTES LIKE THE HOT TUB! WHY CAN'T I HAVE AN ASPIRIN?
AND MAKE SURE THEY KNOW THAT COMPETITION IS A BUMMER.
WHAT'S THE SCORE?
WHO CARES? WE'RE PLAYING TO A THOUS
ARE YOU HIGH?
MAYBE AL
YOUR KIDS SHOULD BE ABLE TO WORK THROUGH ANY OTHER ISSUES THEY HAV AT THE WEEKLY ENCOUNTER GROUP.
THE SHOWER IS NOT A TV CHANNEL. IF I'M IN THERE, JUST KEEP WALKING, UNLESS YOU WANT A KICK IN THE NUTS!
THAT'S REALLY UPTIGHT, HONEY.
WHERE DID ALL THIS VIOLENCE COME FROM?
IF YOUR OPEN-MINDED PARENTING LEADS TO A PROFANITY-LACED TIRADE ABOUT FEELING ABANDONED, DON'T TAKE IT PERSONALLY. THEY'RE JUST ACTING OUT, LIKE ALL KIDS DO.
#@☆!!*?% ◮$&#!!!!
JUST REMEMBER, IT TOOK YEARS OF THERA TO EXPRESS YOURSELF THAT OPENLY, AN YOUR CHILD DOES IT ALREADY. AREN'T YOU PR

ADVERTISEMENT

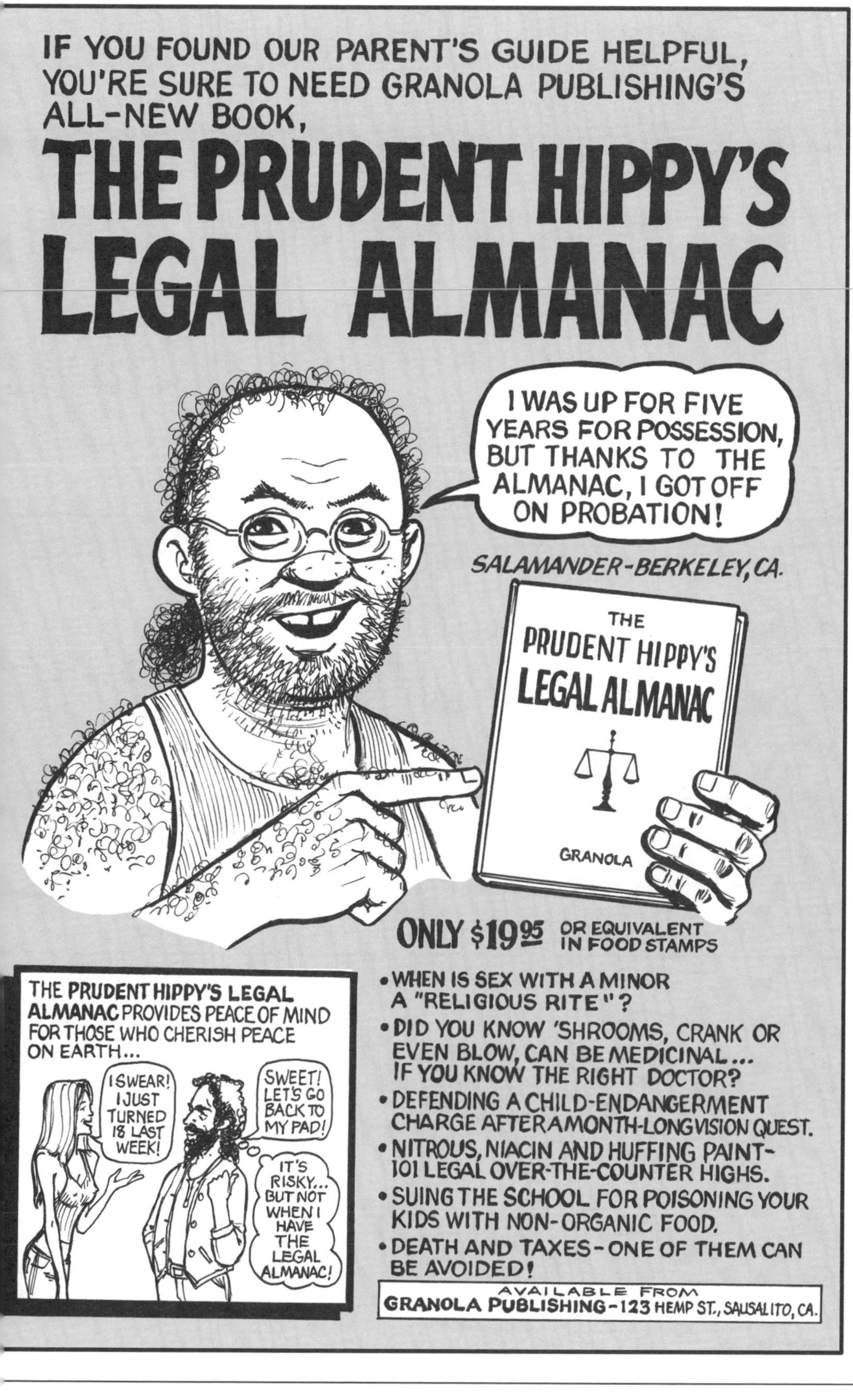
IF YOU FOUND OUR PARENT'S GUIDE HELPFUL, YOU'RE SURE TO NEED GRANOLA PUBLISHING'S ALL-NEW BOOK,
THE PRUDENT HIPPY'S LEGAL ALMANAC
I WAS UP FOR FIVE YEARS FOR POSSESSION, BUT THANKS TO THE ALMANAC, I GOT OFF ON PROBATION!
SALAMANDER-BERKELEY, CA.
THE PRUDENT HIPPY'S LEGAL ALMANAC
GRANOLA
ONLY $19.95 OR EQUIVALENT IN FOOD STAMPS
THE PRUDENT HIPPY'S LEGAL ALMANAC PROVIDES PEACE OF MIND FOR THOSE WHO CHERISH PEACE ON EARTH...
I SWEAR! I JUST TURNED 18 LAST WEEK!
SWEET! LET'S GO BACK TO MY PAD!
IT'S RISKY... BUT NOT WHEN I HAVE THE LEGAL ALMANAC!
• WHEN IS SEX WITH A MINOR A "RELIGIOUS RITE"?
• DID YOU KNOW 'SHROOMS, CRANK OR EVEN BLOW, CAN BE MEDICINAL... IF YOU KNOW THE RIGHT DOCTOR?
• DEFENDING A CHILD-ENDANGERMENT CHARGE AFTER A MONTH-LONG VISION QUEST.
• NITROUS, NIACIN AND HUFFING PAINT- 101 LEGAL OVER-THE-COUNTER HIGHS.
• SUING THE SCHOOL FOR POISONING YOUR KIDS WITH NON-ORGANIC FOOD.
• DEATH AND TAXES - ONE OF THEM CAN BE AVOIDED!
AVAILABLE FROM
GRANOLA PUBLISHING - 123 HEMP ST., SAUSALITO, CA.

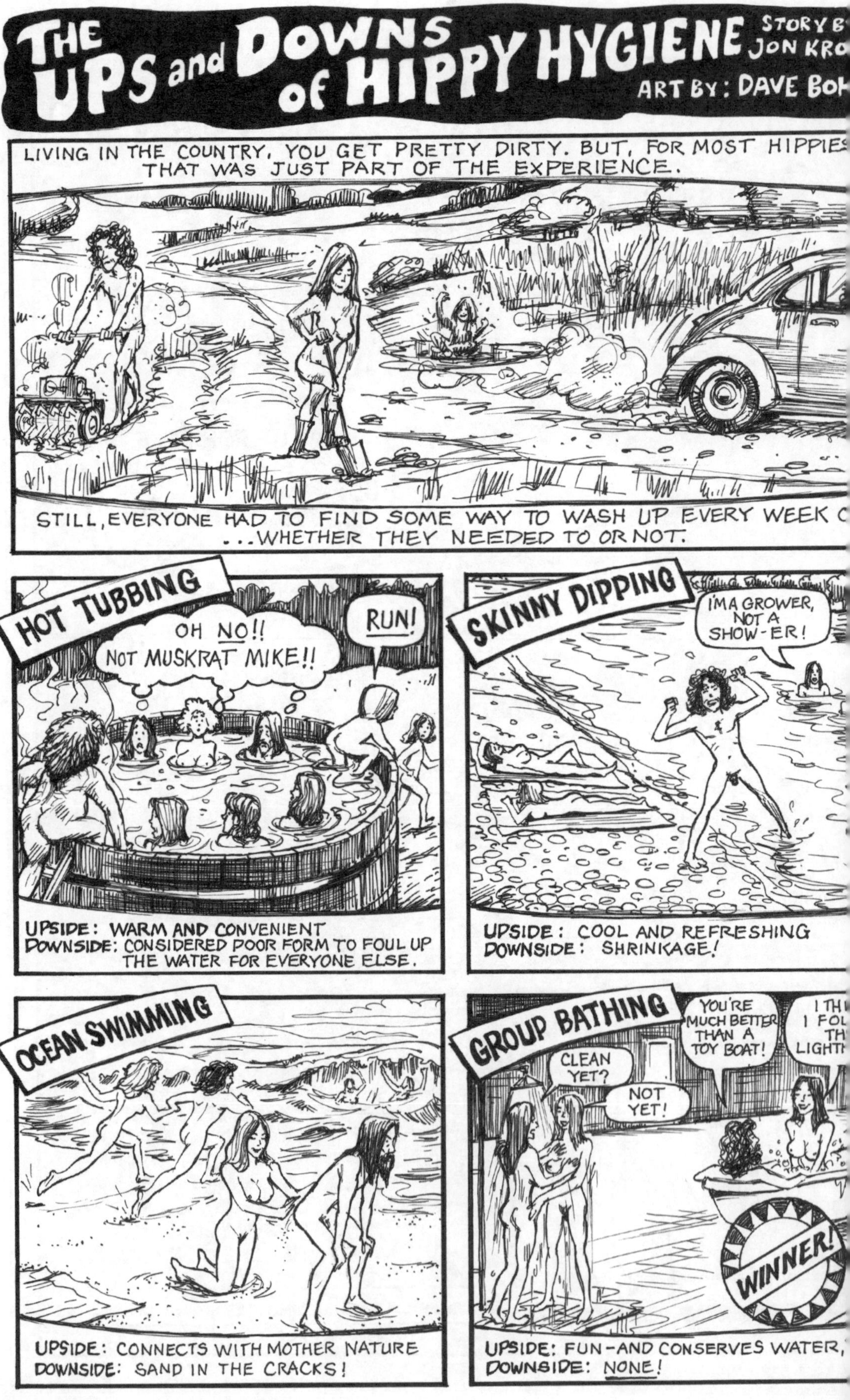

THE UPS and DOWNS of HIPPY HYGIENE
STORY B
JON KRO
ART BY: DAVE BOH
LIVING IN THE COUNTRY, YOU GET PRETTY DIRTY. BUT, FOR MOST HIPPIES THAT WAS JUST PART OF THE EXPERIENCE.
STILL, EVERYONE HAD TO FIND SOME WAY TO WASH UP EVERY WEEK O ...WHETHER THEY NEEDED TO OR NOT.
HOT TUBBING
OH NO!! NOT MUSKRAT MIKE!!
RUN!
UPSIDE: WARM AND CONVENIENT
DOWNSIDE: CONSIDERED POOR FORM TO FOUL UP THE WATER FOR EVERYONE ELSE.
SKINNY DIPPING
I'M A GROWER, NOT A SHOW-ER!
UPSIDE: COOL AND REFRESHING
DOWNSIDE: SHRINKAGE!
OCEAN SWIMMING
UPSIDE: CONNECTS WITH MOTHER NATURE
DOWNSIDE: SAND IN THE CRACKS!
GROUP BATHING
CLEAN YET?
NOT YET!
YOU'RE MUCH BETTER THAN A TOY BOAT!
I TH I FOL TH LIGHT
WINNER!
UPSIDE: FUN-AND CONSERVES WATER,
DOWNSIDE: NONE!

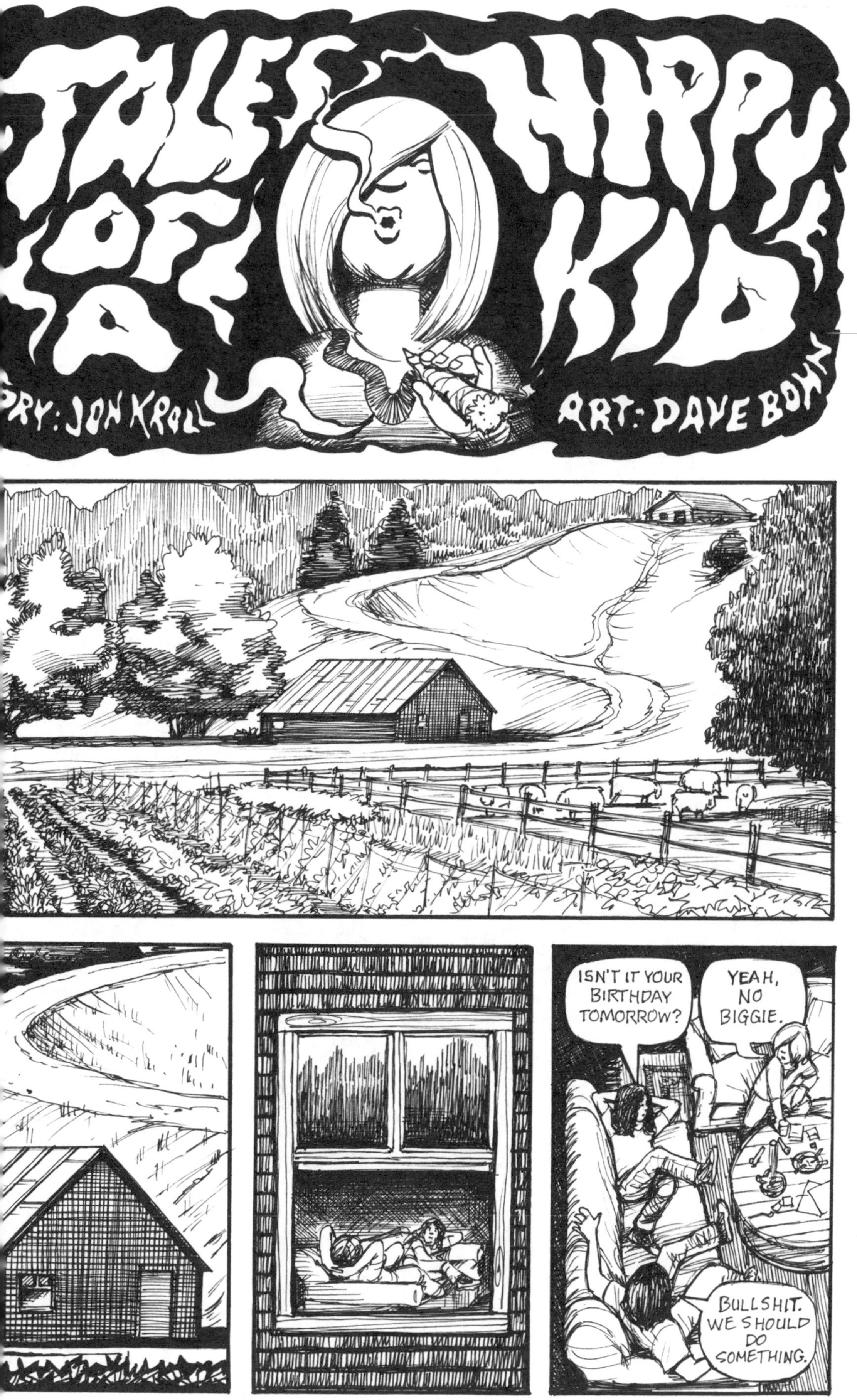
TALES OF A HIPPY KID
RY: JON KROLL
ART: DAVE BOH
ISN'T IT YOUR BIRTHDAY TOMORROW?
YEAH, NO BIGGIE.
BULLSHIT. WE SHOULD DO SOMETHING.

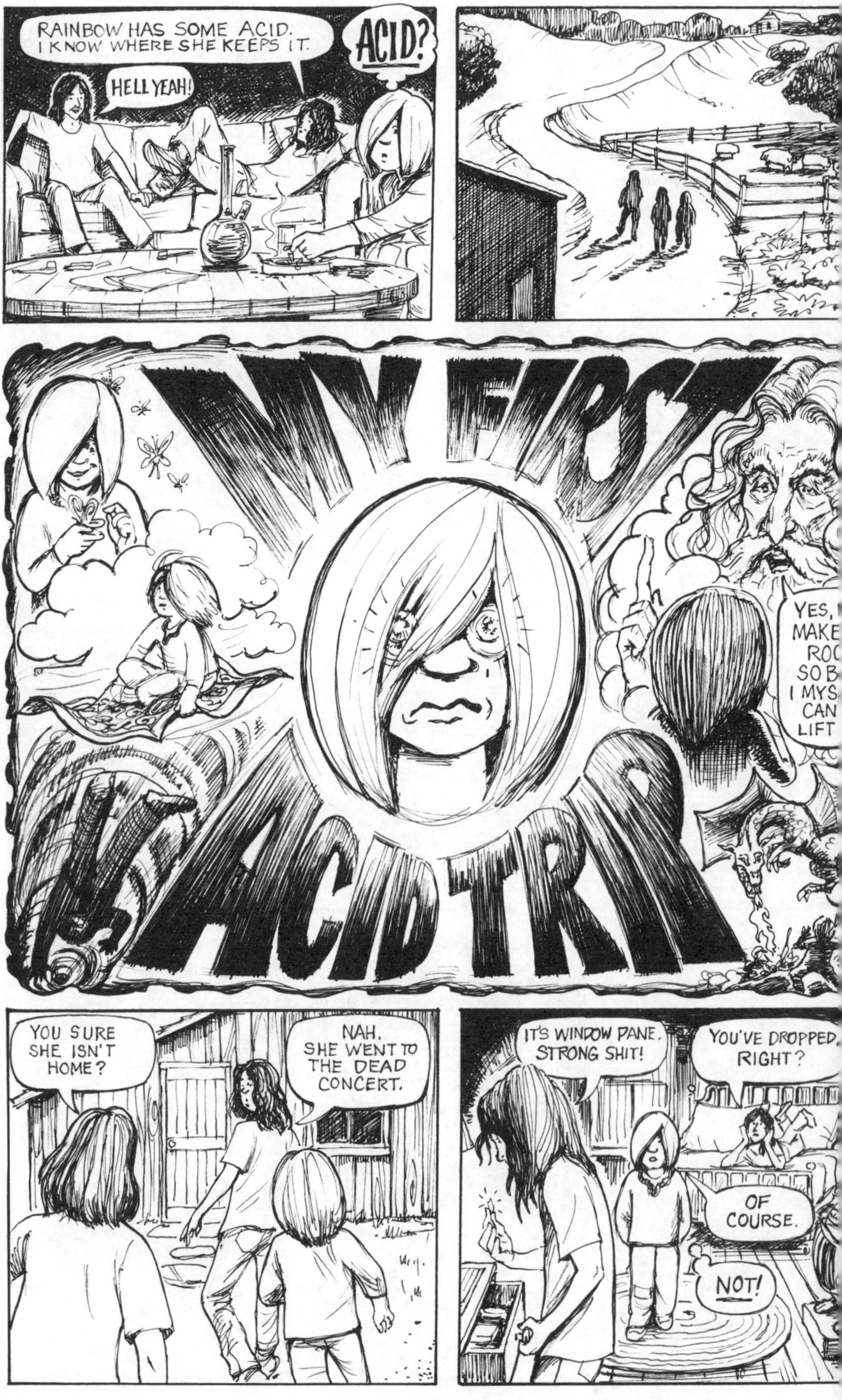

RAINBOW HAS SOME ACID. I KNOW WHERE SHE KEEPS IT.
HELL YEAH!
ACID?
MY FIRST ACID TRIP
YOU SURE SHE ISN'T HOME?
NAH, SHE WENT TO THE DEAD CONCERT.
IT'S WINDOW PANE. STRONG SHIT!
YOU'VE DROPPED, RIGHT?
OF COURSE.
NOT!

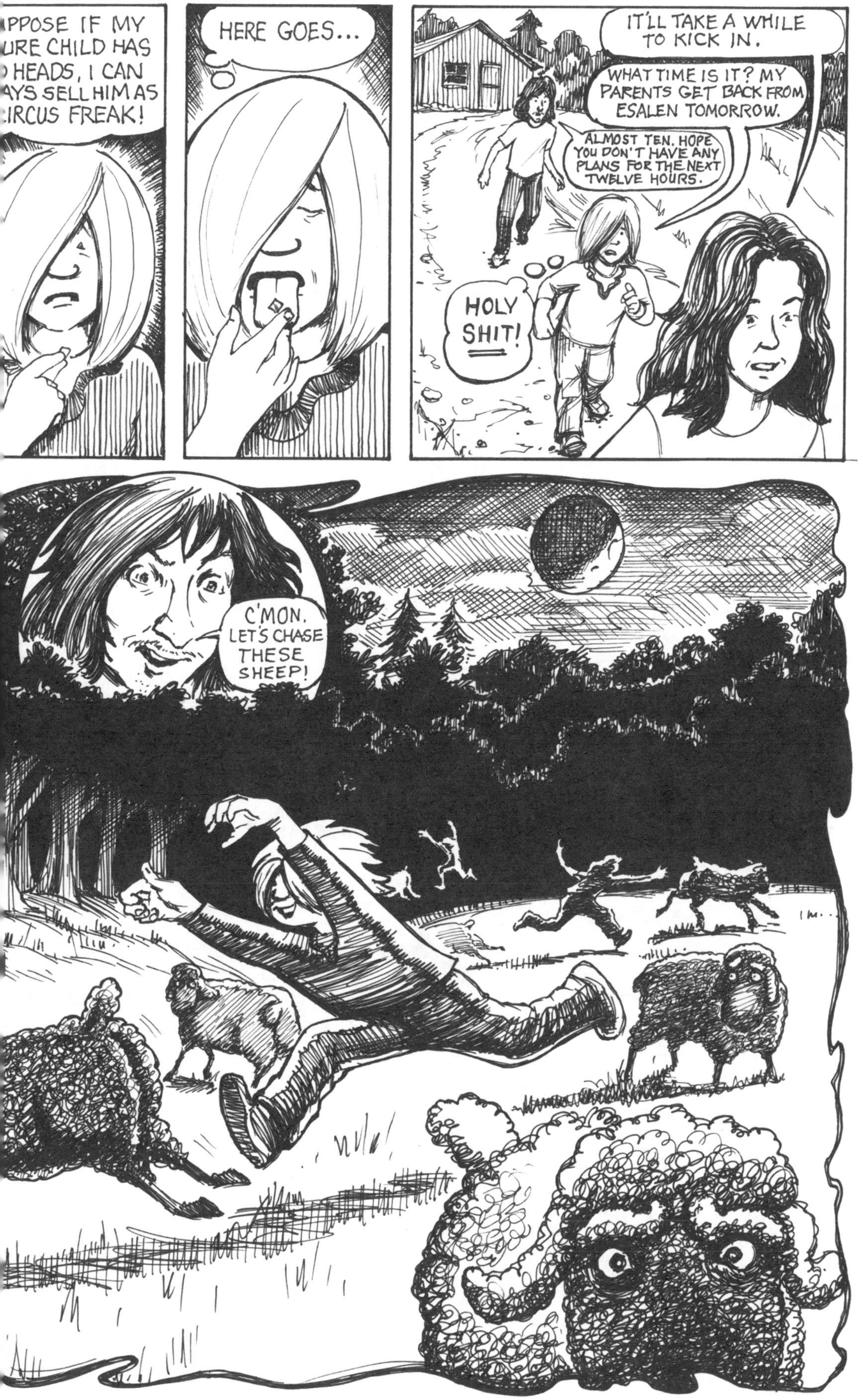
PPOSE IF MY URE CHILD HAS HEADS, I CAN AYS SELL HIM AS IRCUS FREAK!
HERE GOES...
IT'LL TAKE A WHILE TO KICK IN.
WHAT TIME IS IT? MY PARENTS GET BACK FROM ESALEN TOMORROW.
ALMOST TEN. HOPE YOU DON'T HAVE ANY PLANS FOR THE NEXT TWELVE HOURS.
HOLY SHIT!
C'MON. LET'S CHASE THESE SHEEP!

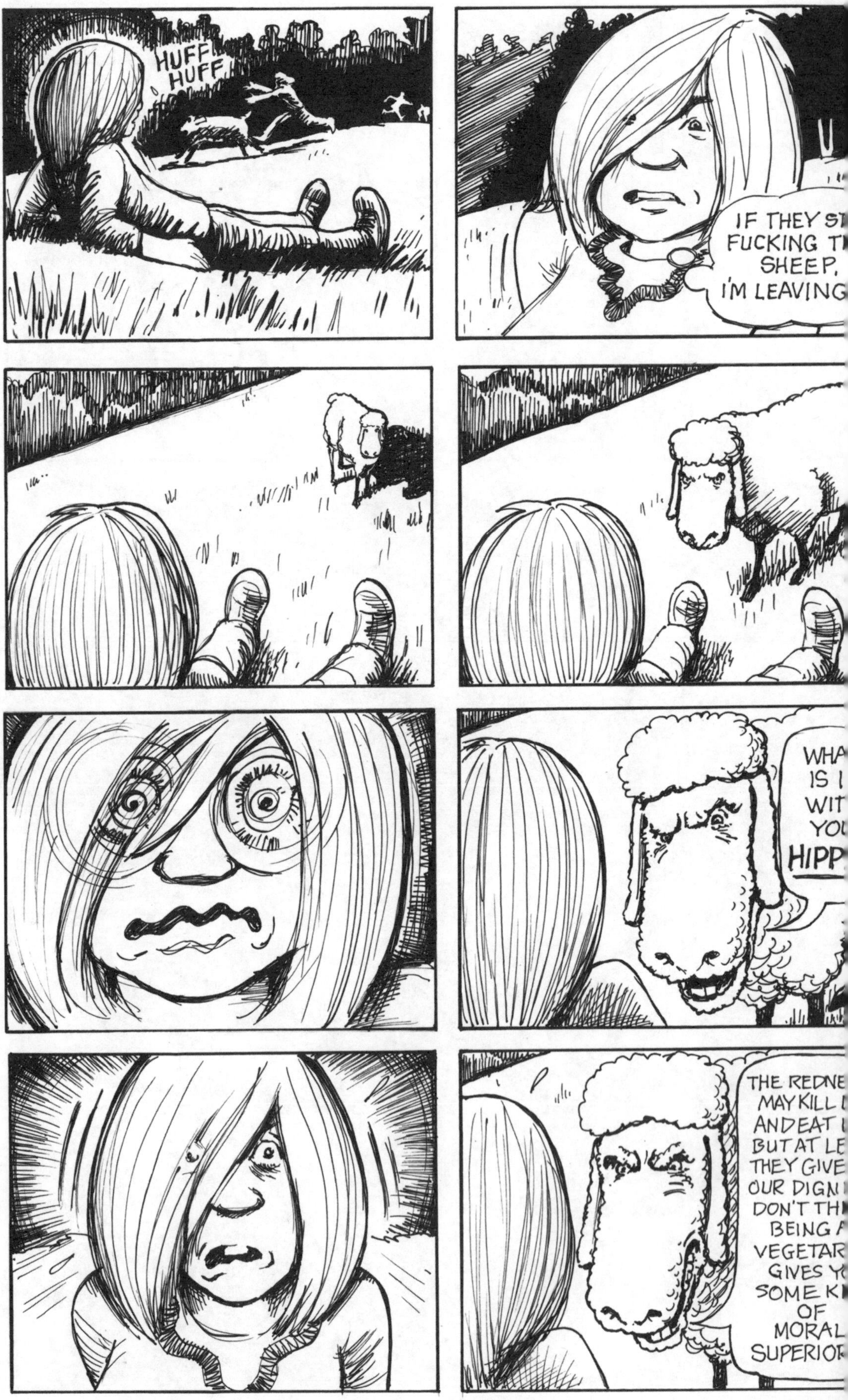
HUFF HUFF
IF THEY ST
FUCKING T
SHEEP,
I'M LEAVING
WHA
IS I
WIT
YOU
HIPP
THE REDNE
MAY KILL
AND EAT
BUT AT LE
THEY GIVE
OUR DIGN
DON'T TH
BEING A
VEGETAR
GIVES Y
SOME K
OF
MORAL
SUPERIOR

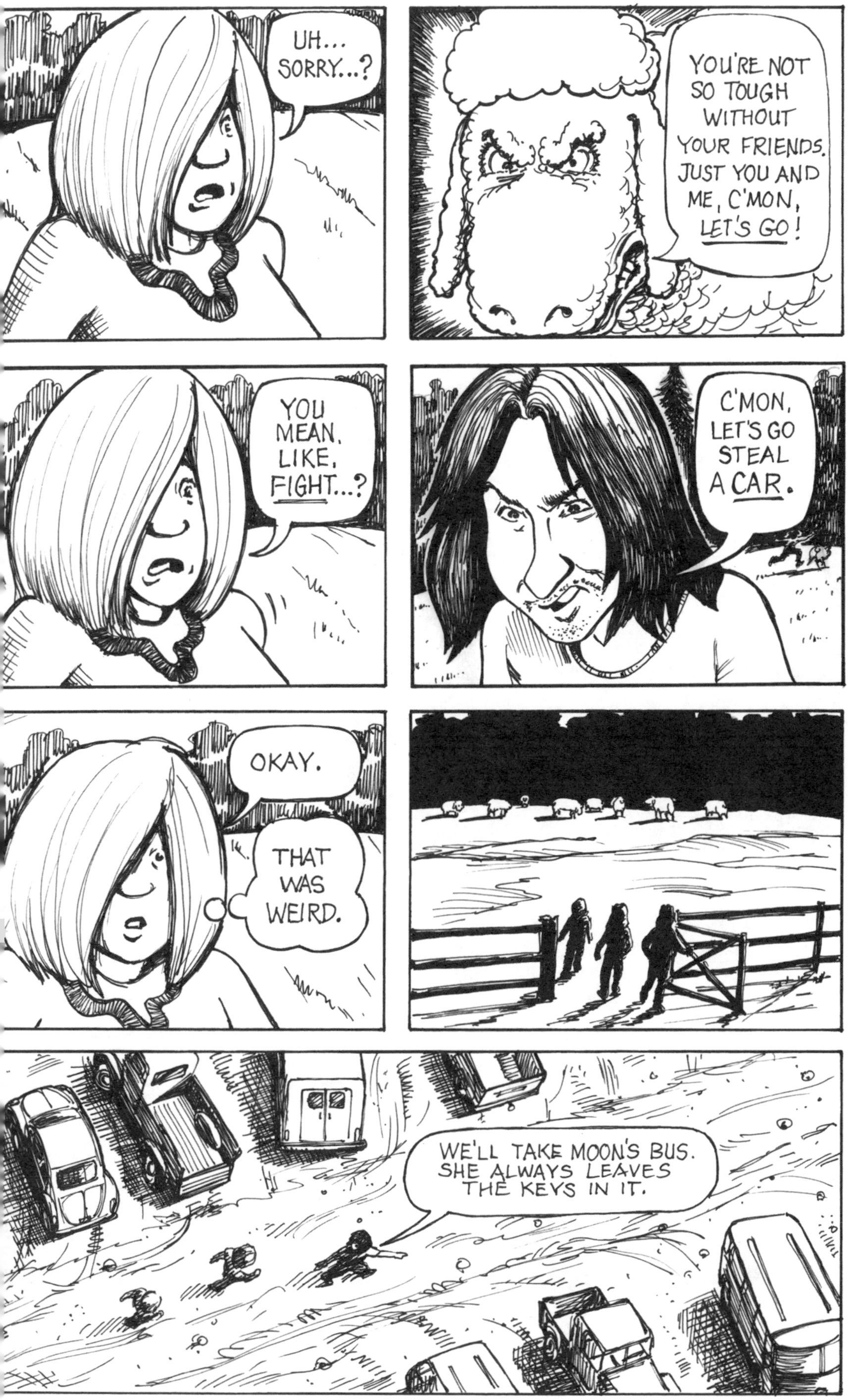
UH... SORRY...?
YOU'RE NOT SO TOUGH WITHOUT YOUR FRIENDS. JUST YOU AND ME, C'MON, LET'S GO!
YOU MEAN, LIKE, FIGHT...?
C'MON, LET'S GO STEAL A CAR.
OKAY.
THAT WAS WEIRD.
WE'LL TAKE MOON'S BUS. SHE ALWAYS LEAVES THE KEYS IN IT.

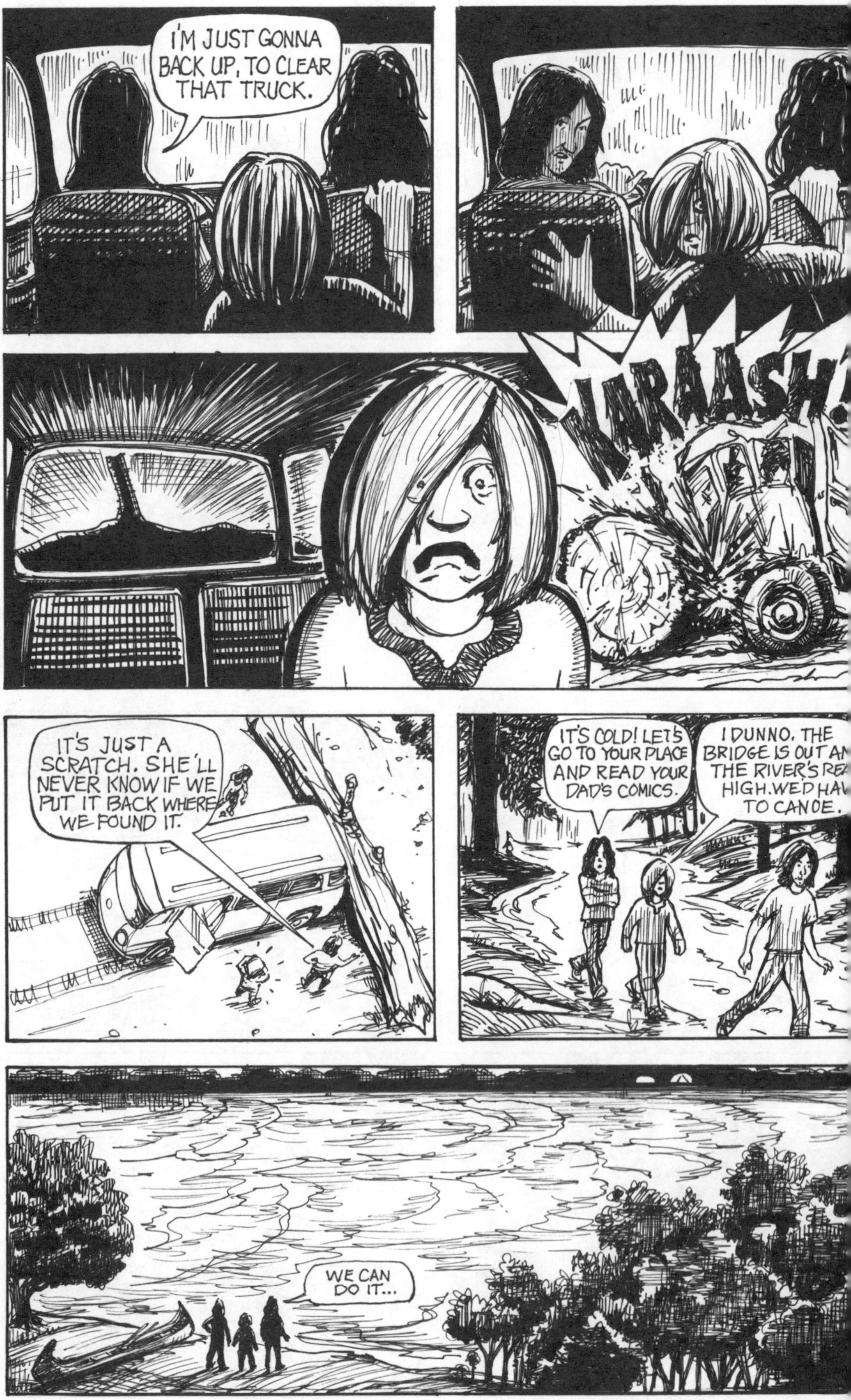
I'M JUST GONNA BACK UP, TO CLEAR THAT TRUCK.
KARAASH!
IT'S JUST A SCRATCH. SHE'LL NEVER KNOW IF WE PUT IT BACK WHERE WE FOUND IT.
IT'S COLD! LET'S GO TO YOUR PLACE AND READ YOUR DAD'S COMICS.
I DUNNO. THE BRIDGE IS OUT AN THE RIVER'S RE HIGH. WE'D HAV TO CANOE.
WE CAN DO IT...

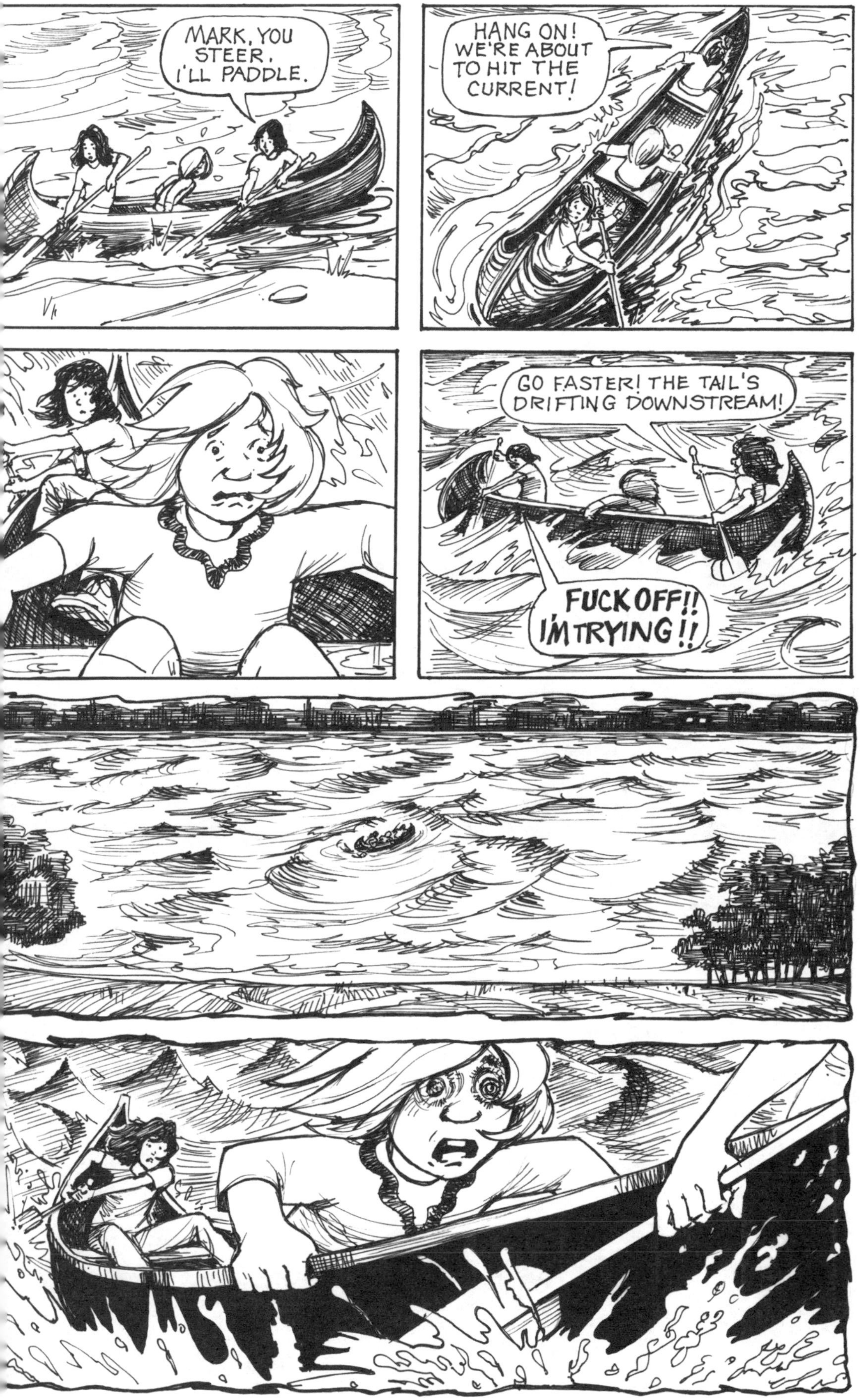
MARK, YOU STEER. I'LL PADDLE.
HANG ON! WE'RE ABOUT TO HIT THE CURRENT!
GO FASTER! THE TAIL'S DRIFTING DOWNSTREAM!
FUCK OFF!! I'M TRYING!!

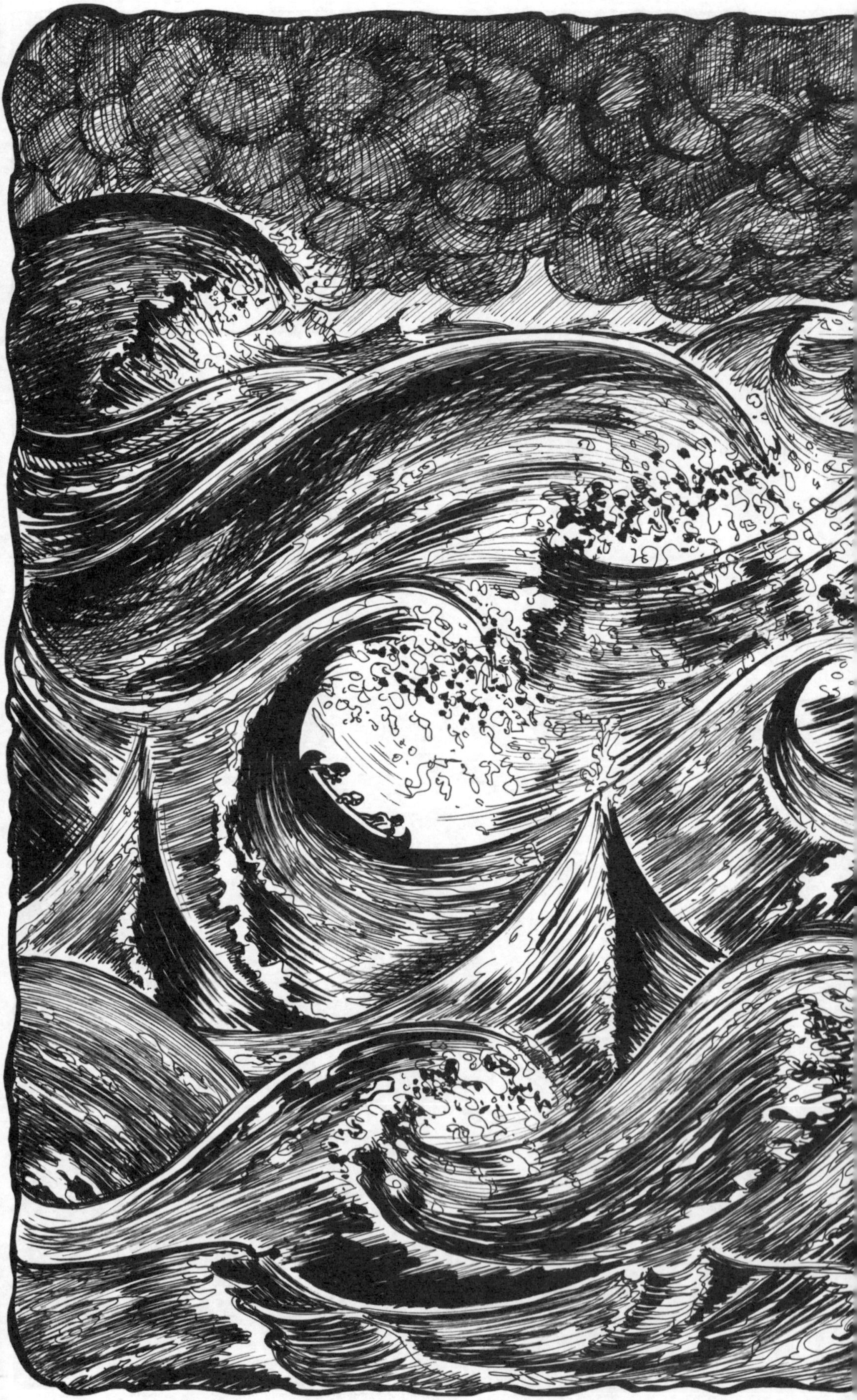

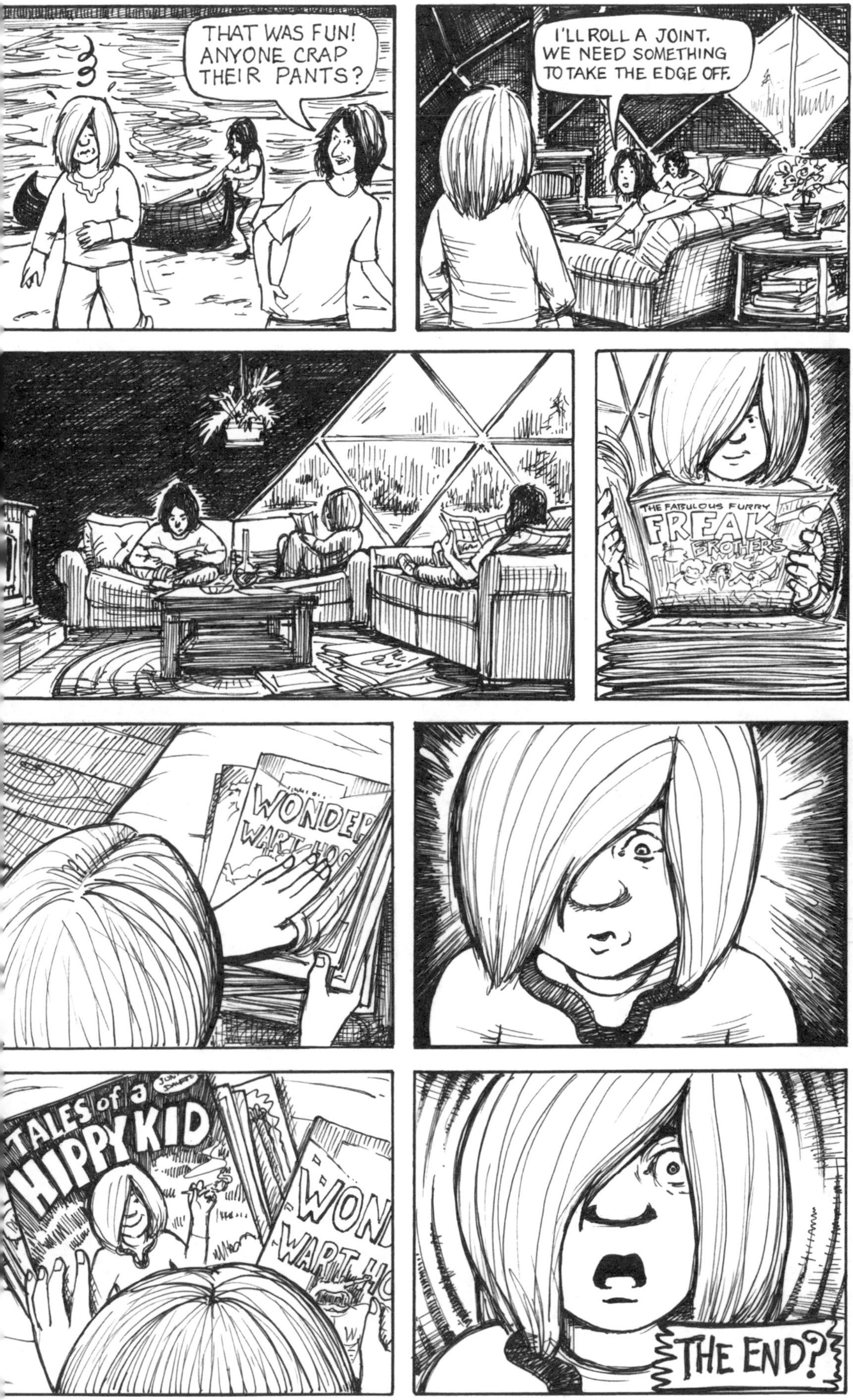
THAT WAS FUN! ANYONE CRAP THEIR PANTS?
I'LL ROLL A JOINT. WE NEED SOMETHING TO TAKE THE EDGE OFF.
THE FABULOUS FURRY FREAK BROTHERS
WONDER WART-HO
TALES of a HIPPY KID
WON WART-HO
THE END?

THE FILM FESTIVAL
STORY: JON KROL
ART: DAVE BOH
MY FRIEND DARRELL'S BRINGING SOME MOVIES UP FROM THE CITY. HE'S GOT "ATTACK OF THE MUSHROOM PEOPLE", "FALL OF THE HOUSE OF USHER" AND "YELLOW SUBMARINE."
BITCHIN'! LET'S HAVE A PARTY!
IF I CALL CHILD SERVICES ON MY PARENTS, CAN I COME TO THE CITY TO LIVE WITH YOU?
AND MOVE IN ON MY ACTION? NO CHANCE, YOU HOR LITTLE FUCKER
THE GENERATOR WILL LAST FOR ALL THREE MOVIES?
YOU BET. CHECK ON THE FOOD.
GAS
CHUG CHUG CHUG
REMEMBER, THESE ARE THE REGULAR BROWNIES AND THOSE ARE THE DOUBLE DOSE SPACE CAKES!
GOD, I'D LI TO MOTORBO THOSE MAMMAR
I'M NOT FEELING ANYTHING. I'D BETTER TAKE A COUPLE MORE.
HMM. WHICH WERE THE STRONG ONES?
BURP!

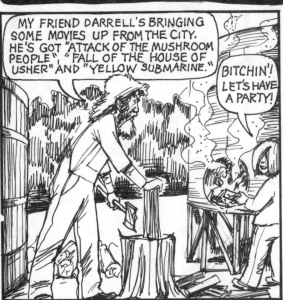

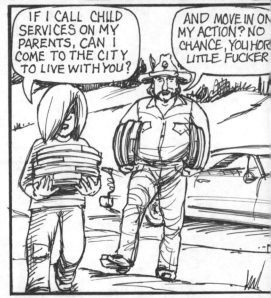

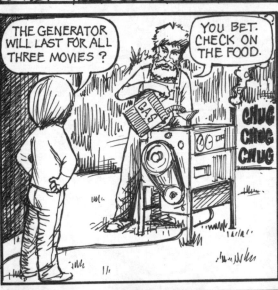

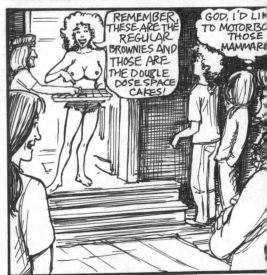

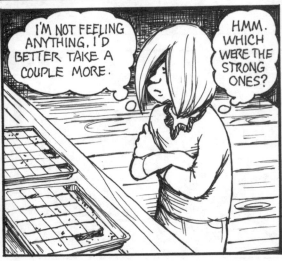

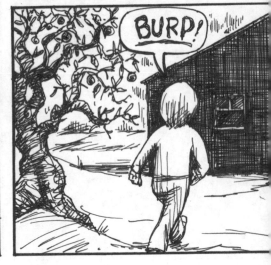

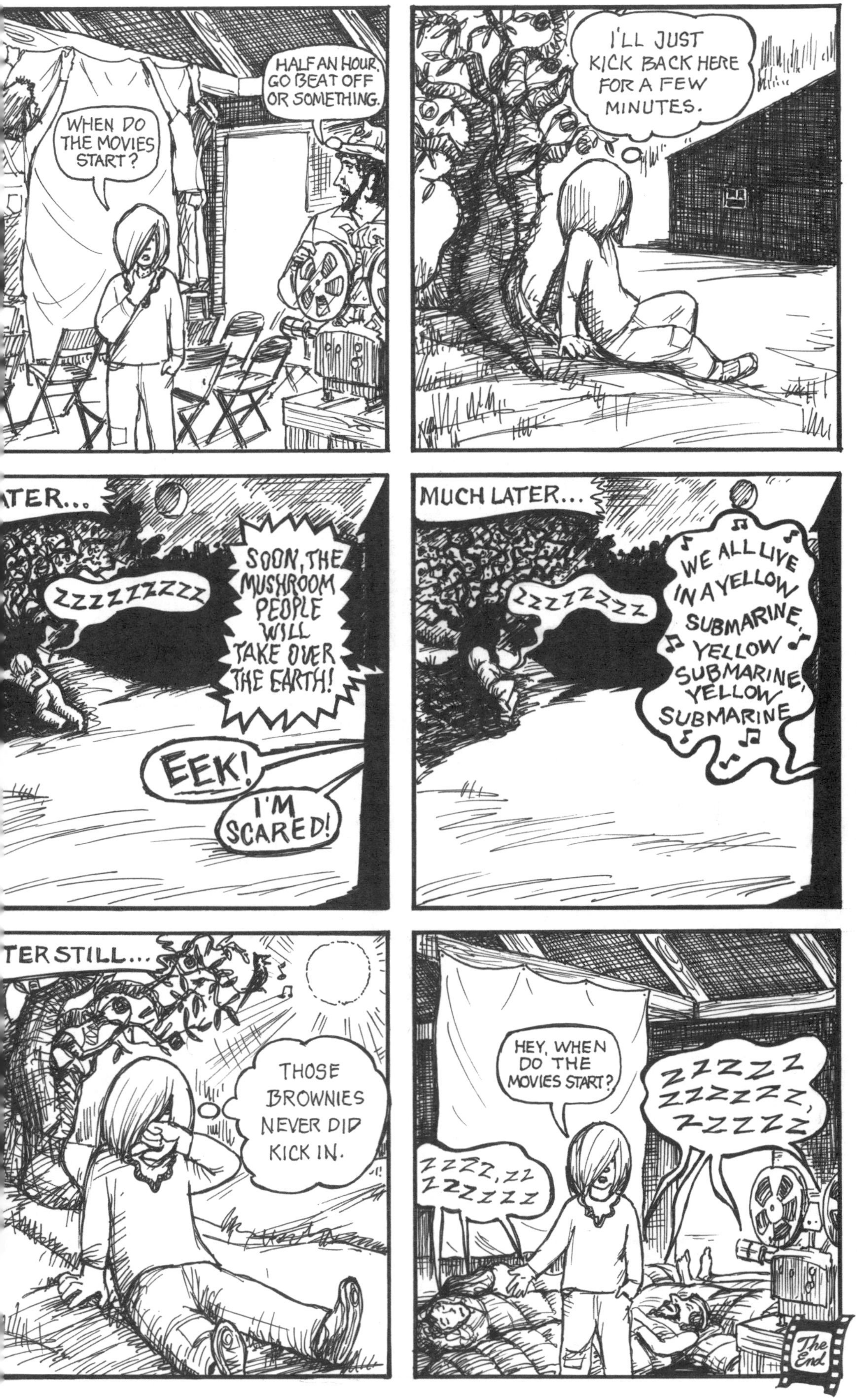
WHEN DO THE MOVIES START?
HALF AN HOUR. GO BEAT OFF OR SOMETHING.
I'LL JUST KICK BACK HERE FOR A FEW MINUTES.
ATER...
ZZZZZZZZZ
SOON, THE MUSHROOM PEOPLE WILL TAKE OVER THE EARTH!
EEK!
I'M SCARED!
MUCH LATER...
ZZZZZZZZ
WE ALL LIVE IN A YELLOW SUBMARINE, YELLOW SUBMARINE, YELLOW SUBMARINE
TER STILL...
THOSE BROWNIES NEVER DID KICK IN.
HEY, WHEN DO THE MOVIES START?
ZZZZ, ZZ ZZZZZZ
ZZZZZ ZZZZZZ, ZZZZZ
The End

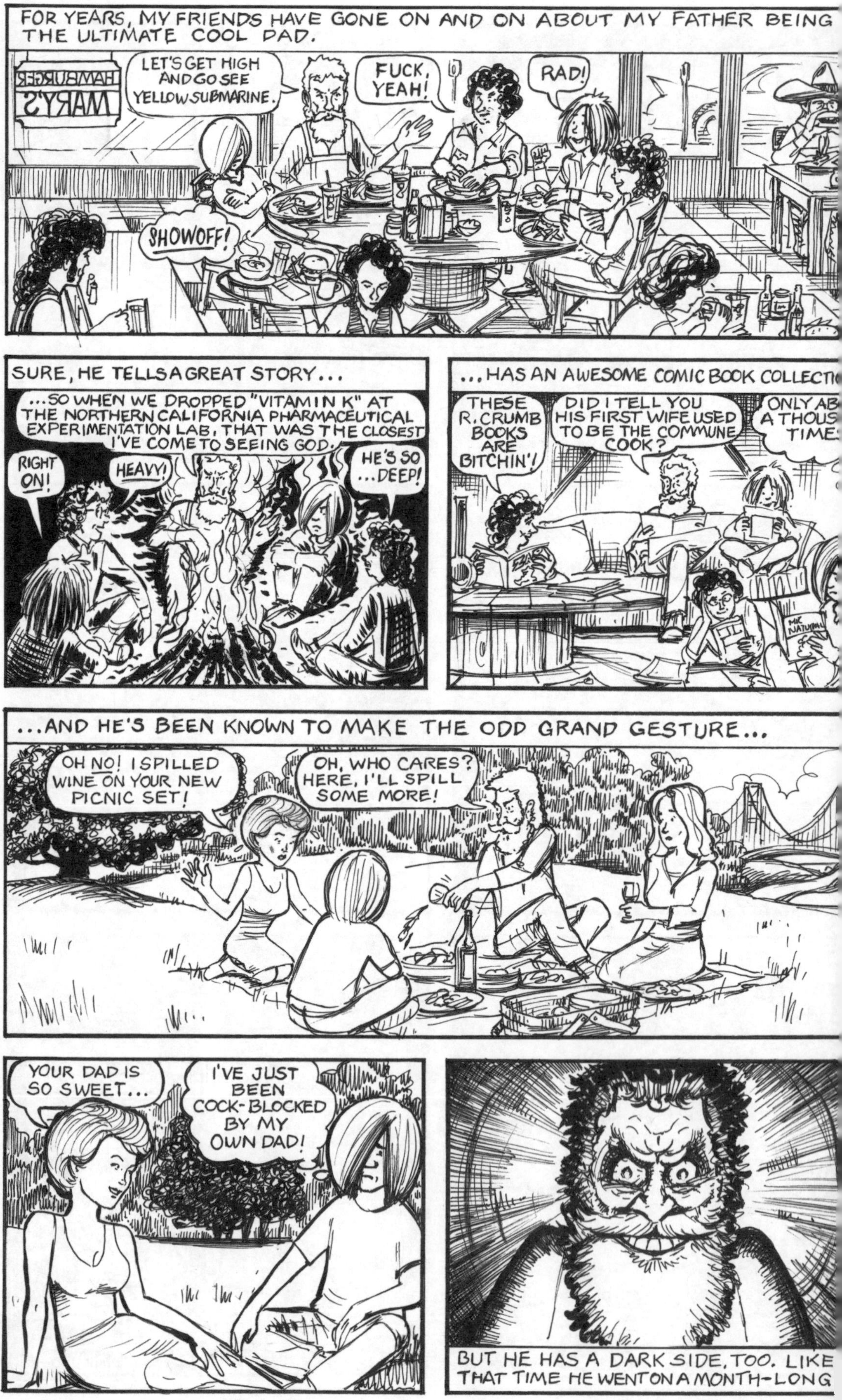
FOR YEARS, MY FRIENDS HAVE GONE ON AND ON ABOUT MY FATHER BEING THE ULTIMATE COOL DAD.
HAMBURGER MARY'S
LET'S GET HIGH AND GO SEE YELLOW SUBMARINE.
FUCK, YEAH!
RAD!
SHOWOFF!
SURE, HE TELLS A GREAT STORY...
...SO WHEN WE DROPPED "VITAMIN K" AT THE NORTHERN CALIFORNIA PHARMACEUTICAL EXPERIMENTATION LAB, THAT WAS THE CLOSEST I'VE COME TO SEEING GOD.
RIGHT ON!
HEAVY!
HE'S SO ...DEEP!
...HAS AN AWESOME COMIC BOOK COLLECTI
THESE R. CRUMB BOOKS ARE BITCHIN'!
DID I TELL YOU HIS FIRST WIFE USED TO BE THE COMMUNE COOK?
ONLY AB A THOUS TIME
...AND HE'S BEEN KNOWN TO MAKE THE ODD GRAND GESTURE...
OH NO! I SPILLED WINE ON YOUR NEW PICNIC SET!
OH, WHO CARES? HERE, I'LL SPILL SOME MORE!
YOUR DAD IS SO SWEET...
I'VE JUST BEEN COCK-BLOCKED BY MY OWN DAD!
BUT HE HAS A DARK SIDE, TOO. LIKE THAT TIME HE WENT ON A MONTH-LONG

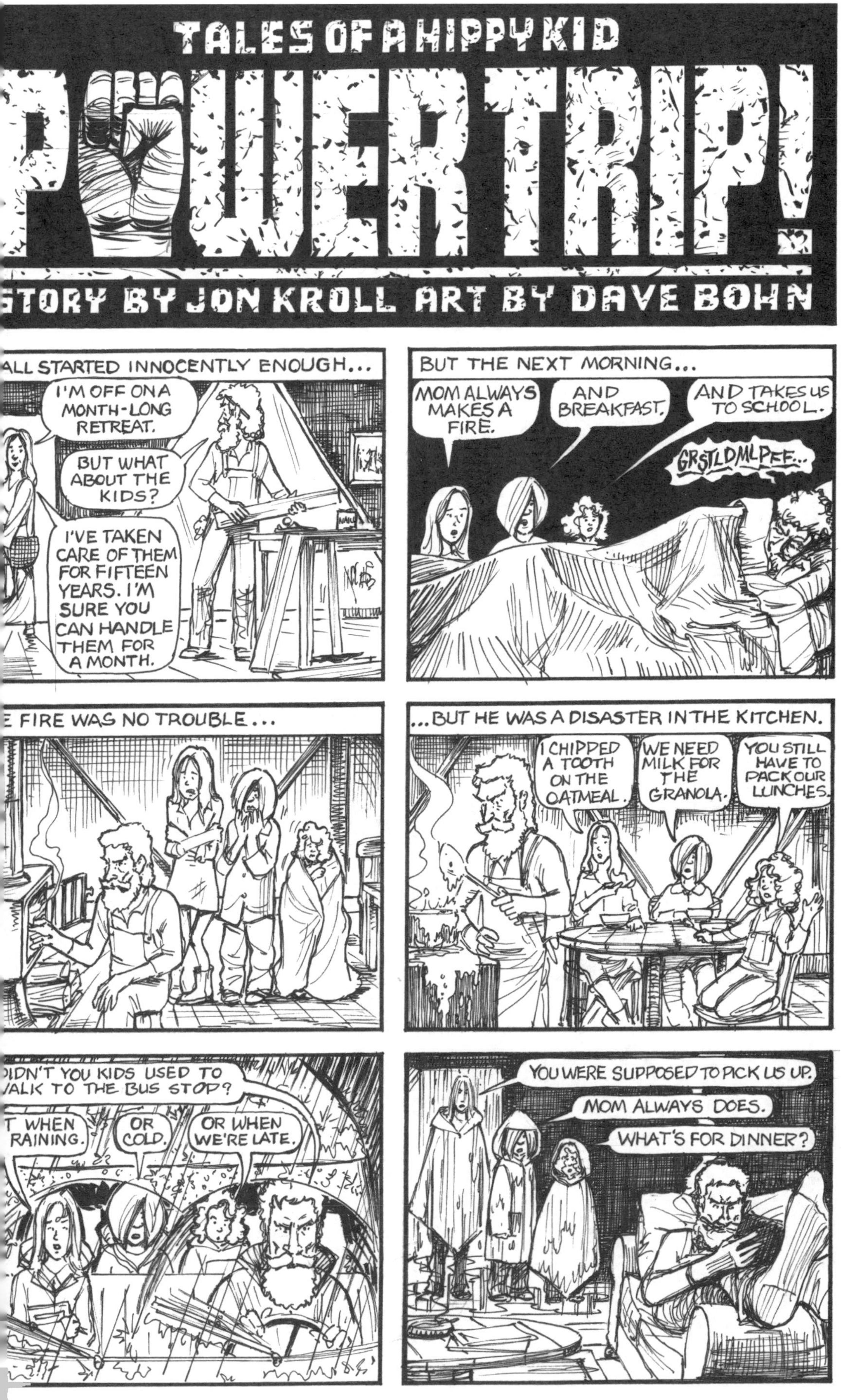
TALES OF A HIPPY KID
POWER TRIP!
STORY BY JON KROLL ART BY DAVE BOHN
ALL STARTED INNOCENTLY ENOUGH...
I'M OFF ON A MONTH-LONG RETREAT.
BUT WHAT ABOUT THE KIDS?
I'VE TAKEN CARE OF THEM FOR FIFTEEN YEARS. I'M SURE YOU CAN HANDLE THEM FOR A MONTH.
BUT THE NEXT MORNING...
MOM ALWAYS MAKES A FIRE.
AND BREAKFAST.
AND TAKES US TO SCHOOL.
GRSTLDMLPFF...
E FIRE WAS NO TROUBLE...
...BUT HE WAS A DISASTER IN THE KITCHEN.
I CHIPPED A TOOTH ON THE OATMEAL.
WE NEED MILK FOR THE GRANOLA.
YOU STILL HAVE TO PACK OUR LUNCHES.
IDN'T YOU KIDS USED TO VALK TO THE BUS STOP?
T WHEN RAINING.
OR COLD.
OR WHEN WE'RE LATE.
YOU WERE SUPPOSED TO PICK US UP.
MOM ALWAYS DOES.
WHAT'S FOR DINNER?

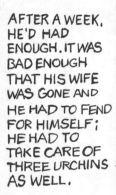

AFTER A WEEK, HE'D HAD ENOUGH. IT WAS BAD ENOUGH THAT HIS WIFE WAS GONE AND HE HAD TO FEND FOR HIMSELF; HE HAD TO TAKE CARE OF THREE URCHINS AS WELL.

I'M TIRED OF TAKING CARE OF YOU. IN FACT, I'M THE ONE WHO WORKS AROUND HERE. SO MAYBE IT'S TIME FOR YOU TO START TAKING CARE OF ME!

BUT YOU DON'T WORK! YOU JUST HANG AROUND HERE ALL DAY!

YEAH, OUR SCHOOL IS MORE LIKE WORK THAN WHAT YOU

YEA

I WORK HARD EVERY DAY. I WORK IN THE GARDEN. I FIX THE PLUMBING. I BUILT THIS HOUSE!!

I MILK THE GOATS!

AND I BRING IN THE FIREWOOD

YEAH!

FROM NOW ON, IT'S GOING TO BE DIFFERENT AROUND HERE. FROM NOW ON YOU MAKE YOUR OWN FIRE IN THE MORNING. IN FACT, I WANT YOU TO MAKE MINE, TOO! AND BRING ME A CUP OF TEA. THEN MAYBE I'LL GIVE YOU A RIDE TO SCHOOL!

I'VE GOT SOME POPCORN AND SOME CHOCOLATE, SO I'M GOING TO HAVE DINNER BY MYSELF TONIGHT. YOU GUYS ARE ON YOUR OWN!

SLAM!

FUCK YOU!

THIS IS BULLSHIT!

BRICKH

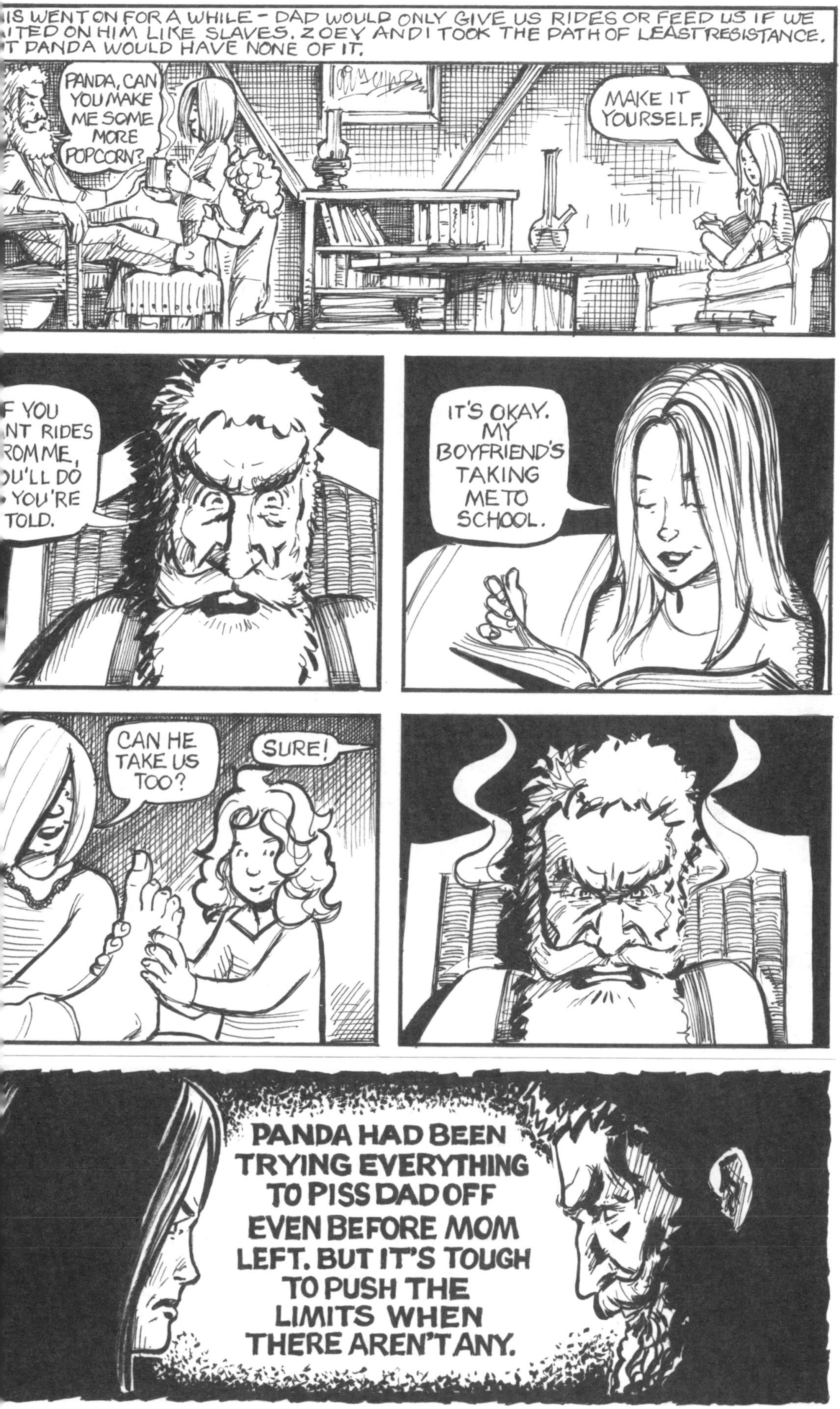
IS WENT ON FOR A WHILE - DAD WOULD ONLY GIVE US RIDES OR FEED US IF WE
ITED ON HIM LIKE SLAVES. ZOEY AND I TOOK THE PATH OF LEAST RESISTANCE.
T PANDA WOULD HAVE NONE OF IT.
PANDA, CAN YOU MAKE ME SOME MORE POPCORN?
MAKE IT YOURSELF.
F YOU NT RIDES ROM ME, OU'LL DO YOU'RE TOLD.
IT'S OKAY. MY BOYFRIEND'S TAKING ME TO SCHOOL.
CAN HE TAKE US TOO?
SURE!
PANDA HAD BEEN TRYING EVERYTHING TO PISS DAD OFF EVEN BEFORE MOM LEFT. BUT IT'S TOUGH TO PUSH THE LIMITS WHEN THERE AREN'T ANY.

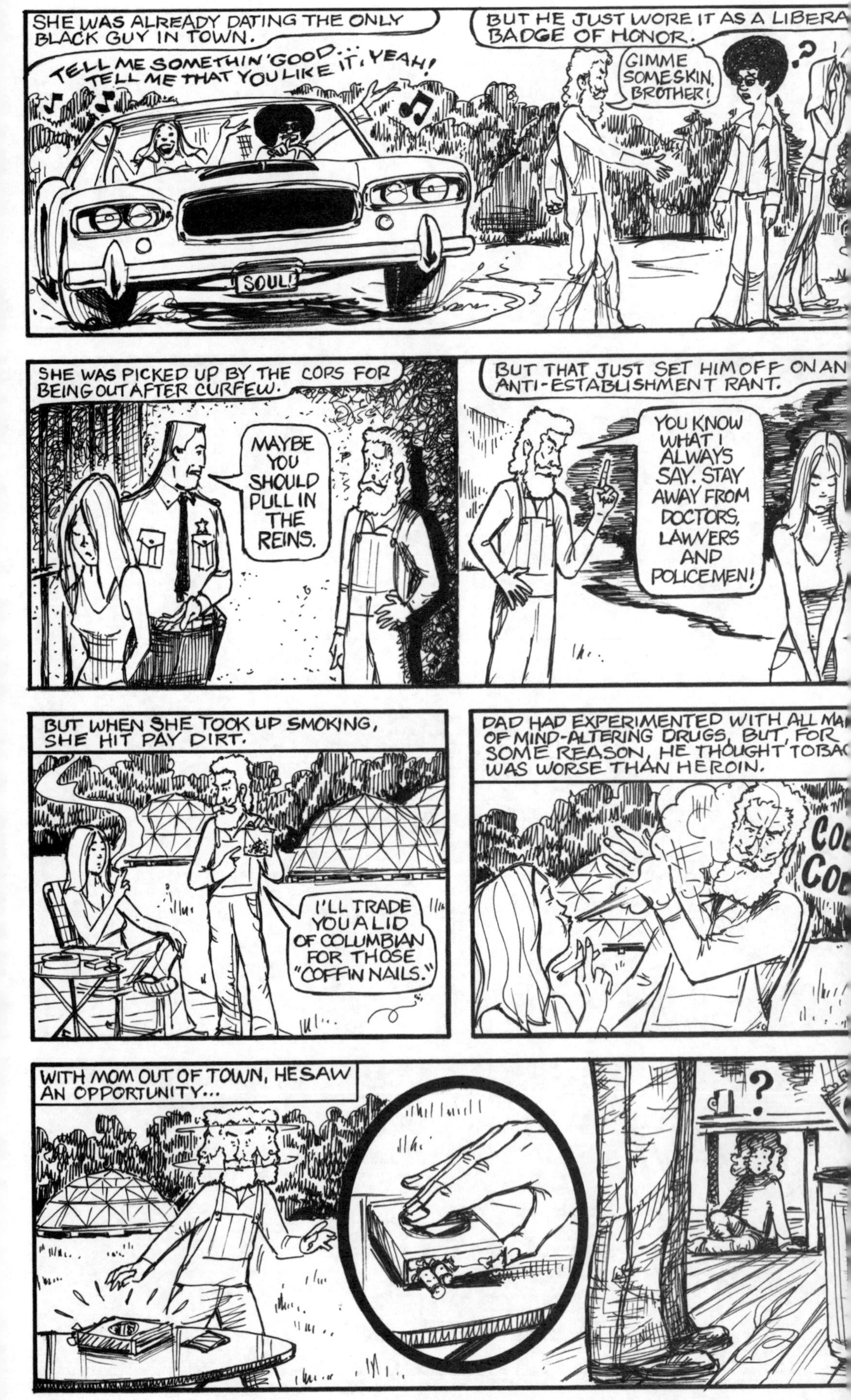
SHE WAS ALREADY DATING THE ONLY BLACK GUY IN TOWN.
TELL ME SOMETHIN' GOOD... TELL ME THAT YOU LIKE IT, YEAH!
SOUL!
BUT HE JUST WORE IT AS A LIBERA
BADGE OF HONOR.
GIMME SOME SKIN, BROTHER!
?
SHE WAS PICKED UP BY THE COPS FOR BEING OUT AFTER CURFEW.
MAYBE YOU SHOULD PULL IN THE REINS.
BUT THAT JUST SET HIM OFF ON AN
ANTI-ESTABLISHMENT RANT.
YOU KNOW WHAT I ALWAYS SAY. STAY AWAY FROM DOCTORS, LAWYERS AND POLICEMEN!
BUT WHEN SHE TOOK UP SMOKING, SHE HIT PAY DIRT.
I'LL TRADE YOU A LID OF COLUMBIAN FOR THOSE "COFFIN NAILS."
DAD HAD EXPERIMENTED WITH ALL MA
OF MIND-ALTERING DRUGS, BUT, FOR
SOME REASON, HE THOUGHT TOBAC
WAS WORSE THAN HEROIN.
WITH MOM OUT OF TOWN, HE SAW AN OPPORTUNITY...
?

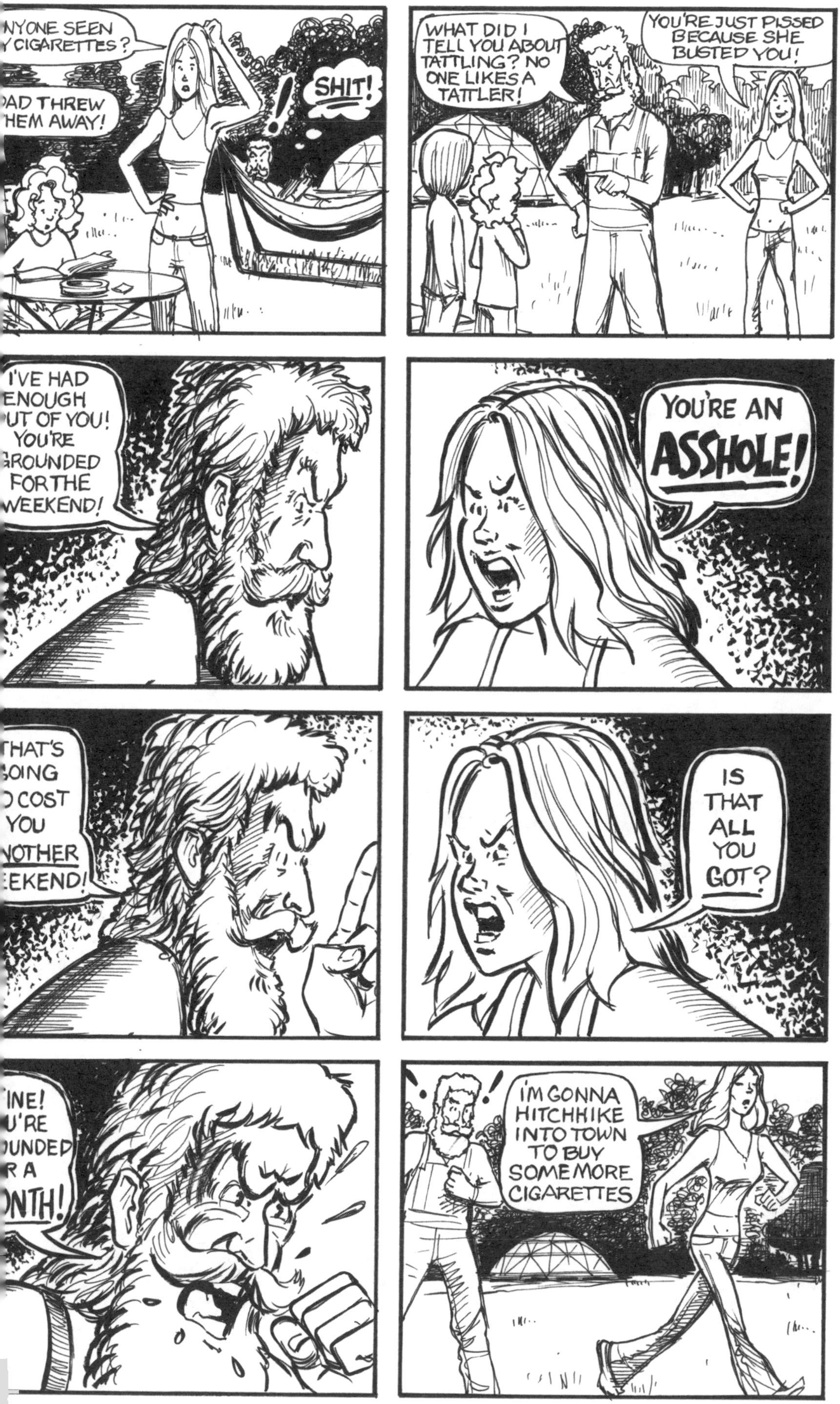
NYONE SEEN Y CIGARETTES?
AD THREW HEM AWAY!
SHIT!
WHAT DID I TELL YOU ABOUT TATTLING? NO ONE LIKES A TATTLER!
YOU'RE JUST PISSED BECAUSE SHE BUSTED YOU!
I'VE HAD ENOUGH UT OF YOU! YOU'RE ROUNDED FOR THE WEEKEND!
YOU'RE AN ASSHOLE!
THAT'S OING O COST YOU NOTHER EEKEND!
IS THAT ALL YOU GOT?
INE! U'RE UNDED R A NTH!
I'M GONNA HITCHHIKE INTO TOWN TO BUY SOME MORE CIGARETTES

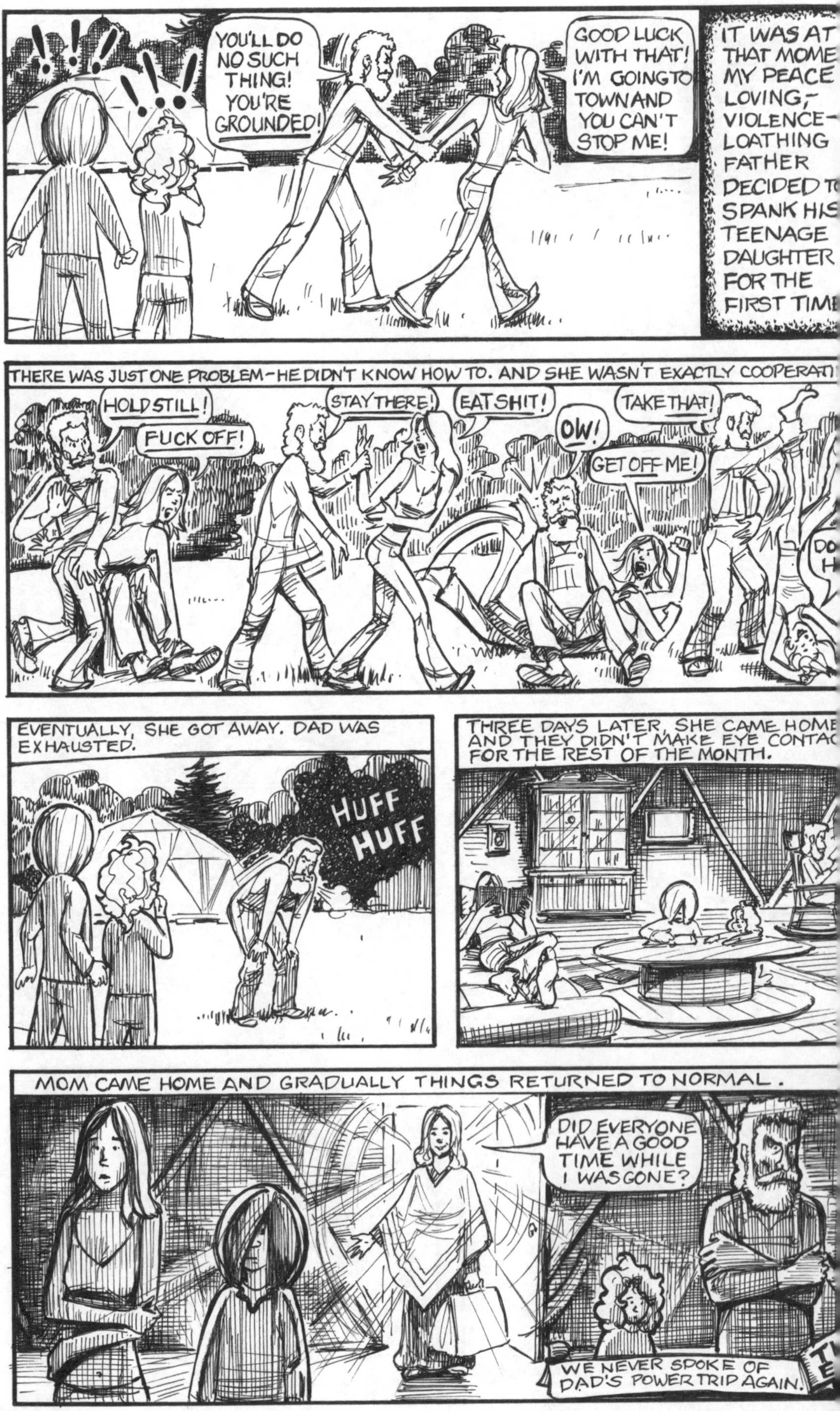

!!!
!!!
YOU'LL DO NO SUCH THING! YOU'RE GROUNDED!
GOOD LUCK WITH THAT! I'M GOING TO TOWN AND YOU CAN'T STOP ME!
IT WAS AT THAT MOME MY PEACE LOVING,- VIOLENCE- LOATHING FATHER DECIDED T SPANK HIS TEENAGE DAUGHTER FOR THE FIRST TIM
THERE WAS JUST ONE PROBLEM-HE DIDN'T KNOW HOW TO. AND SHE WASN'T EXACTLY COOPERATI
HOLD STILL!
FUCK OFF!
STAY THERE!
EAT SHIT!
OW!
GET OFF ME!
TAKE THAT!
EVENTUALLY, SHE GOT AWAY. DAD WAS EXHAUSTED.
HUFF HUFF
THREE DAYS LATER, SHE CAME HOME AND THEY DIDN'T MAKE EYE CONTA FOR THE REST OF THE MONTH.
MOM CAME HOME AND GRADUALLY THINGS RETURNED TO NORMAL.
DID EVERYONE HAVE A GOOD TIME WHILE I WAS GONE?
WE NEVER SPOKE OF DAD'S POWER TRIP AGAIN.

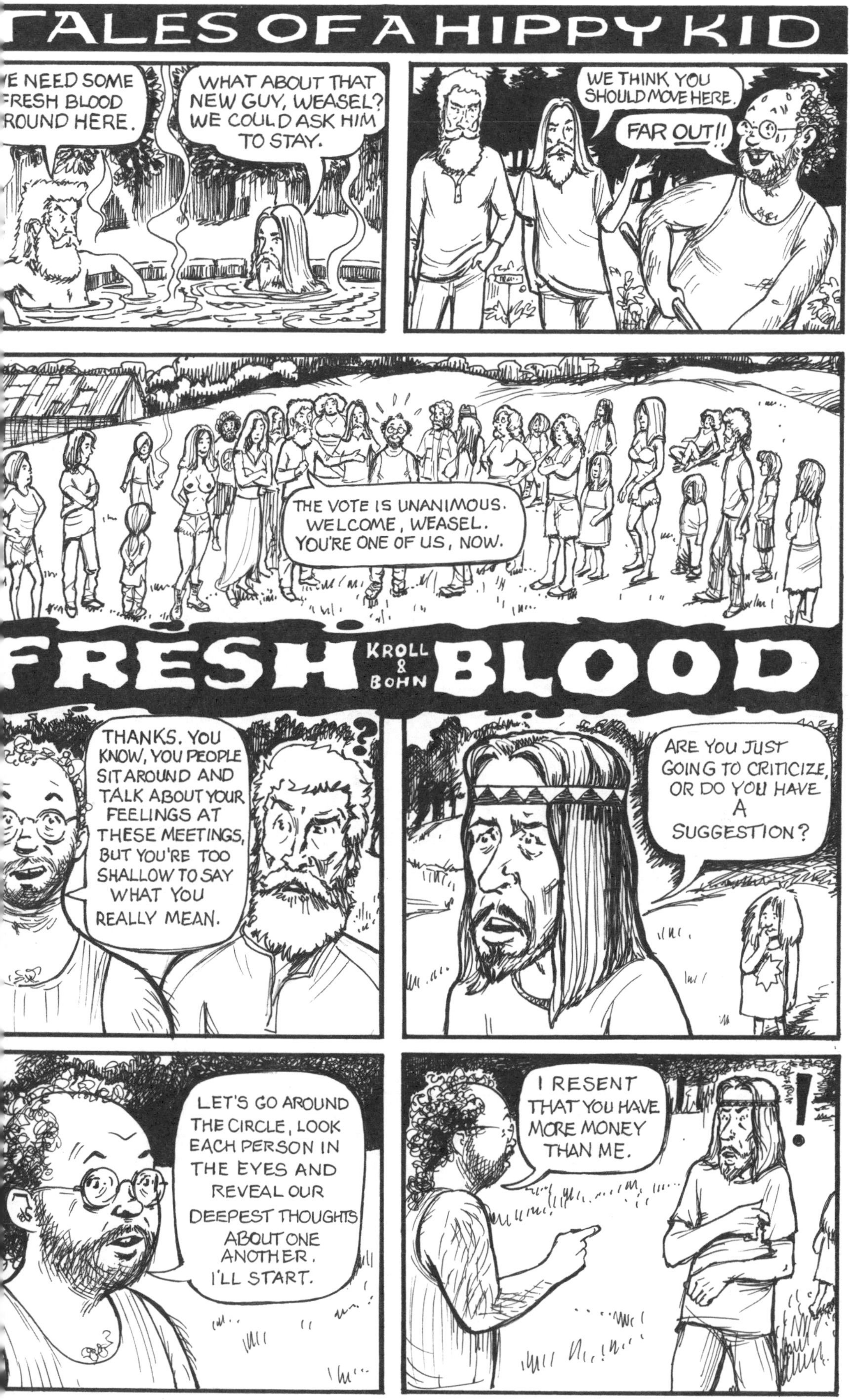
TALES OF A HIPPY KID
WE NEED SOME FRESH BLOOD AROUND HERE.
WHAT ABOUT THAT NEW GUY, WEASEL? WE COULD ASK HIM TO STAY.
WE THINK YOU SHOULD MOVE HERE.
FAR OUT!!
THE VOTE IS UNANIMOUS. WELCOME, WEASEL. YOU'RE ONE OF US, NOW.
FRESH BLOOD
KROLL & BOHN
THANKS. YOU KNOW, YOU PEOPLE SIT AROUND AND TALK ABOUT YOUR FEELINGS AT THESE MEETINGS, BUT YOU'RE TOO SHALLOW TO SAY WHAT YOU REALLY MEAN.
?
ARE YOU JUST GOING TO CRITICIZE, OR DO YOU HAVE A SUGGESTION?
LET'S GO AROUND THE CIRCLE, LOOK EACH PERSON IN THE EYES AND REVEAL OUR DEEPEST THOUGHTS ABOUT ONE ANOTHER. I'LL START.
I RESENT THAT YOU HAVE MORE MONEY THAN ME.
!

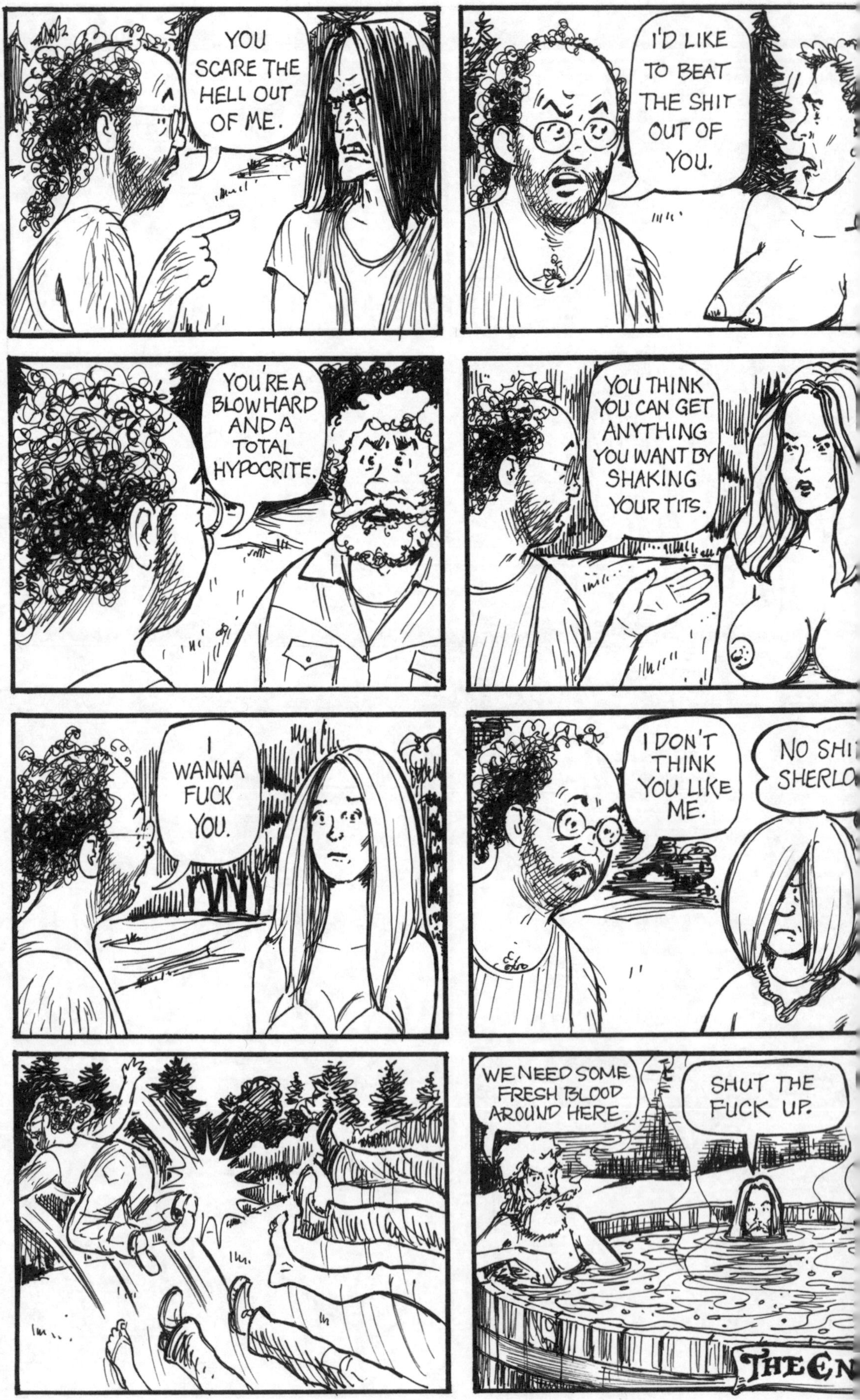
YOU SCARE THE HELL OUT OF ME.
I'D LIKE TO BEAT THE SHIT OUT OF YOU.
YOU'RE A BLOWHARD AND A TOTAL HYPOCRITE.
YOU THINK YOU CAN GET ANYTHING YOU WANT BY SHAKING YOUR TITS.
I WANNA FUCK YOU.
I DON'T THINK YOU LIKE ME.
NO SHI
SHERLO
WE NEED SOME FRESH BLOOD AROUND HERE.
SHUT THE FUCK UP.
THE EN

TALES of a HIPPY KID

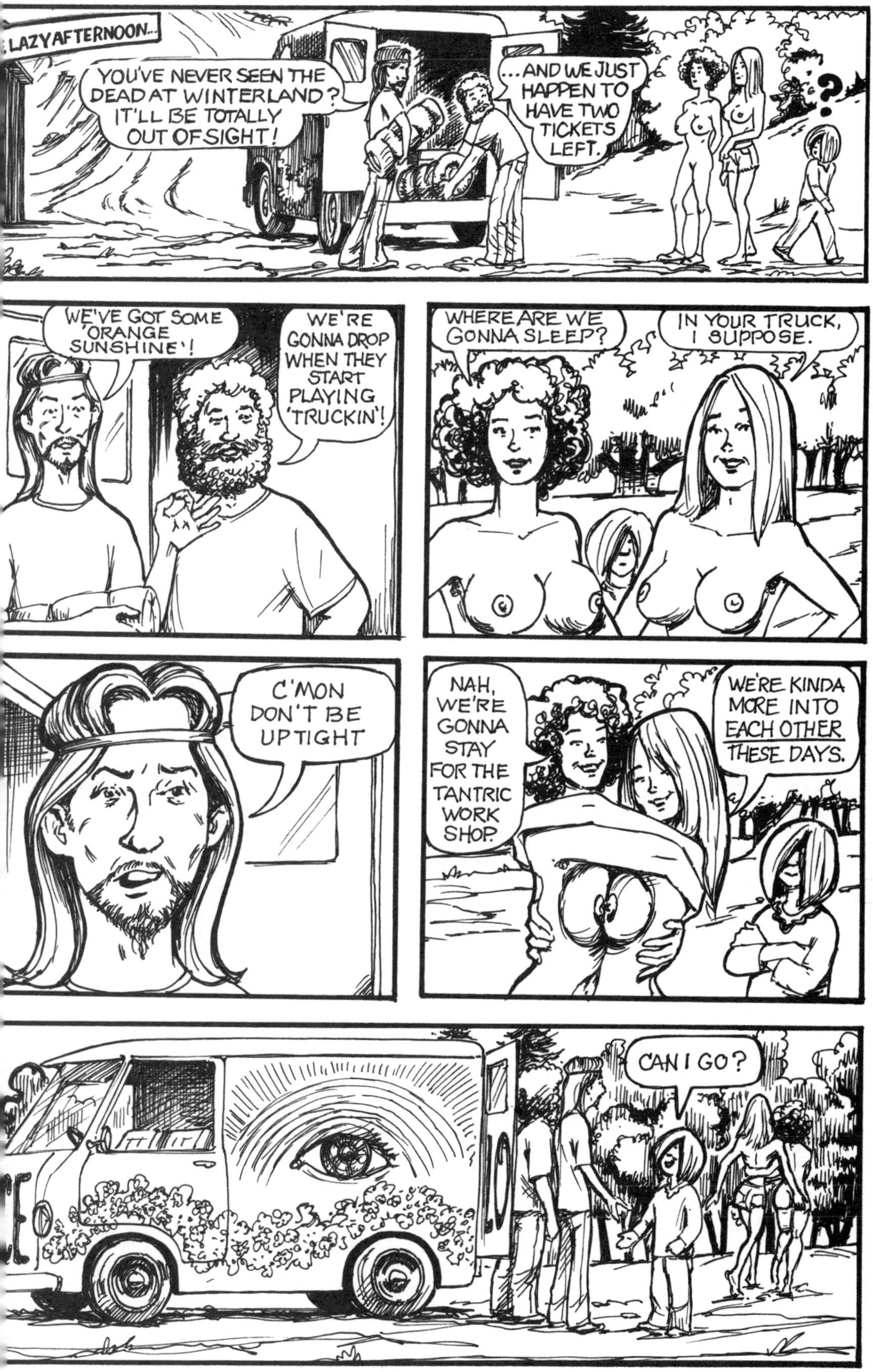

LAZY AFTERNOON..
YOU'VE NEVER SEEN THE DEAD AT WINTERLAND? IT'LL BE TOTALLY OUT OF SIGHT!
...AND WE JUST HAPPEN TO HAVE TWO TICKETS LEFT.
?
WE'VE GOT SOME 'ORANGE SUNSHINE'!
WE'RE GONNA DROP WHEN THEY START PLAYING 'TRUCKIN'!
WHERE ARE WE GONNA SLEEP?
IN YOUR TRUCK, I SUPPOSE.
C'MON DON'T BE UPTIGHT
NAH, WE'RE GONNA STAY FOR THE TANTRIC WORK SHOP.
WE'RE KINDA MORE INTO EACH OTHER THESE DAYS.
CAN I GO?

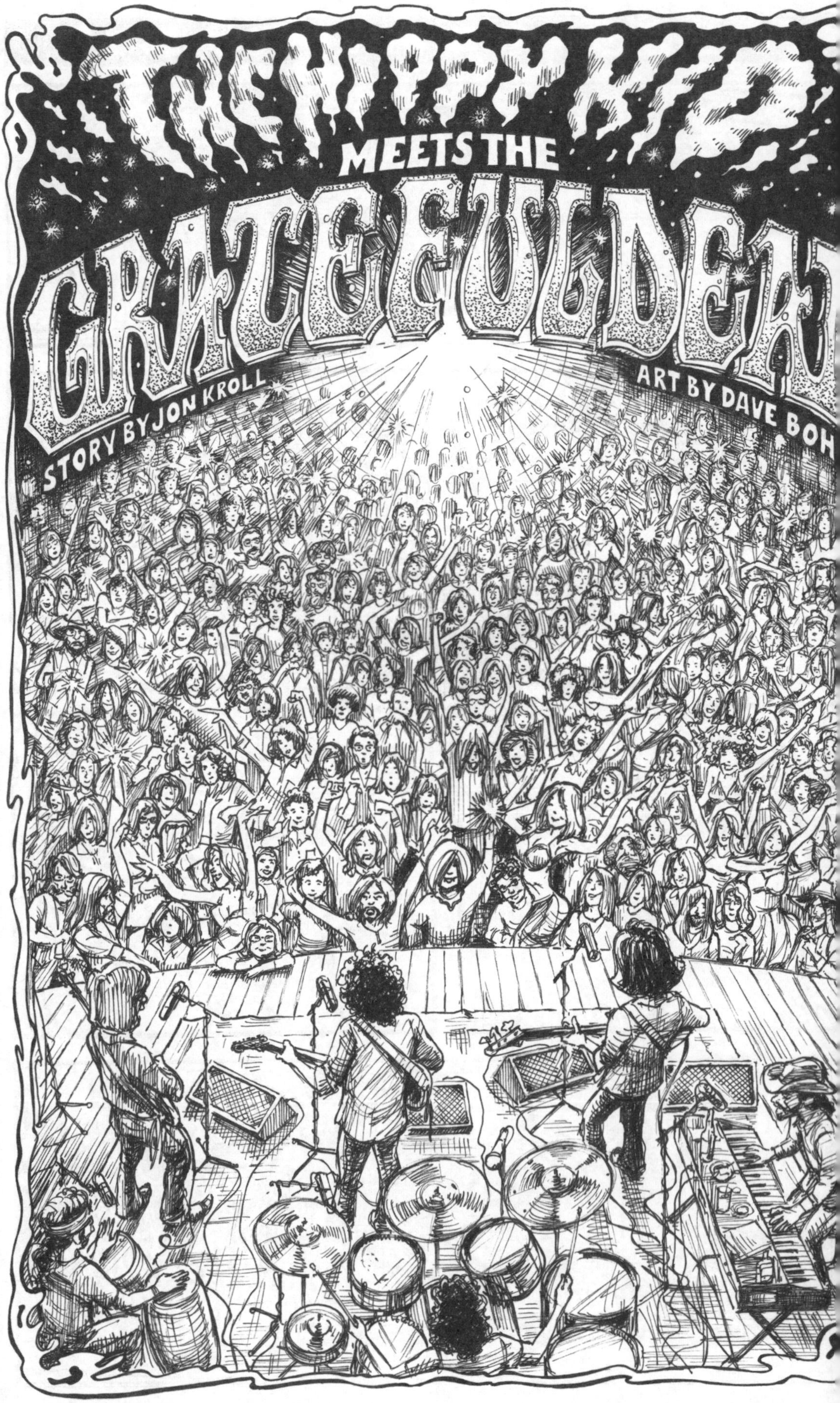
THE HIPPY KID
MEETS THE
GRATEFUL DEA
STORY BY JON KROLL
ART BY DAVE BOH

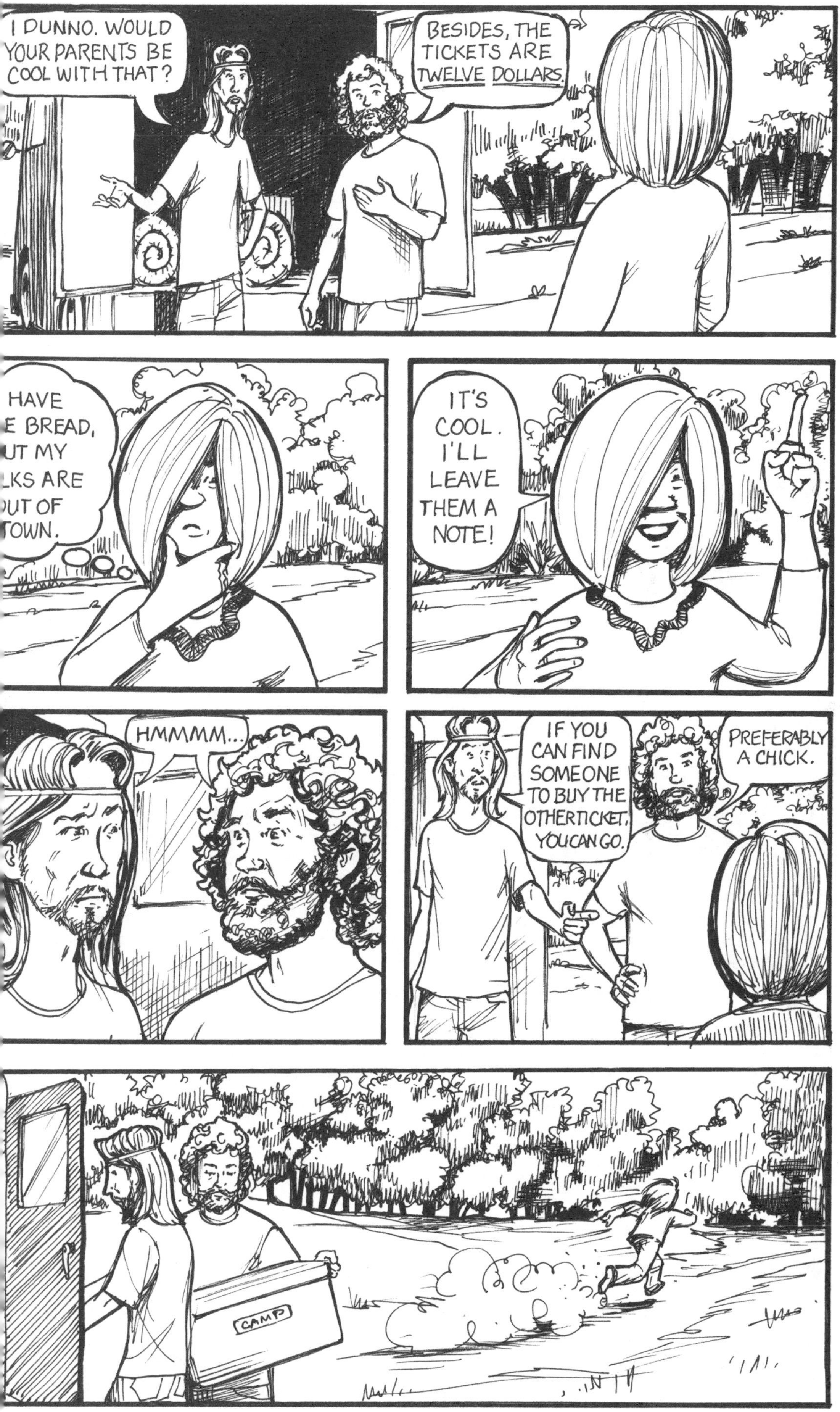
I DUNNO. WOULD YOUR PARENTS BE COOL WITH THAT?
BESIDES, THE TICKETS ARE TWELVE DOLLARS.
HAVE E BREAD, UT MY LKS ARE UT OF TOWN.
IT'S COOL. I'LL LEAVE THEM A NOTE!
HMMMM...
IF YOU CAN FIND SOMEONE TO BUY THE OTHER TICKET, YOU CAN GO.
PREFERABLY A CHICK.
CAMP

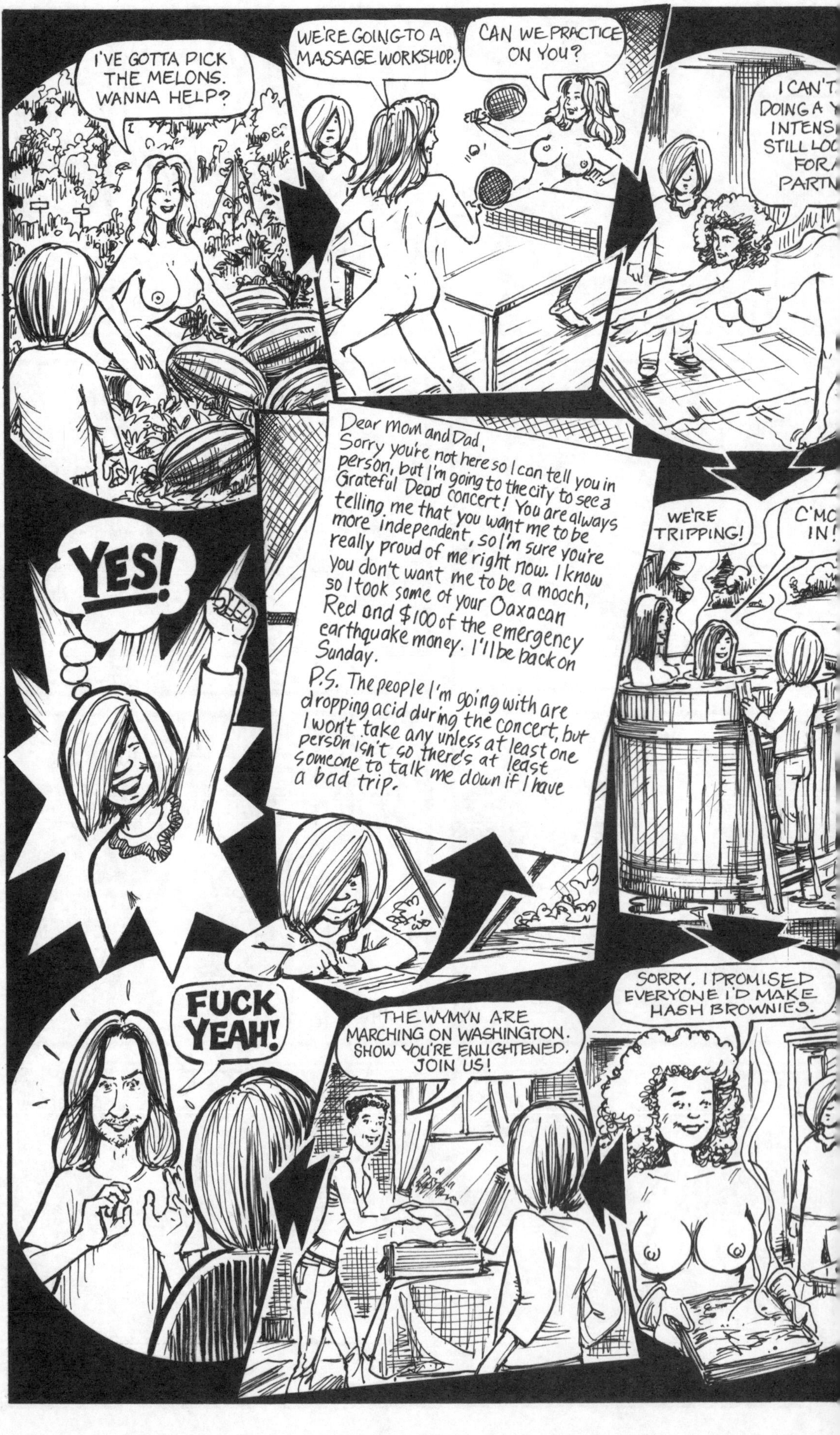
I'VE GOTTA PICK THE MELONS. WANNA HELP?
WE'RE GOING TO A MASSAGE WORKSHOP.
CAN WE PRACTICE ON YOU?
I CAN'T
DOING A
INTENS
STILL LOO
FOR A
PARTN
WE'RE TRIPPING!
C'MO
IN!
SORRY. I PROMISED EVERYONE I'D MAKE HASH BROWNIES.
THE WYMYN ARE MARCHING ON WASHINGTON. SHOW YOU'RE ENLIGHTENED. JOIN US!
FUCK YEAH!
YES!
Dear mom and Dad,
Sorry you're not here so I can tell you in person, but I'm going to the city to see a Grateful Dead concert! You are always telling me that you want me to be more independent, so I'm sure you're really proud of me right now. I know you don't want me to be a mooch, so I took some of your Oaxacan Red and $100 of the emergency earthquake money. I'll be back on Sunday.
P.S. The people I'm going with are dropping acid during the concert, but I won't take any unless at least one person isn't so there's at least someone to talk me down if I have a bad trip.

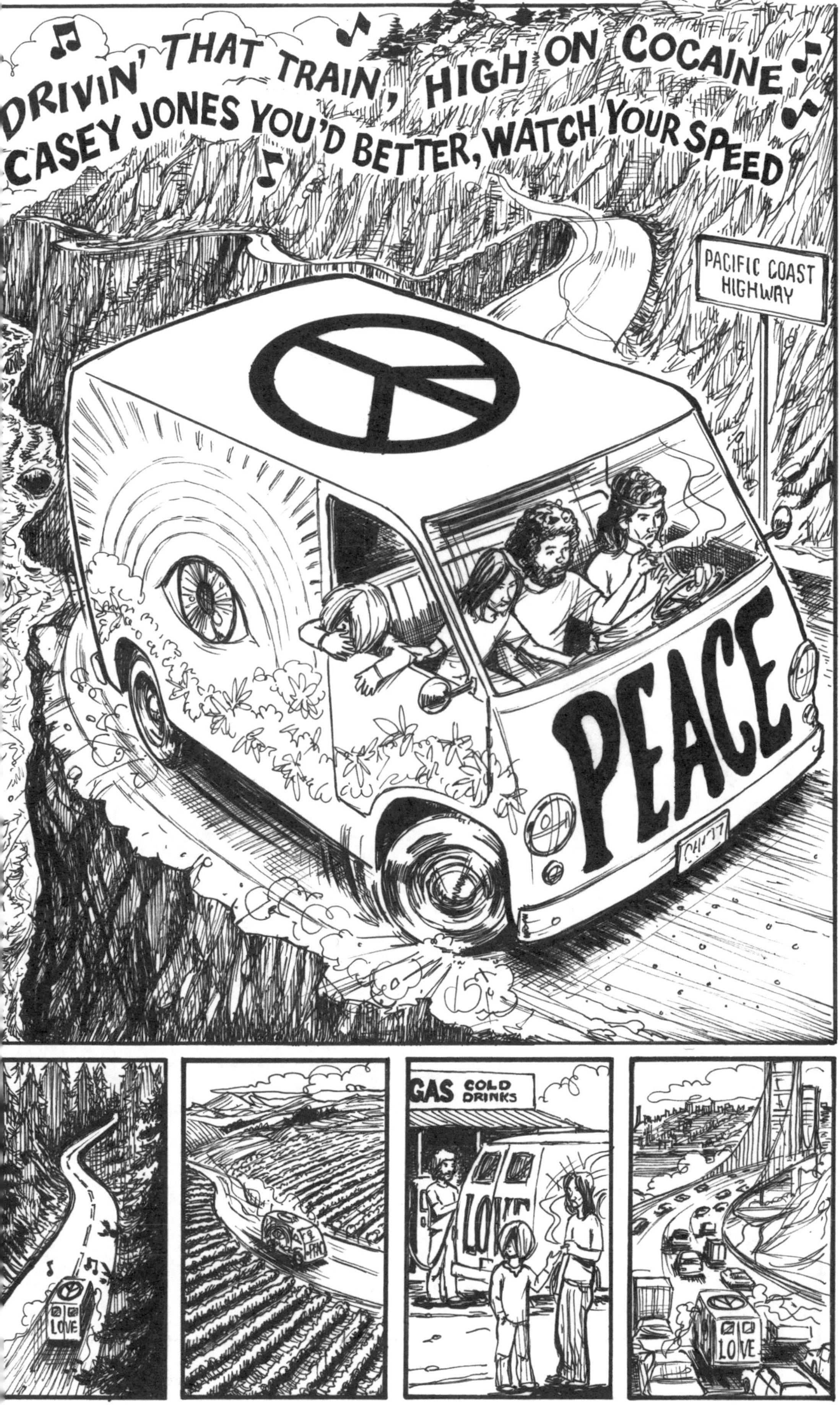
DRIVIN' THAT TRAIN, HIGH ON COCAINE
CASEY JONES YOU'D BETTER, WATCH YOUR SPEED
PACIFIC COAST HIGHWAY
PEACE
LOVE
GAS COLD DRINKS
LOVE
LOVE

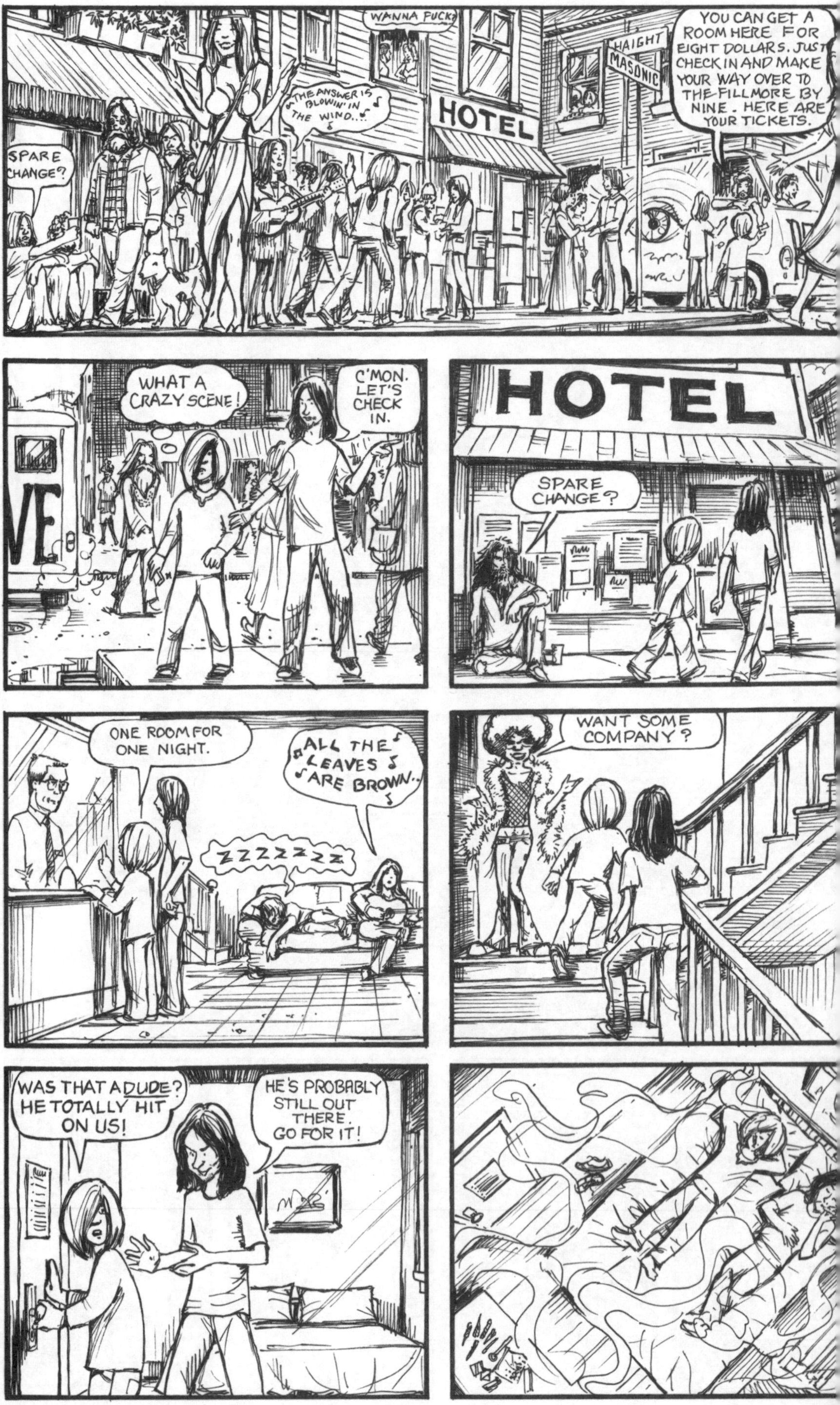
SPARE CHANGE?
WANNA FUCK?
THE ANSWER IS BLOWIN' IN THE WIND...
HOTEL
HAIGHT
MASONIC
YOU CAN GET A ROOM HERE FOR EIGHT DOLLARS. JUST CHECK IN AND MAKE YOUR WAY OVER TO THE FILLMORE BY NINE. HERE ARE YOUR TICKETS.
WHAT A CRAZY SCENE!
C'MON. LET'S CHECK IN.
HOTEL
SPARE CHANGE?
ONE ROOM FOR ONE NIGHT.
ZZZZZZZ
ALL THE LEAVES ARE BROWN..
WANT SOME COMPANY?
WAS THAT A DUDE? HE TOTALLY HIT ON US!
HE'S PROBABLY STILL OUT THERE. GO FOR IT!

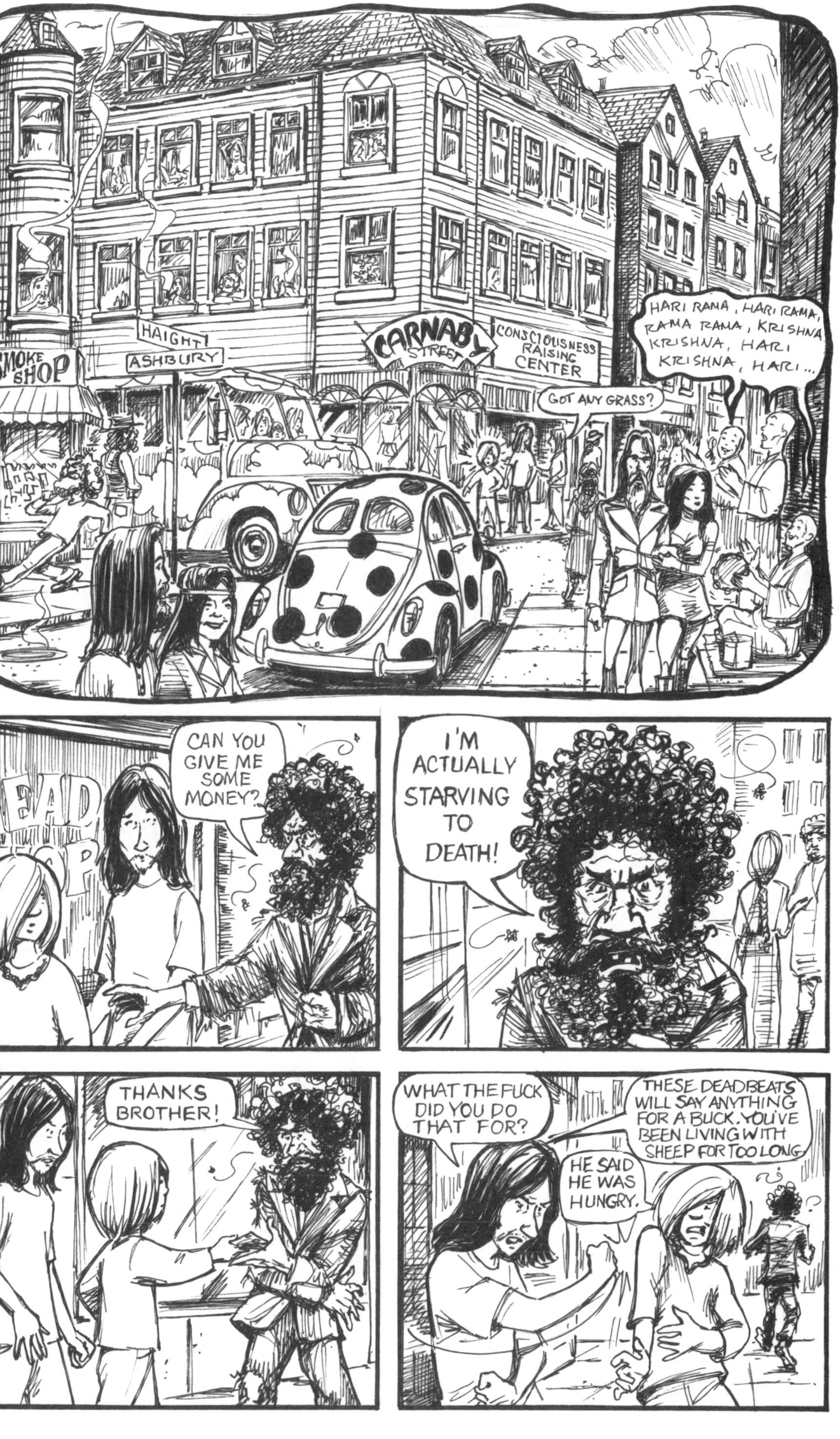
HAIGHT
ASHBURY
SMOKE SHOP
CARNABY STREET
CONSCIOUSNESS RAISING CENTER
GOT ANY GRASS?
HARI RAMA, HARI RAMA, RAMA RAMA, KRISHNA KRISHNA, HARI KRISHNA, HARI...
CAN YOU GIVE ME SOME MONEY?
I'M ACTUALLY STARVING TO DEATH!
THANKS BROTHER!
WHAT THE FUCK DID YOU DO THAT FOR?
HE SAID HE WAS HUNGRY.
THESE DEADBEATS WILL SAY ANYTHING FOR A BUCK. YOU'VE BEEN LIVING WITH SHEEP FOR TOO LONG.

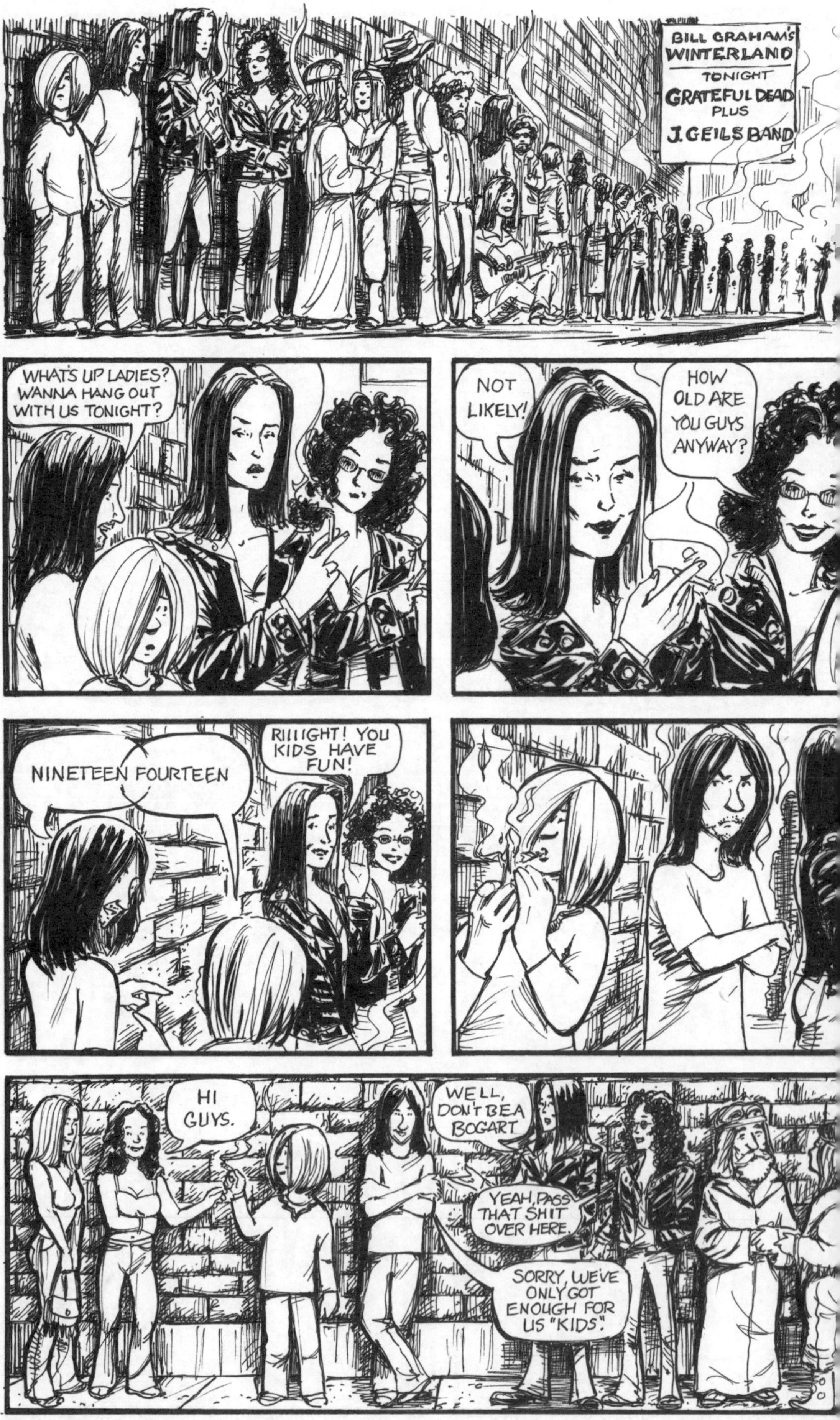
BILL GRAHAM'S WINTERLAND
TONIGHT
GRATEFUL DEAD
PLUS
J. GEILS BAND
WHAT'S UP LADIES? WANNA HANG OUT WITH US TONIGHT?
NOT LIKELY!
HOW OLD ARE YOU GUYS ANYWAY?
NINETEEN FOURTEEN
RIIIIGHT! YOU KIDS HAVE FUN!
HI GUYS.
WELL, DON'T BE A BOGART
YEAH, PASS THAT SHIT OVER HERE.
SORRY, WE'VE ONLY GOT ENOUGH FOR US "KIDS".

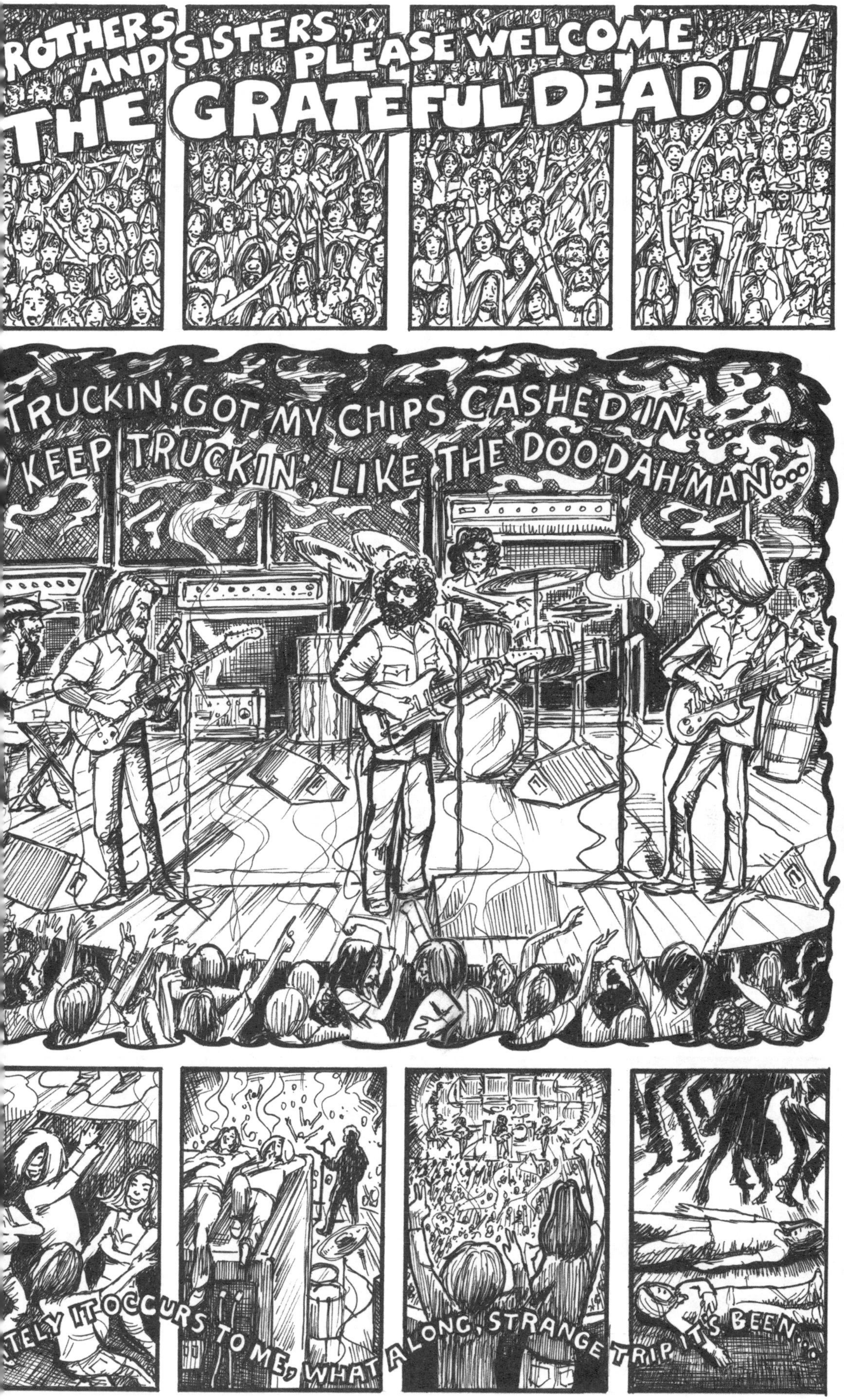
ROTHERS, AND SISTERS, PLEASE WELCOME
THE GRATEFUL DEAD!!!
TRUCKIN', GOT MY CHIPS CASHED IN...
KEEP TRUCKIN', LIKE THE DOODAH MAN...
TELY IT OCCURS TO ME, WHAT A LONG, STRANGE TRIP IT'S BEEN...

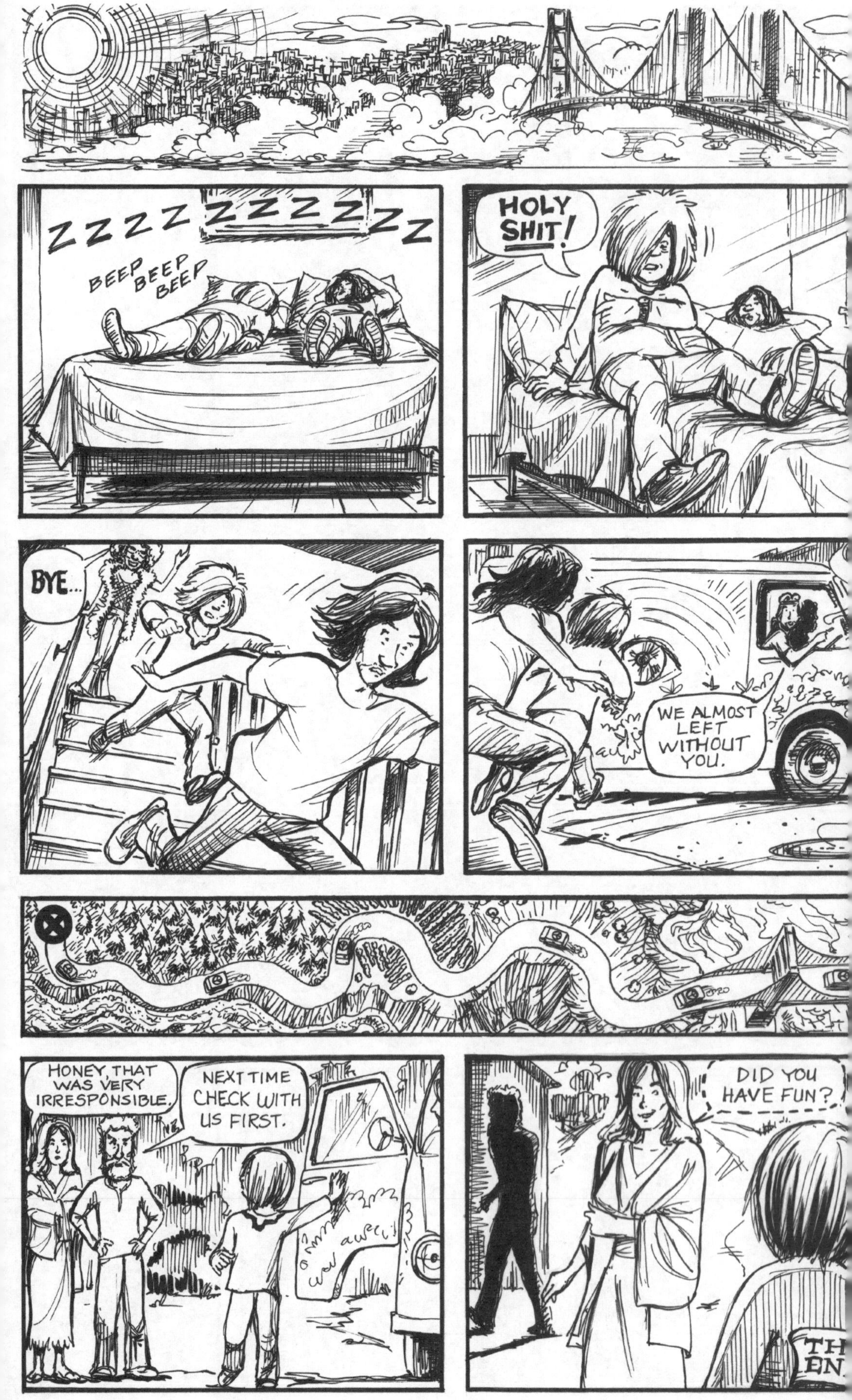
ZZZZZZZZZZZ
BEEP BEEP BEEP
HOLY SHIT!
BYE...
WE ALMOST LEFT WITHOUT YOU.
HONEY, THAT WAS VERY IRRESPONSIBLE.
NEXT TIME CHECK WITH US FIRST.
DID YOU HAVE FUN?
TH
EN.

TALES of a HIPPY KID

J. KROLL
D. BOHN

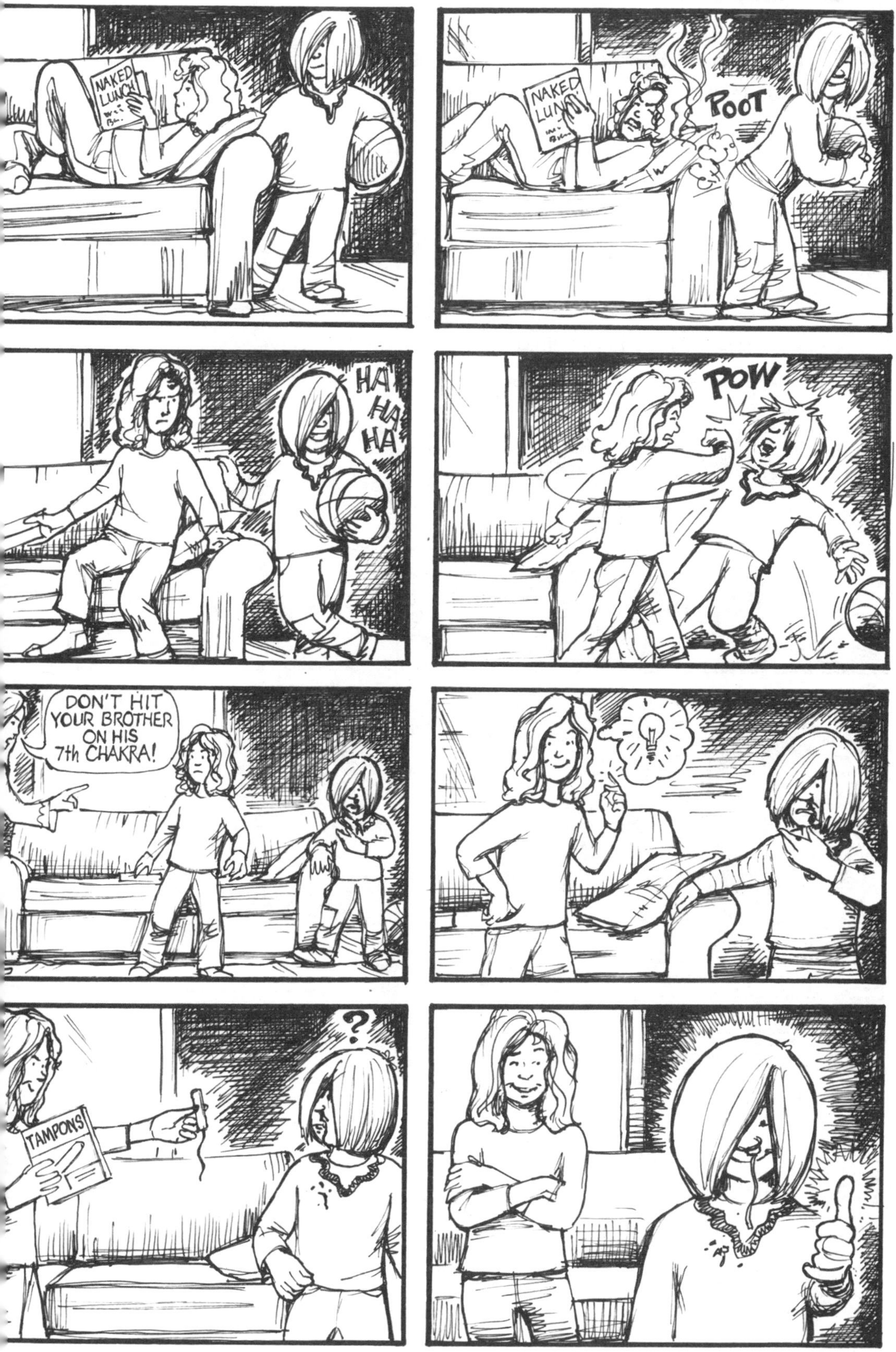
NAKED LUNCH
NAKED LUN
POOT
HA HA HA
POW
DON'T HIT YOUR BROTHER ON HIS 7th CHAKRA!
?
TAMPONS

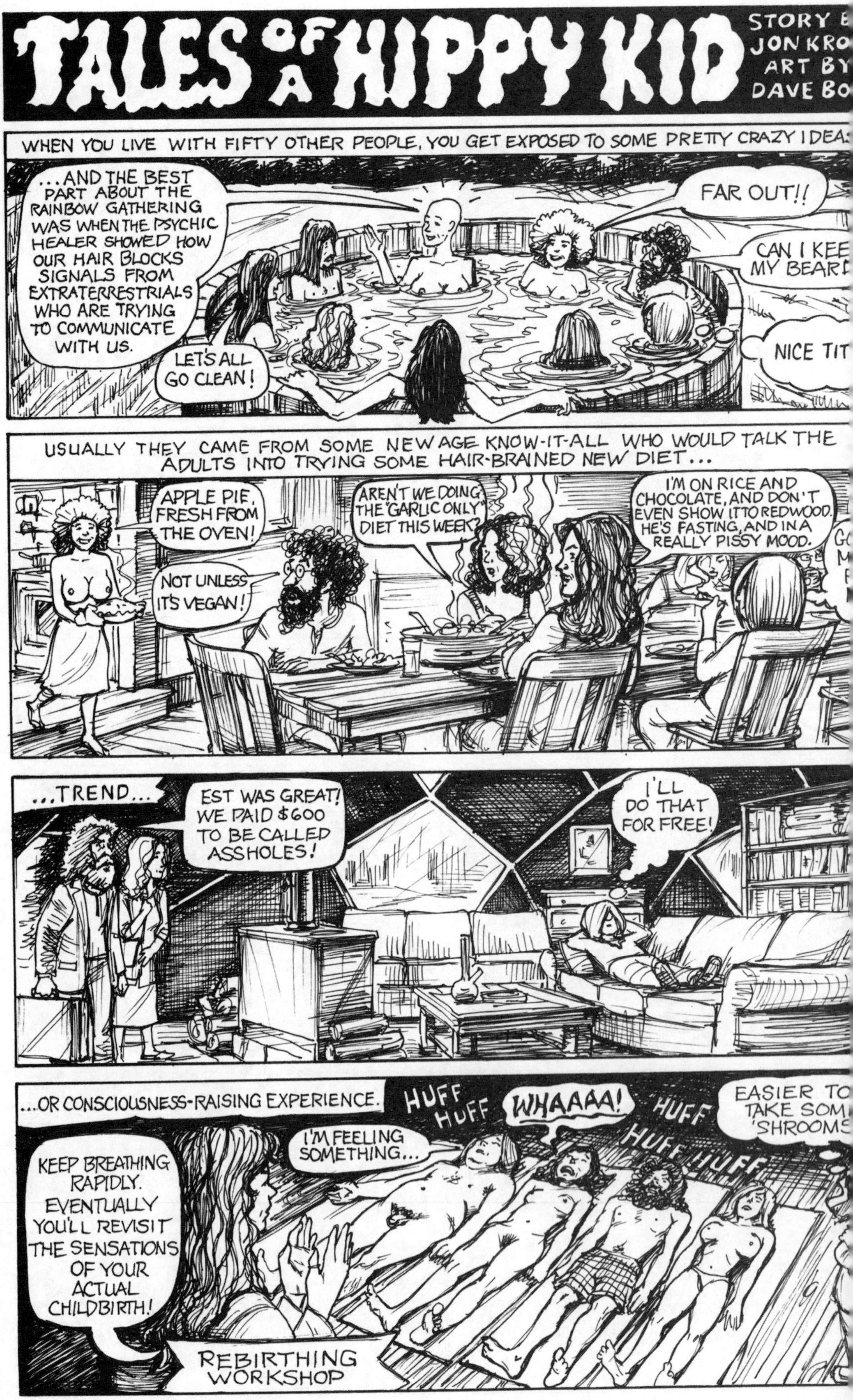
TALES OF A HIPPY KID
STORY B
JON KRO
ART BY
DAVE BO
WHEN YOU LIVE WITH FIFTY OTHER PEOPLE, YOU GET EXPOSED TO SOME PRETTY CRAZY IDEAS
...AND THE BEST PART ABOUT THE RAINBOW GATHERING WAS WHEN THE PSYCHIC HEALER SHOWED HOW OUR HAIR BLOCKS SIGNALS FROM EXTRATERRESTRIALS WHO ARE TRYING TO COMMUNICATE WITH US.
FAR OUT!!
CAN I KEE MY BEARD
LET'S ALL GO CLEAN!
NICE TIT
USUALLY THEY CAME FROM SOME NEW AGE KNOW-IT-ALL WHO WOULD TALK THE ADULTS INTO TRYING SOME HAIR-BRAINED NEW DIET...
APPLE PIE, FRESH FROM THE OVEN!
NOT UNLESS IT'S VEGAN!
AREN'T WE DOING THE "GARLIC ONLY" DIET THIS WEEK?
I'M ON RICE AND CHOCOLATE, AND DON'T EVEN SHOW IT TO REDWOOD. HE'S FASTING, AND IN A REALLY PISSY MOOD.
...TREND...
EST WAS GREAT! WE PAID $600 TO BE CALLED ASSHOLES!
I'LL DO THAT FOR FREE!
...OR CONSCIOUSNESS-RAISING EXPERIENCE.
HUFF HUFF
WHAAAA!
HUFF
HUFF HUFF
EASIER TO TAKE SOM 'SHROOMS
I'M FEELING SOMETHING...
KEEP BREATHING RAPIDLY. EVENTUALLY YOU'LL REVISIT THE SENSATIONS OF YOUR ACTUAL CHILDBIRTH!
REBIRTHING WORKSHOP

E KIDS WEREN'T AS EASILY SWAYED.

WANNA JOIN OUR MEDITATION CIRCLE?

MEDITATION'S BORING.

SO WE STARTED A REVOLT. WE DECIDED THAT SOME HIPPY THINGS WERE OK...

BUT THE REST WERE...

HIPPY BULLSHIT

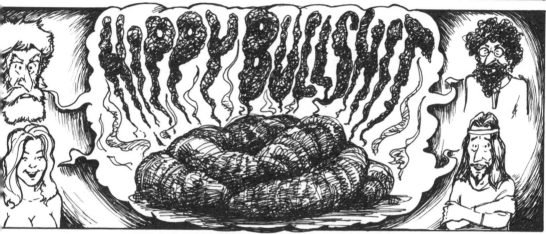

Y BULLSHIT" BECAME OUR BATTLE CRY, IF WE WERE FORCED TO EAT SOMETHING GROSS...

PUSH!

RIGHT AFTER PATCHOULI GIVES BIRTH, WE CAN ALL EAT THE PLACENTA!

SOUNDS LIKE HIPPY BULLSHIT TO ME!

EW!

GOT ANY "PLACENTA HELPER"?

BELIEVE SOMETHING STUPID.

YOU KNOW, SOME NATIVE AMERICAN TRIBES BELIEVE IT'S THE RESPONSIBILITY OF THE OLDER MEN TO USHER YOUNG GIRLS INTO WOMANHOOD.

THAT'S HIPPY BULLSHIT, YOU PERVERT!

HEH HEH HEH

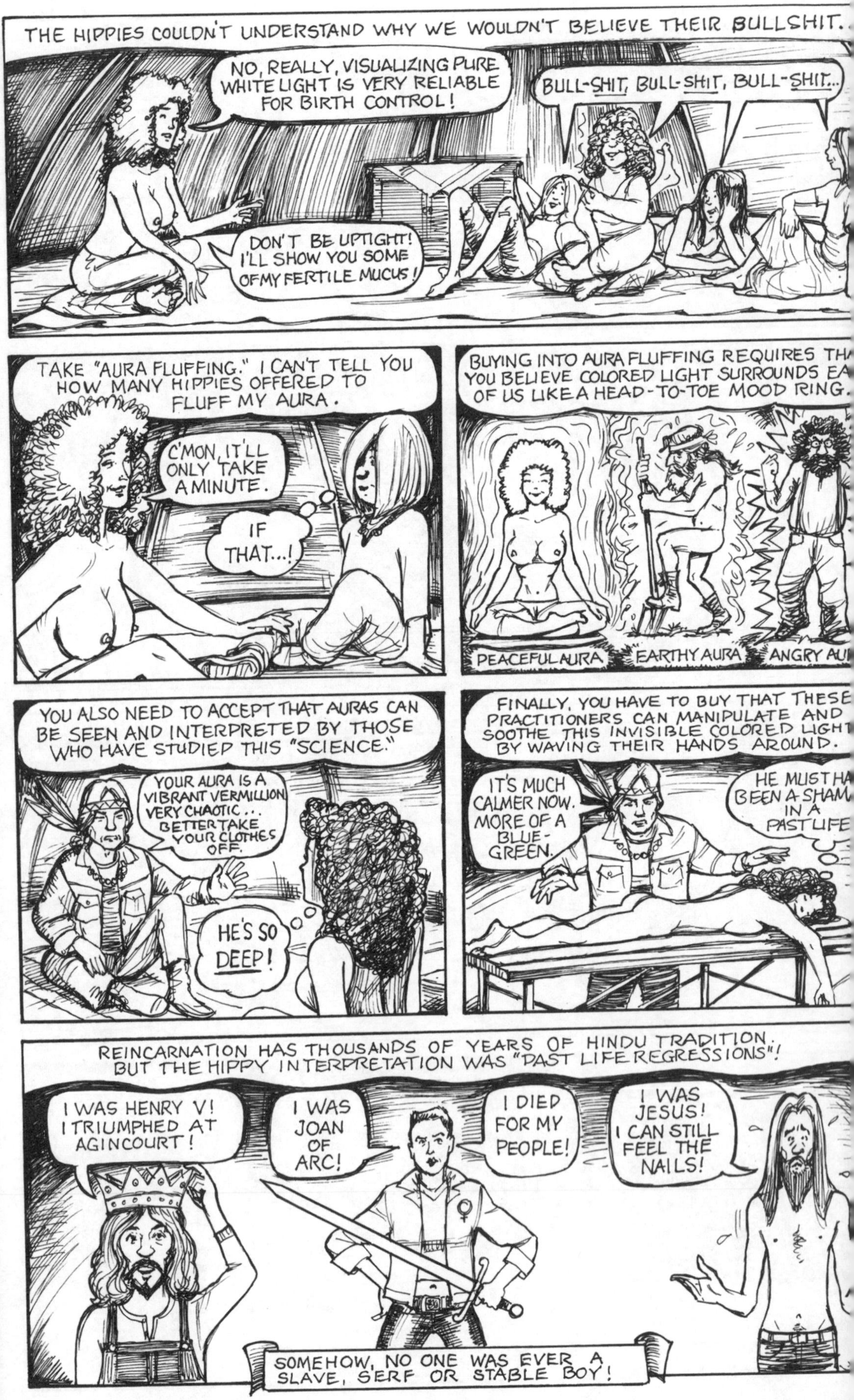
THE HIPPIES COULDN'T UNDERSTAND WHY WE WOULDN'T BELIEVE THEIR BULLSHIT...
NO, REALLY, VISUALIZING PURE WHITE LIGHT IS VERY RELIABLE FOR BIRTH CONTROL!
BULL-SHIT, BULL-SHIT, BULL-SHIT...
DON'T BE UPTIGHT! I'LL SHOW YOU SOME OF MY FERTILE MUCUS!
TAKE "AURA FLUFFING." I CAN'T TELL YOU HOW MANY HIPPIES OFFERED TO FLUFF MY AURA.
C'MON, IT'LL ONLY TAKE A MINUTE.
IF THAT...!
BUYING INTO AURA FLUFFING REQUIRES THA
YOU BELIEVE COLORED LIGHT SURROUNDS EA
OF US LIKE A HEAD-TO-TOE MOOD RING.
PEACEFUL AURA
EARTHY AURA
ANGRY AU
YOU ALSO NEED TO ACCEPT THAT AURAS CAN BE SEEN AND INTERPRETED BY THOSE WHO HAVE STUDIED THIS "SCIENCE."
YOUR AURA IS A VIBRANT VERMILLION, VERY CHAOTIC... BETTER TAKE YOUR CLOTHES OFF.
HE'S SO DEEP!
FINALLY, YOU HAVE TO BUY THAT THESE PRACTITIONERS CAN MANIPULATE AND SOOTHE THIS INVISIBLE COLORED LIGHT BY WAVING THEIR HANDS AROUND.
IT'S MUCH CALMER NOW. MORE OF A BLUE-GREEN.
HE MUST HA
BEEN A SHAM
IN A
PAST LIFE
REINCARNATION HAS THOUSANDS OF YEARS OF HINDU TRADITION. BUT THE HIPPY INTERPRETATION WAS "PAST LIFE REGRESSIONS"!
I WAS HENRY V! I TRIUMPHED AT AGINCOURT!
I WAS JOAN OF ARC!
I DIED FOR MY PEOPLE!
I WAS JESUS! I CAN STILL FEEL THE NAILS!
SOMEHOW, NO ONE WAS EVER A SLAVE, SERF OR STABLE BOY!

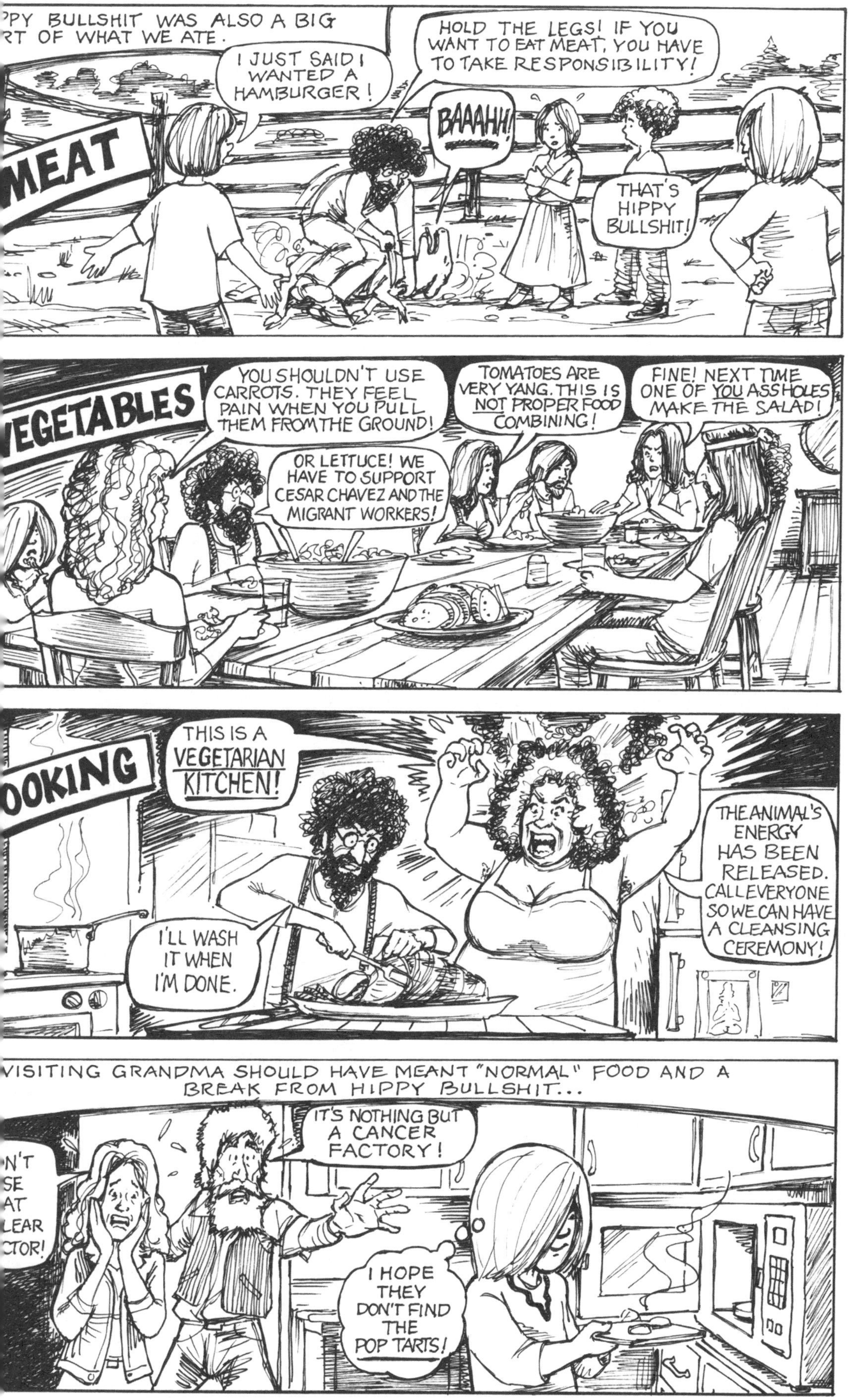

PPY BULLSHIT WAS ALSO A BIG
RT OF WHAT WE ATE.
MEAT
I JUST SAID I WANTED A HAMBURGER!
HOLD THE LEGS! IF YOU WANT TO EAT MEAT, YOU HAVE TO TAKE RESPONSIBILITY!
BAAAHH!
THAT'S HIPPY BULLSHIT!
VEGETABLES
YOU SHOULDN'T USE CARROTS. THEY FEEL PAIN WHEN YOU PULL THEM FROM THE GROUND!
OR LETTUCE! WE HAVE TO SUPPORT CESAR CHAVEZ AND THE MIGRANT WORKERS!
TOMATOES ARE VERY YANG. THIS IS NOT PROPER FOOD COMBINING!
FINE! NEXT TIME ONE OF YOU ASSHOLES MAKE THE SALAD!
OOKING
THIS IS A VEGETARIAN KITCHEN!
I'LL WASH IT WHEN I'M DONE.
THE ANIMAL'S ENERGY HAS BEEN RELEASED. CALL EVERYONE SO WE CAN HAVE A CLEANSING CEREMONY!
VISITING GRANDMA SHOULD HAVE MEANT "NORMAL" FOOD AND A BREAK FROM HIPPY BULLSHIT...
N'T SE AT LEAR CTOR!
IT'S NOTHING BUT A CANCER FACTORY!
I HOPE THEY DON'T FIND THE POP TARTS!

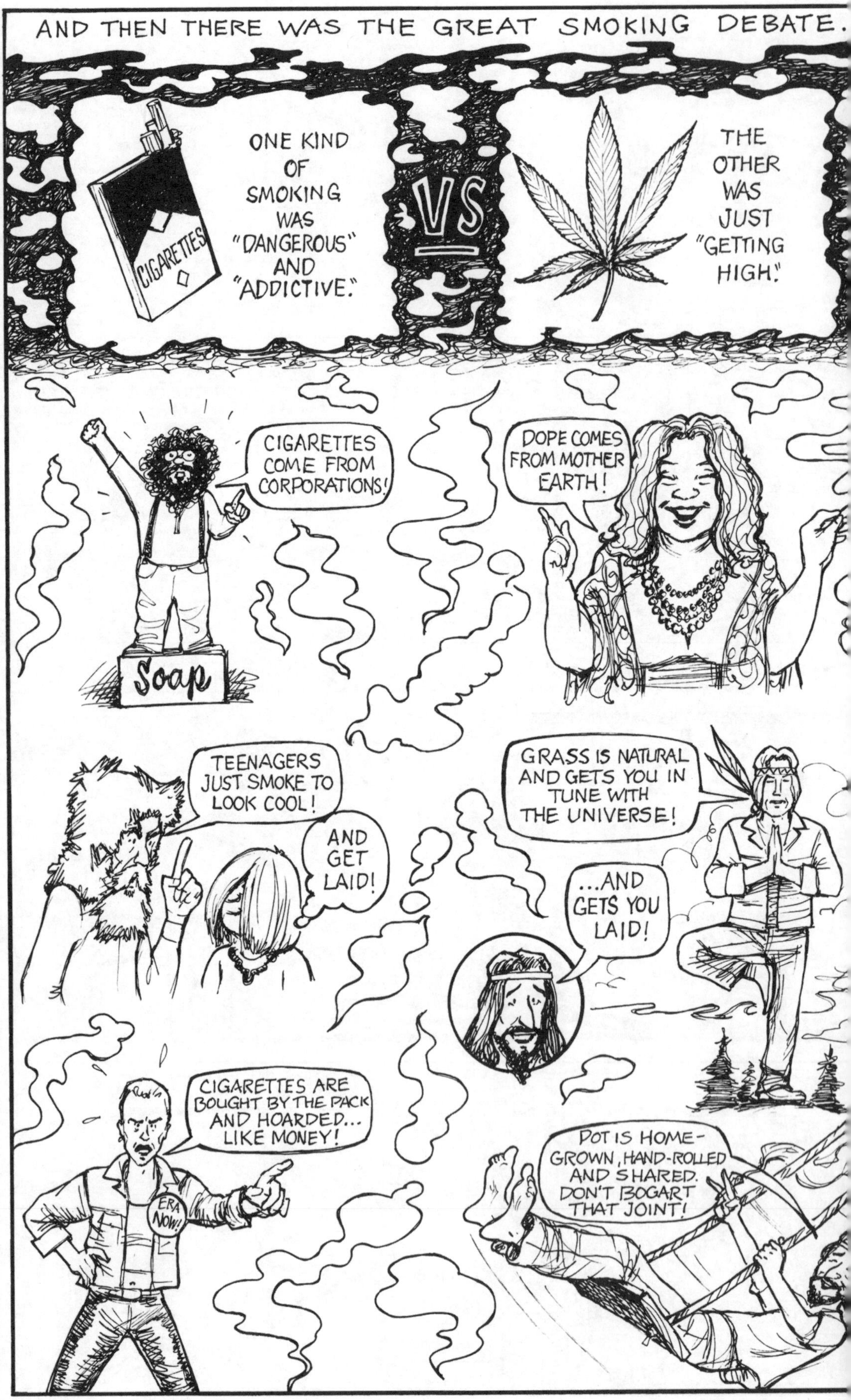

AND THEN THERE WAS THE GREAT SMOKING DEBATE.
CIGARETTES
ONE KIND OF SMOKING WAS "DANGEROUS" AND "ADDICTIVE."
VS
THE OTHER WAS JUST "GETTING HIGH."
CIGARETTES COME FROM CORPORATIONS!
Soap
DOPE COMES FROM MOTHER EARTH!
TEENAGERS JUST SMOKE TO LOOK COOL!
AND GET LAID!
GRASS IS NATURAL AND GETS YOU IN TUNE WITH THE UNIVERSE!
...AND GETS YOU LAID!
CIGARETTES ARE BOUGHT BY THE PACK AND HOARDED... LIKE MONEY!
ERA NOW!
POT IS HOME-GROWN, HAND-ROLLED AND SHARED. DON'T BOGART THAT JOINT!

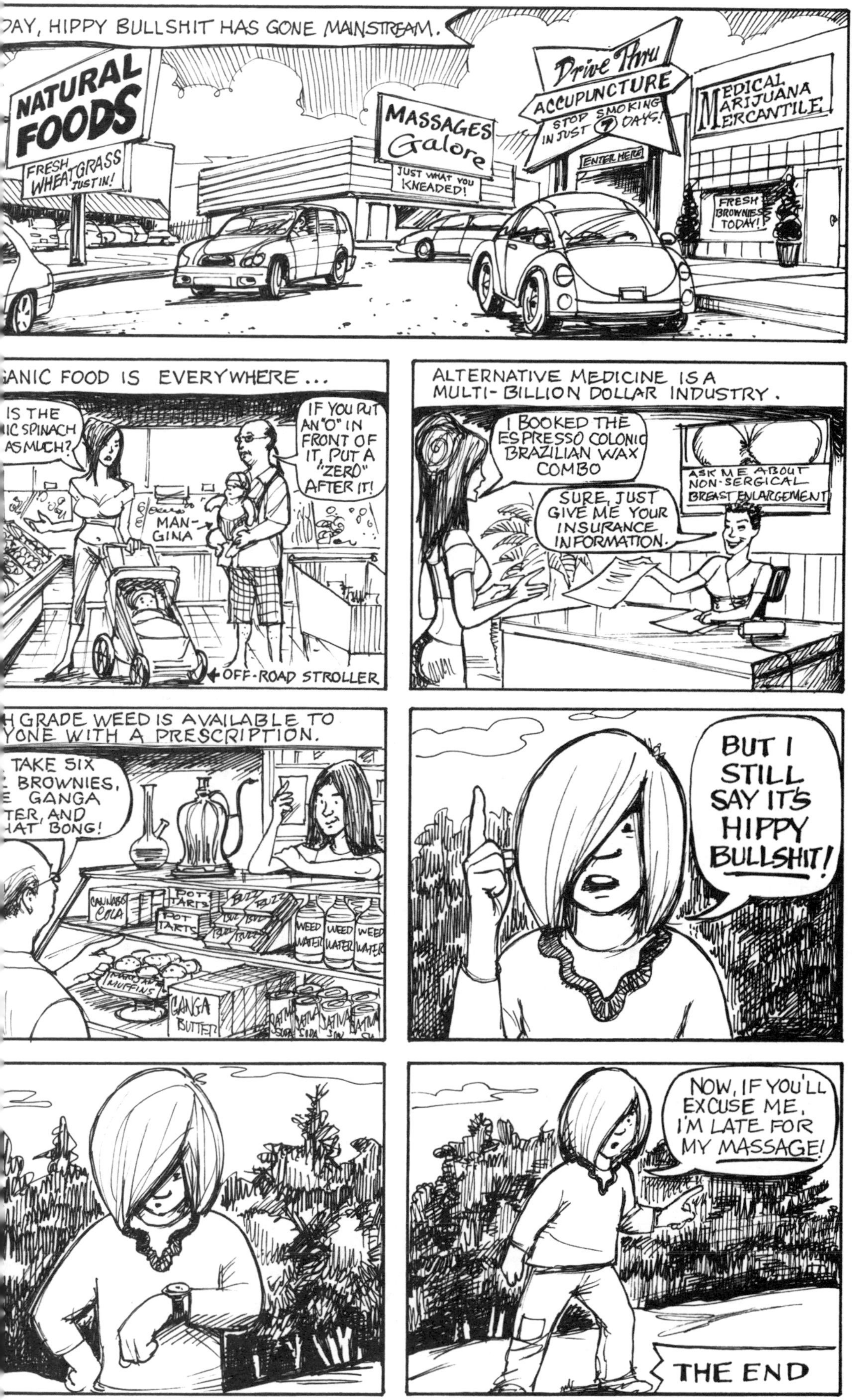

DAY, HIPPY BULLSHIT HAS GONE MAINSTREAM.
NATURAL FOODS
FRESH WHEATGRASS JUST IN!
MASSAGES Galore
JUST WHAT YOU KNEADED!
Drive Thru ACCUPUNCTURE
STOP SMOKING IN JUST 7 DAYS!
ENTER HERE
MEDICAL MARIJUANA MERCANTILE
FRESH BROWNIES TODAY!
GANIC FOOD IS EVERYWHERE...
IS THE
IC SPINACH
AS MUCH?
IF YOU PUT AN "O" IN FRONT OF IT, PUT A "ZERO" AFTER IT!
MAN-GINA
OFF-ROAD STROLLER
ALTERNATIVE MEDICINE IS A MULTI-BILLION DOLLAR INDUSTRY.
I BOOKED THE ESPRESSO COLONIC BRAZILIAN WAX COMBO
ASK ME ABOUT NON-SERGICAL BREAST ENLARGEMENT
SURE, JUST GIVE ME YOUR INSURANCE INFORMATION.
H GRADE WEED IS AVAILABLE TO
YONE WITH A PRESCRIPTION.
TAKE SIX
BROWNIES,
E GANGA
TER, AND
HAT BONG!
CANNABIS COLA
POT TARTS
WEED WATER
MUFFINS
GANGA BUTTER
SATIVA SODA
BUT I STILL SAY IT'S HIPPY BULLSHIT!
NOW, IF YOU'LL EXCUSE ME, I'M LATE FOR MY MASSAGE!
THE END

ADVERTISEMENT

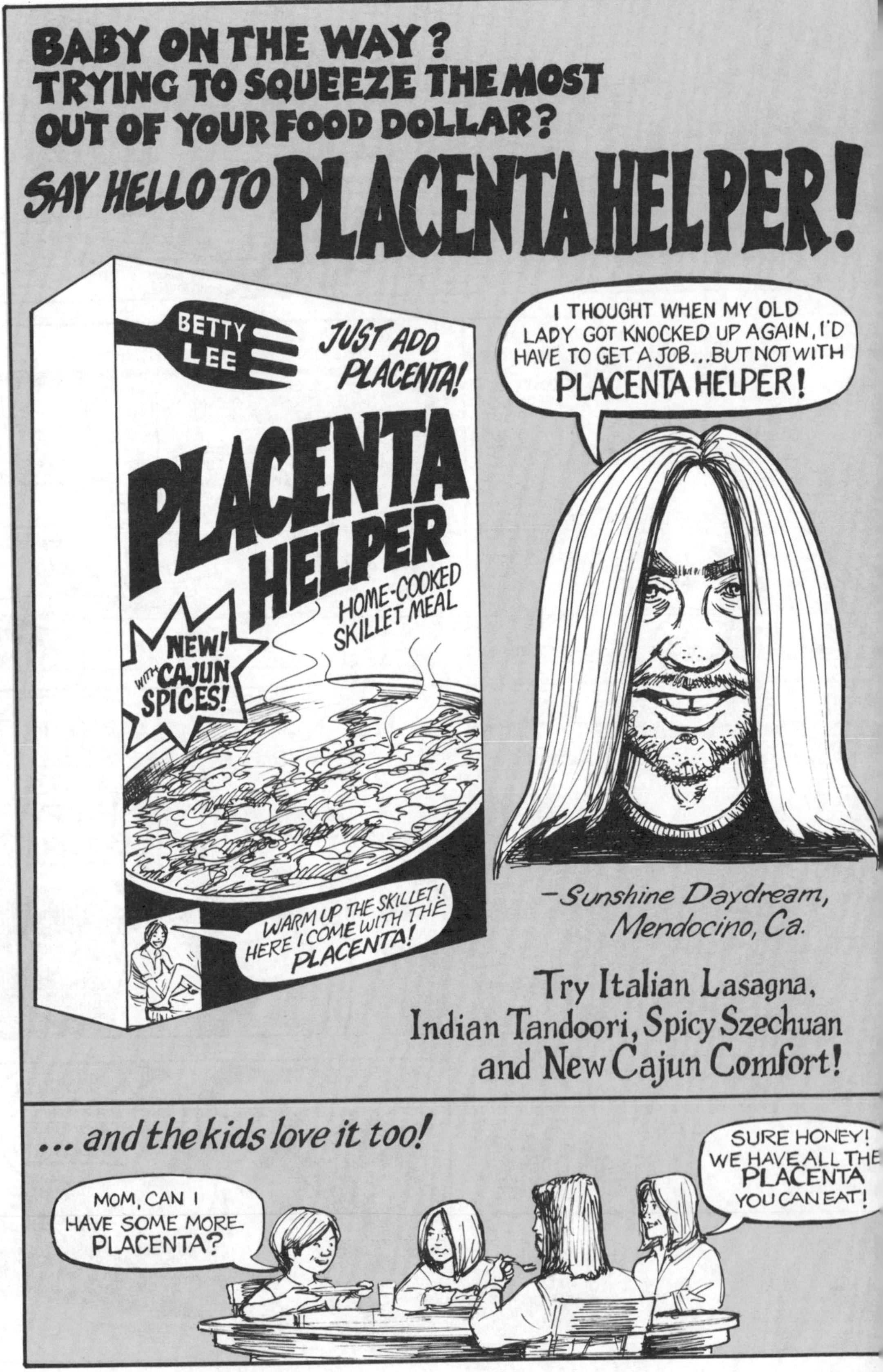

BABY ON THE WAY?
TRYING TO SQUEEZE THE MOST OUT OF YOUR FOOD DOLLAR?
SAY HELLO TO PLACENTA HELPER!
BETTY LEE
JUST ADD PLACENTA!
PLACENTA HELPER
HOME-COOKED SKILLET MEAL
NEW! WITH CAJUN SPICES!
WARM UP THE SKILLET! HERE I COME WITH THE PLACENTA!
I THOUGHT WHEN MY OLD LADY GOT KNOCKED UP AGAIN, I'D HAVE TO GET A JOB...BUT NOT WITH PLACENTA HELPER!
—Sunshine Daydream, Mendocino, Ca.
Try Italian Lasagna, Indian Tandoori, Spicy Szechuan and New Cajun Comfort!
... and the kids love it too!
MOM, CAN I HAVE SOME MORE PLACENTA?
SURE HONEY! WE HAVE ALL THE PLACENTA YOU CAN EAT!

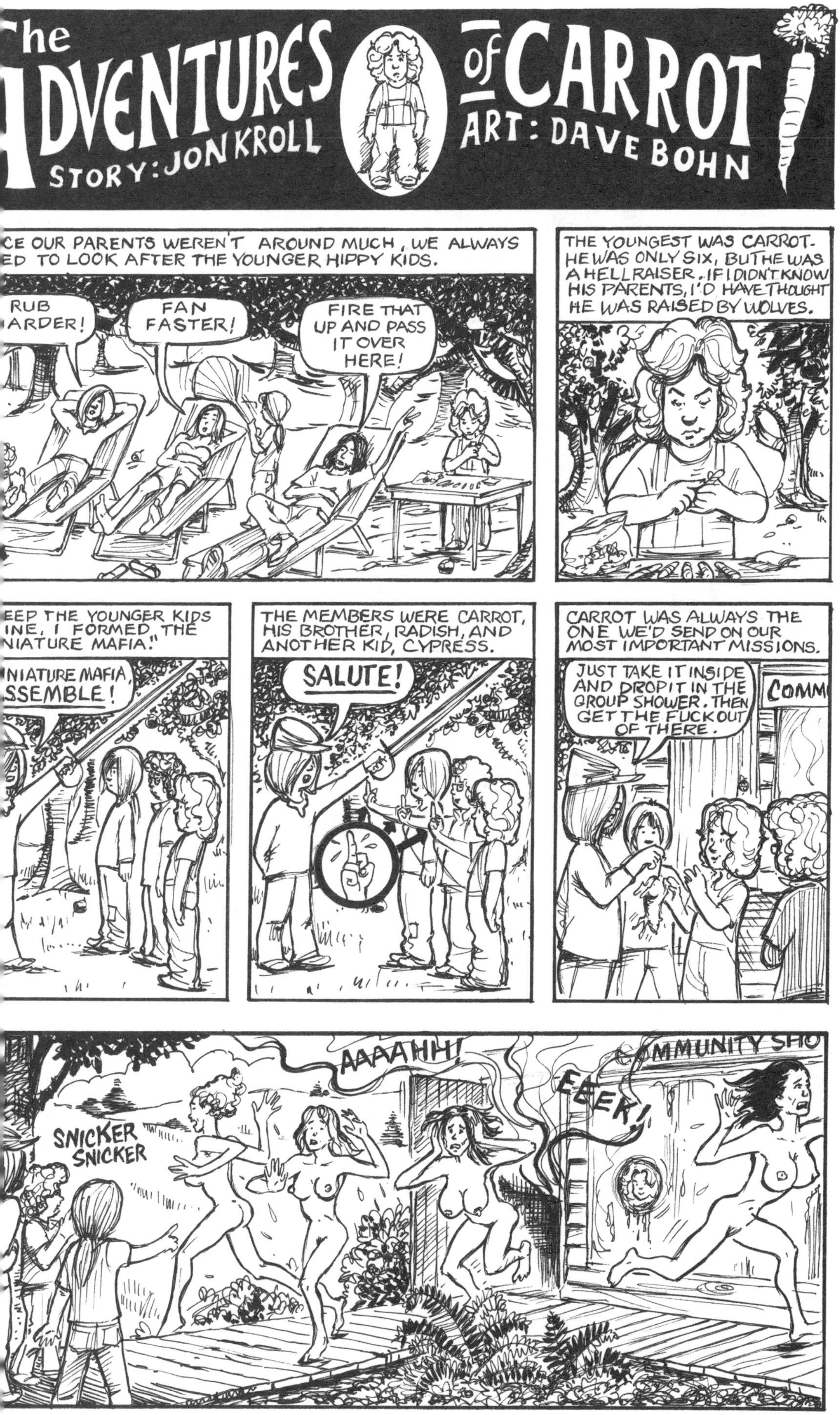
The ADVENTURES of CARROT
STORY: JON KROLL
ART: DAVE BOHN
CE OUR PARENTS WEREN'T AROUND MUCH, WE ALWAYS ED TO LOOK AFTER THE YOUNGER HIPPY KIDS.
RUB ARDER!
FAN FASTER!
FIRE THAT UP AND PASS IT OVER HERE!
THE YOUNGEST WAS CARROT- HE WAS ONLY SIX, BUT HE WAS A HELLRAISER. IF I DIDN'T KNOW HIS PARENTS, I'D HAVE THOUGHT HE WAS RAISED BY WOLVES.
EEP THE YOUNGER KIDS INE, I FORMED THE NIATURE MAFIA."
NIATURE MAFIA, SSEMBLE!
THE MEMBERS WERE CARROT, HIS BROTHER, RADISH, AND ANOTHER KID, CYPRESS.
SALUTE!
CARROT WAS ALWAYS THE ONE WE'D SEND ON OUR MOST IMPORTANT MISSIONS.
JUST TAKE IT INSIDE AND DROP IT IN THE GROUP SHOWER. THEN GET THE FUCK OUT OF THERE.
COMM
AAAAHH!
COMMUNITY SHO
EEEK!
SNICKER SNICKER

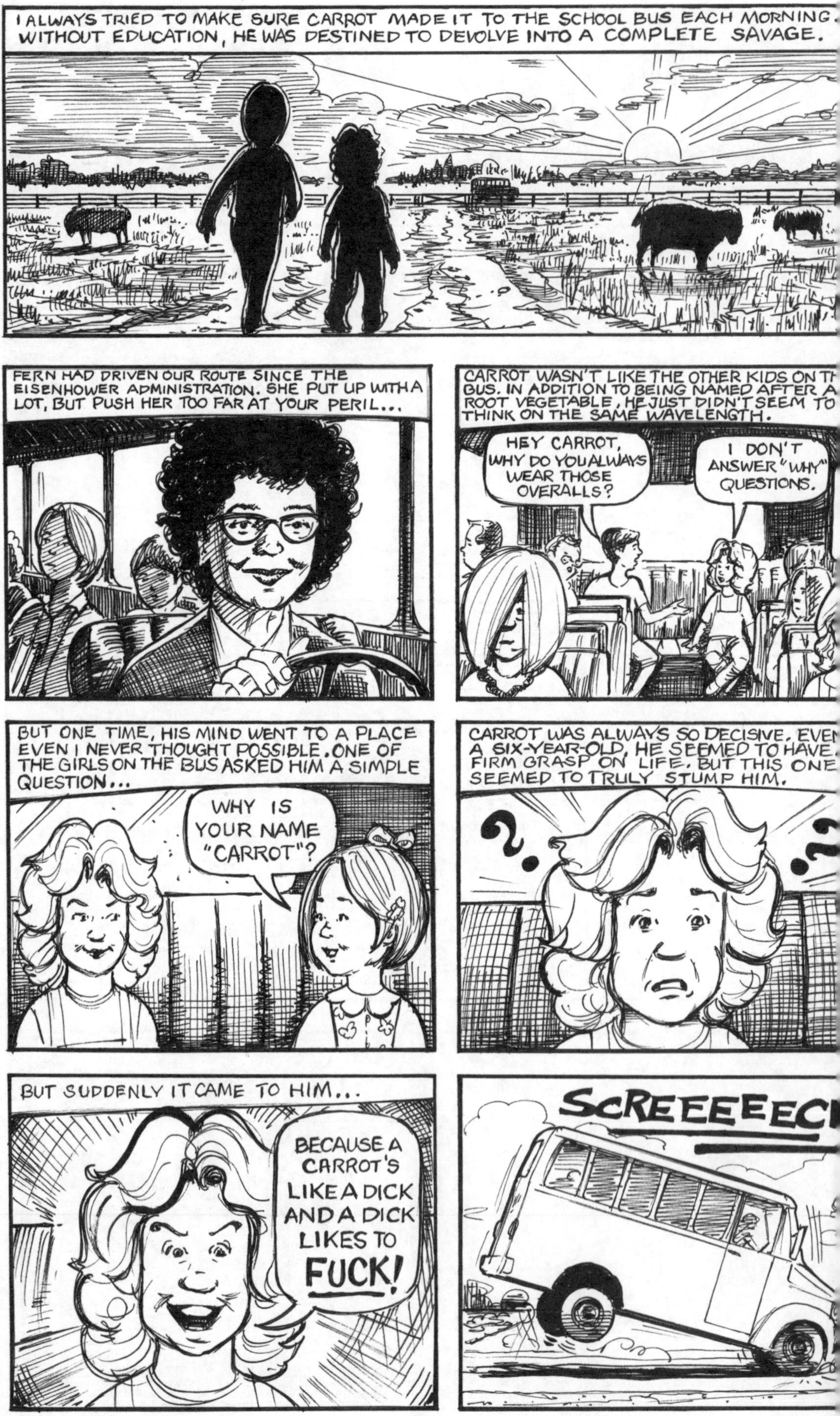
I ALWAYS TRIED TO MAKE SURE CARROT MADE IT TO THE SCHOOL BUS EACH MORNING. WITHOUT EDUCATION, HE WAS DESTINED TO DEVOLVE INTO A COMPLETE SAVAGE.
FERN HAD DRIVEN OUR ROUTE SINCE THE EISENHOWER ADMINISTRATION. SHE PUT UP WITH A LOT, BUT PUSH HER TOO FAR AT YOUR PERIL...
CARROT WASN'T LIKE THE OTHER KIDS ON TH BUS. IN ADDITION TO BEING NAMED AFTER A ROOT VEGETABLE, HE JUST DIDN'T SEEM TO THINK ON THE SAME WAVELENGTH.
HEY CARROT, WHY DO YOU ALWAYS WEAR THOSE OVERALLS?
I DON'T ANSWER "WHY" QUESTIONS.
BUT ONE TIME, HIS MIND WENT TO A PLACE EVEN I NEVER THOUGHT POSSIBLE. ONE OF THE GIRLS ON THE BUS ASKED HIM A SIMPLE QUESTION...
WHY IS YOUR NAME "CARROT"?
CARROT WAS ALWAYS SO DECISIVE. EVEN A SIX-YEAR-OLD, HE SEEMED TO HAVE FIRM GRASP ON LIFE. BUT THIS ONE SEEMED TO TRULY STUMP HIM.
BUT SUDDENLY IT CAME TO HIM...
BECAUSE A CARROT'S LIKE A DICK AND A DICK LIKES TO FUCK!
SCREEEEEC

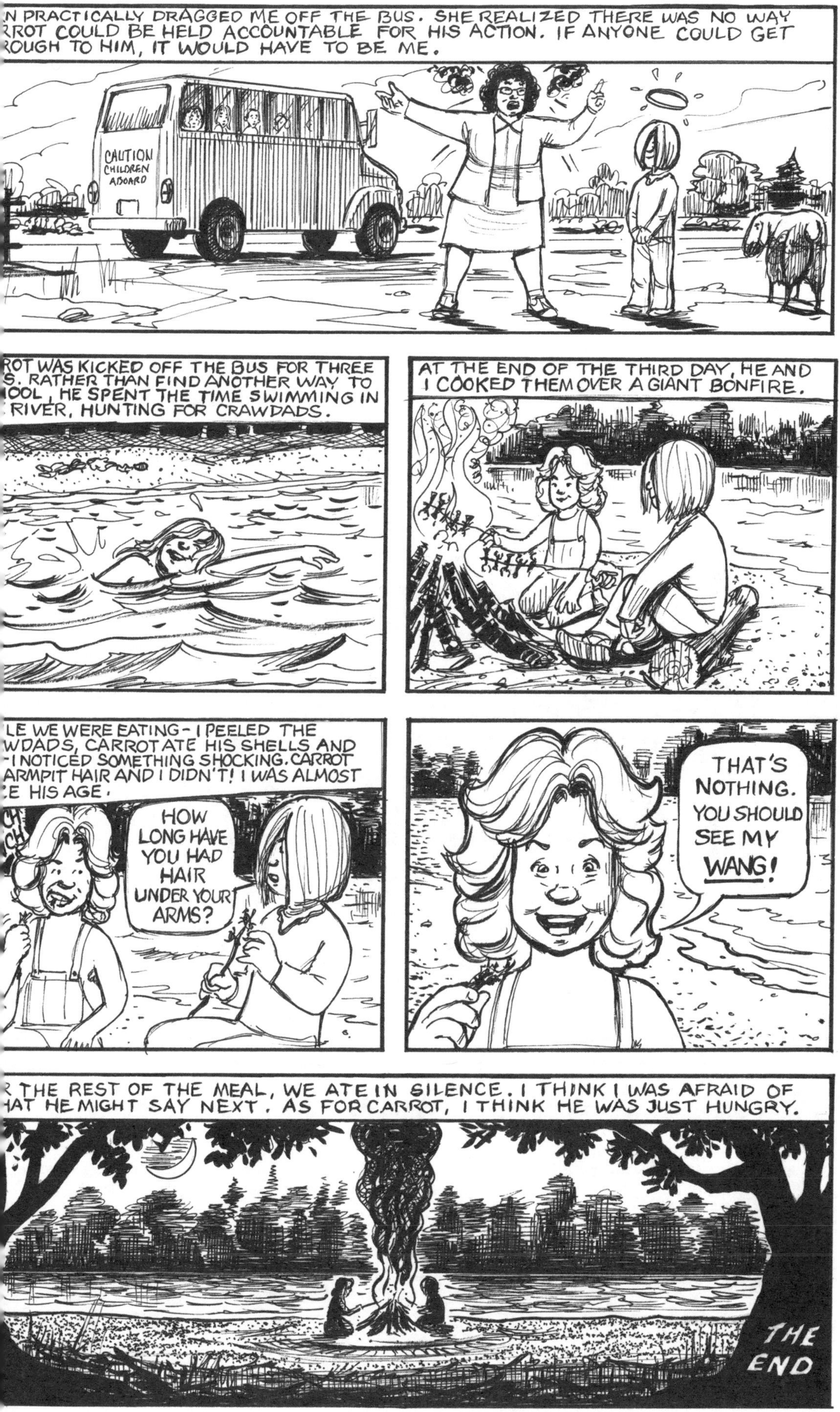
N PRACTICALLY DRAGGED ME OFF THE BUS. SHE REALIZED THERE WAS NO WAY RROT COULD BE HELD ACCOUNTABLE FOR HIS ACTION. IF ANYONE COULD GET ROUGH TO HIM, IT WOULD HAVE TO BE ME.
CAUTION CHILDREN ABOARD
ROT WAS KICKED OFF THE BUS FOR THREE S. RATHER THAN FIND ANOTHER WAY TO IOOL, HE SPENT THE TIME SWIMMING IN RIVER, HUNTING FOR CRAWDADS.
AT THE END OF THE THIRD DAY, HE AND I COOKED THEM OVER A GIANT BONFIRE.
LE WE WERE EATING - I PEELED THE WDADS, CARROT ATE HIS SHELLS AND - I NOTICED SOMETHING SHOCKING. CARROT ARMPIT HAIR AND I DIDN'T! I WAS ALMOST E HIS AGE.
HOW LONG HAVE YOU HAD HAIR UNDER YOUR ARMS?
THAT'S NOTHING. YOU SHOULD SEE MY WANG!
R THE REST OF THE MEAL, WE ATE IN SILENCE. I THINK I WAS AFRAID OF HAT HE MIGHT SAY NEXT. AS FOR CARROT, I THINK HE WAS JUST HUNGRY.
THE END

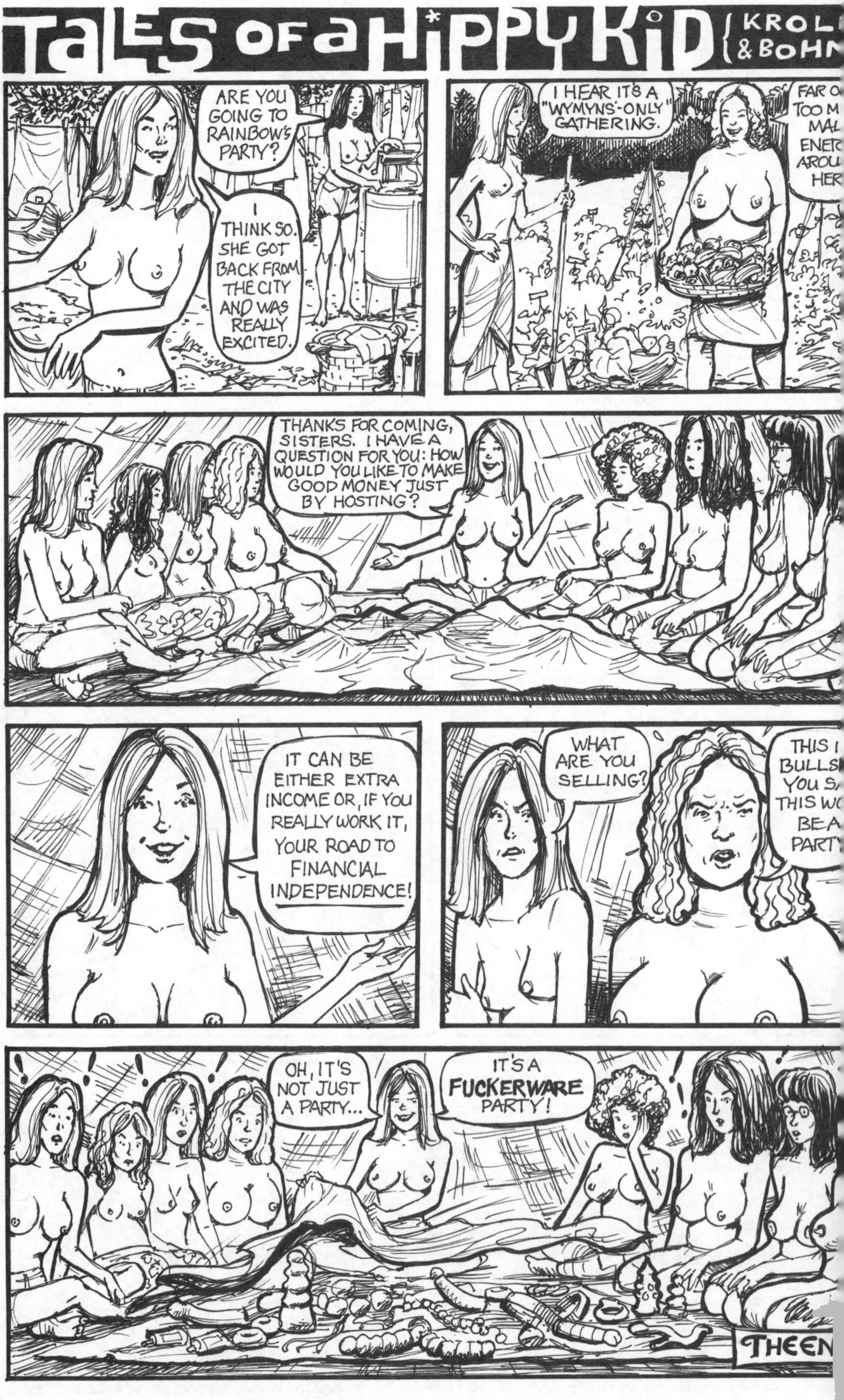
TALES OF A HIPPY KID
ARE YOU GOING TO RAINBOW'S PARTY?
I THINK SO. SHE GOT BACK FROM THE CITY AND WAS REALLY EXCITED.
I HEAR IT'S A "WYMYNS'-ONLY" GATHERING.
THANKS FOR COMING, SISTERS. I HAVE A QUESTION FOR YOU: HOW WOULD YOU LIKE TO MAKE GOOD MONEY JUST BY HOSTING?
IT CAN BE EITHER EXTRA INCOME OR, IF YOU REALLY WORK IT, YOUR ROAD TO FINANCIAL INDEPENDENCE!
WHAT ARE YOU SELLING?
OH, IT'S NOT JUST A PARTY...
IT'S A FUCKERWARE PARTY!

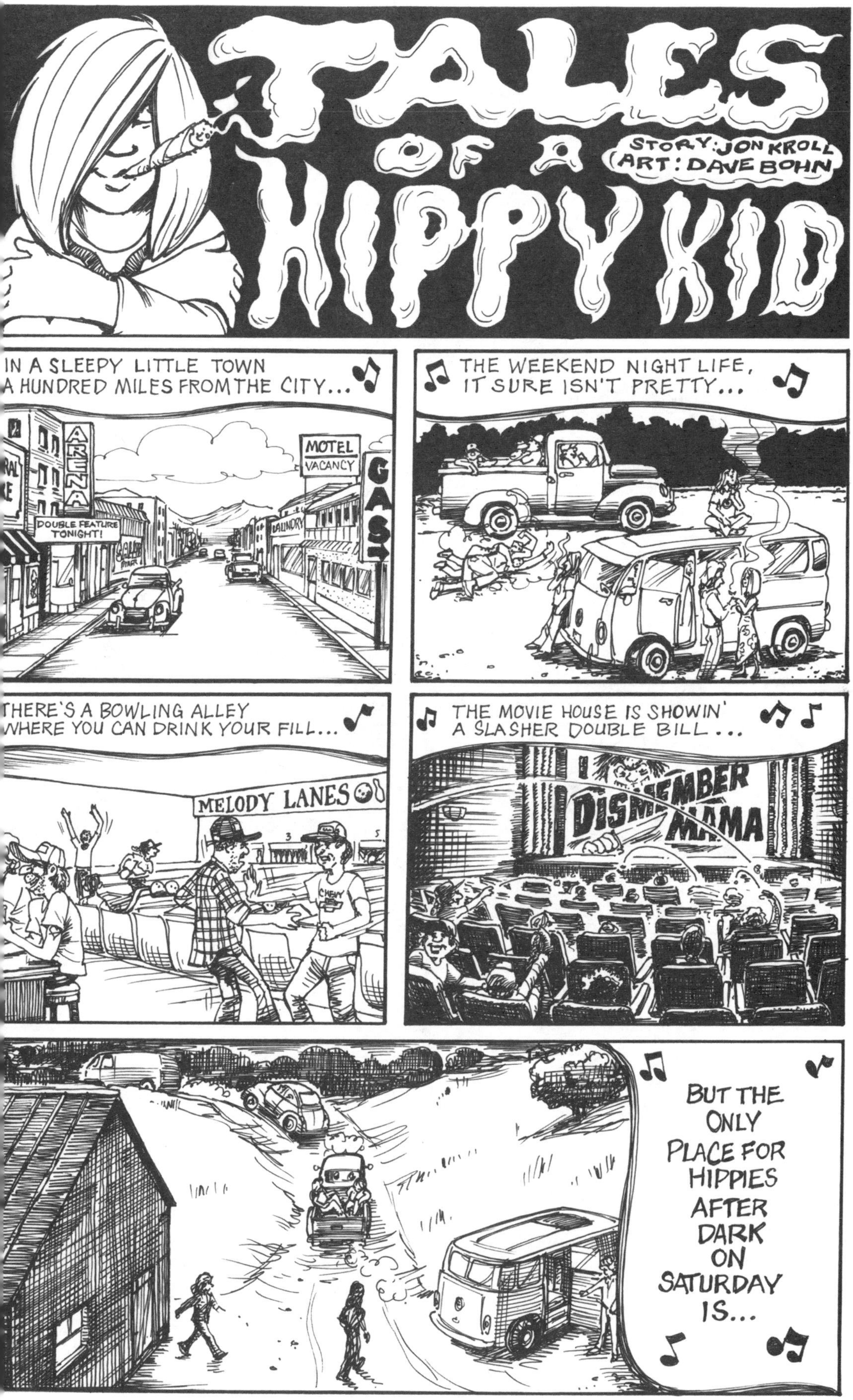
TALES OF A HIPPY KID
STORY: JON KROLL
ART: DAVE BOHN
IN A SLEEPY LITTLE TOWN
A HUNDRED MILES FROM THE CITY...
ARENA
DOUBLE FEATURE TONIGHT!
MOTEL
VACANCY
GAS
LAUNDRY
THE WEEKEND NIGHT LIFE,
IT SURE ISN'T PRETTY...
THERE'S A BOWLING ALLEY
WHERE YOU CAN DRINK YOUR FILL...
MELODY LANES
CHEVY
THE MOVIE HOUSE IS SHOWIN'
A SLASHER DOUBLE BILL...
DISMEMBER MAMA
BUT THE ONLY PLACE FOR HIPPIES AFTER DARK ON SATURDAY IS...

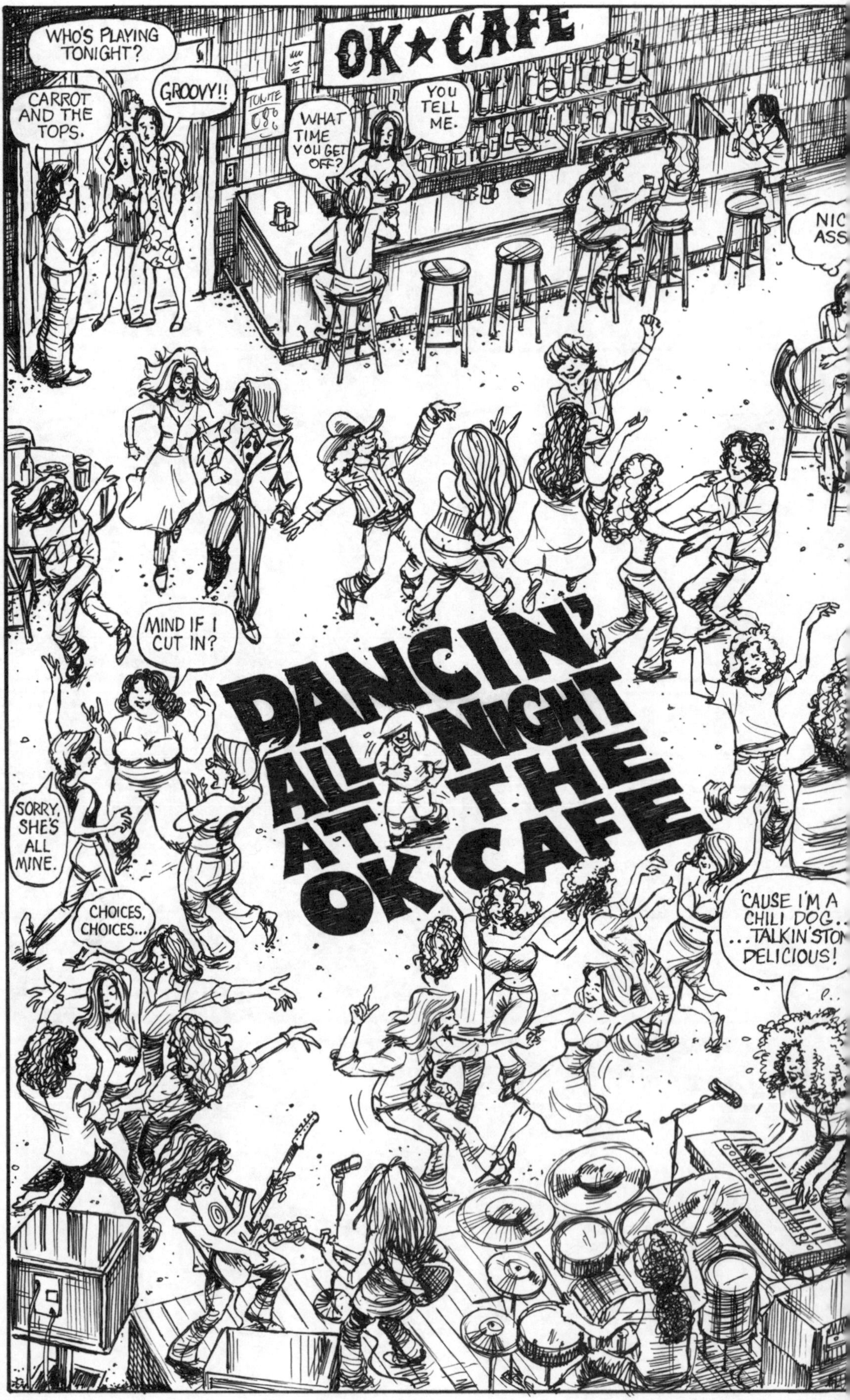

OK★CAFE
WHO'S PLAYING TONIGHT?
CARROT AND THE TOPS.
GROOVY!!
TONITE
WHAT TIME YOU GET OFF?
YOU TELL ME.
MIND IF I CUT IN?
DANCIN' ALL NIGHT AT THE OK CAFE
SORRY, SHE'S ALL MINE.
CHOICES, CHOICES...
'CAUSE I'M A CHILI DOG... ...TALKIN'STON DELICIOUS!

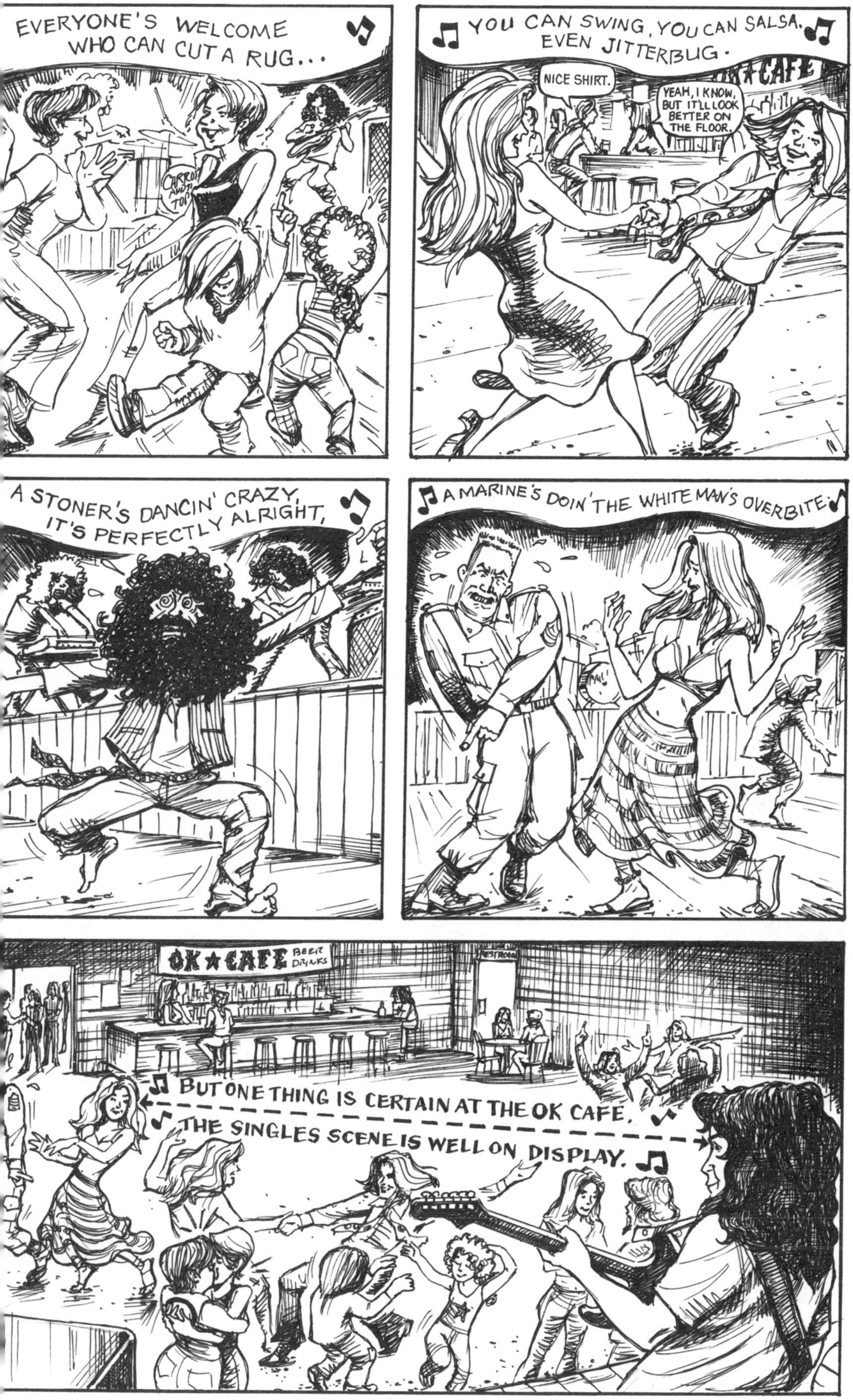
EVERYONE'S WELCOME WHO CAN CUT A RUG...
YOU CAN SWING, YOU CAN SALSA, EVEN JITTERBUG.
NICE SHIRT.
YEAH, I KNOW, BUT IT'LL LOOK BETTER ON THE FLOOR.
A STONER'S DANCIN' CRAZY, IT'S PERFECTLY ALRIGHT,
A MARINE'S DOIN' THE WHITE MAN'S OVERBITE.
OK ★ CAFE
BEER DRINKS
RESTROOM
BUT ONE THING IS CERTAIN AT THE OK CAFE,
THE SINGLES SCENE IS WELL ON DISPLAY.

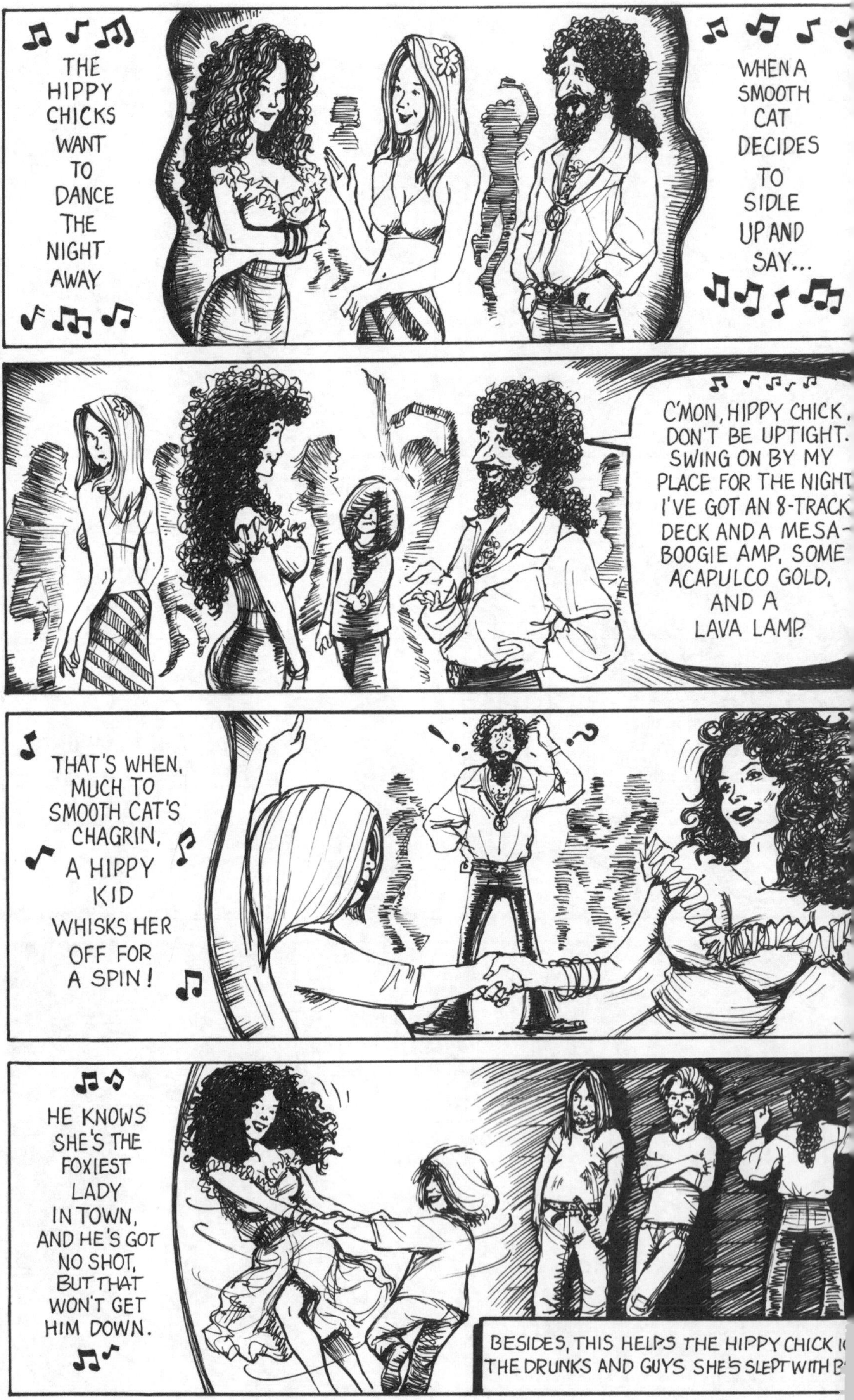
THE HIPPY CHICKS WANT TO DANCE THE NIGHT AWAY
WHEN A SMOOTH CAT DECIDES TO SIDLE UP AND SAY...
C'MON, HIPPY CHICK, DON'T BE UPTIGHT. SWING ON BY MY PLACE FOR THE NIGHT. I'VE GOT AN 8-TRACK DECK AND A MESA-BOOGIE AMP, SOME ACAPULCO GOLD, AND A LAVA LAMP.
!
?
THAT'S WHEN, MUCH TO SMOOTH CAT'S CHAGRIN, A HIPPY KID WHISKS HER OFF FOR A SPIN!
HE KNOWS SHE'S THE FOXIEST LADY IN TOWN, AND HE'S GOT NO SHOT, BUT THAT WON'T GET HIM DOWN.
BESIDES, THIS HELPS THE HIPPY CHICK I
THE DRUNKS AND GUYS SHE'S SLEPT WITH B

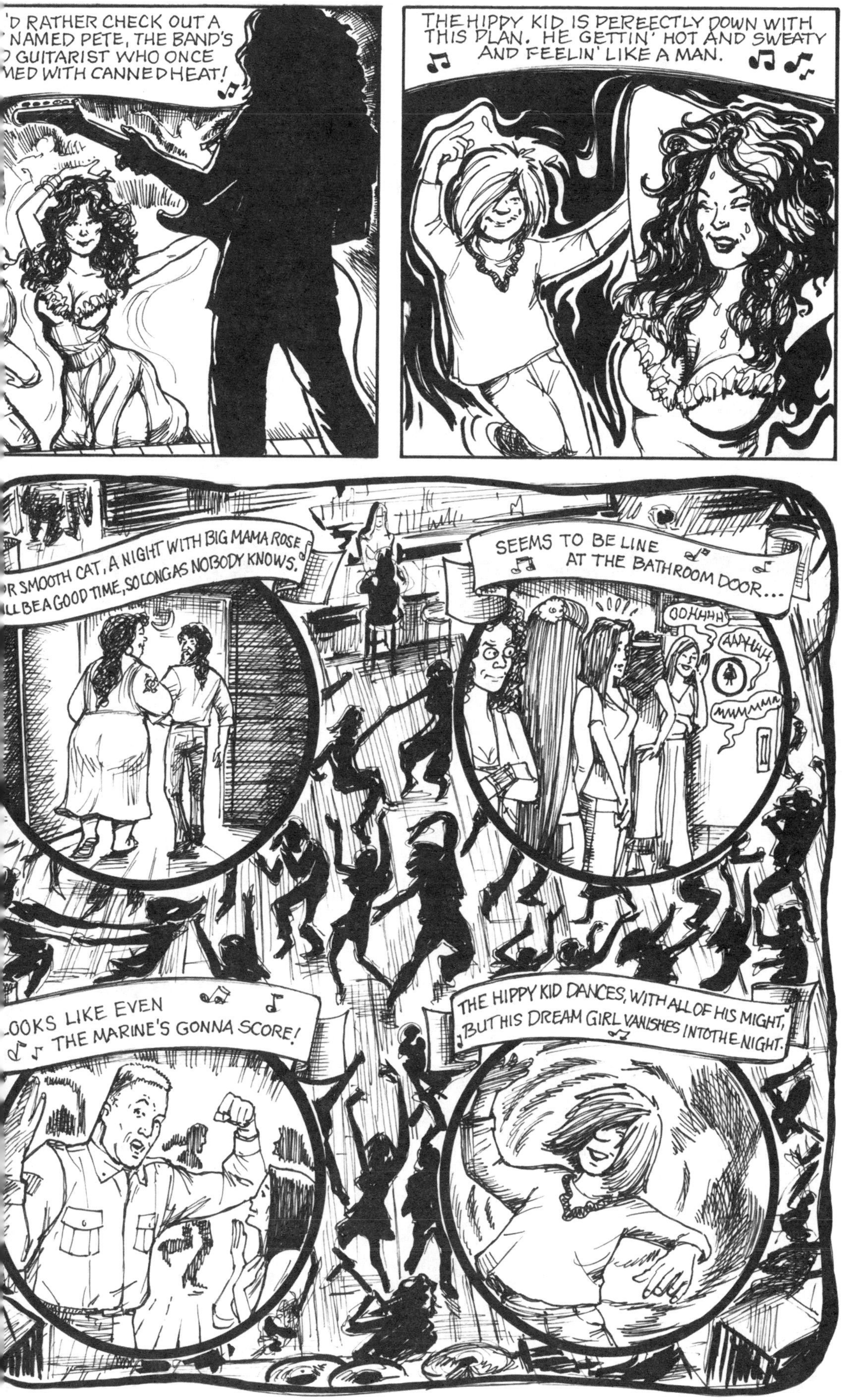
'D RATHER CHECK OUT A
NAMED PETE, THE BAND'S
D GUITARIST WHO ONCE
MED WITH CANNED HEAT!
THE HIPPY KID IS PEREECTLY DOWN WITH THIS PLAN. HE GETTIN' HOT AND SWEATY AND FEELIN' LIKE A MAN.
R SMOOTH CAT, A NIGHT WITH BIG MAMA ROSE
LL BE A GOOD TIME, SO LONG AS NOBODY KNOWS.
SEEMS TO BE LINE AT THE BATHROOM DOOR...
OOHHHH
AAAHHHH
MMMMMMA
OOKS LIKE EVEN THE MARINE'S GONNA SCORE!
THE HIPPY KID DANCES, WITH ALL OF HIS MIGHT,
BUT HIS DREAM GIRL VANISHES INTO THE NIGHT.

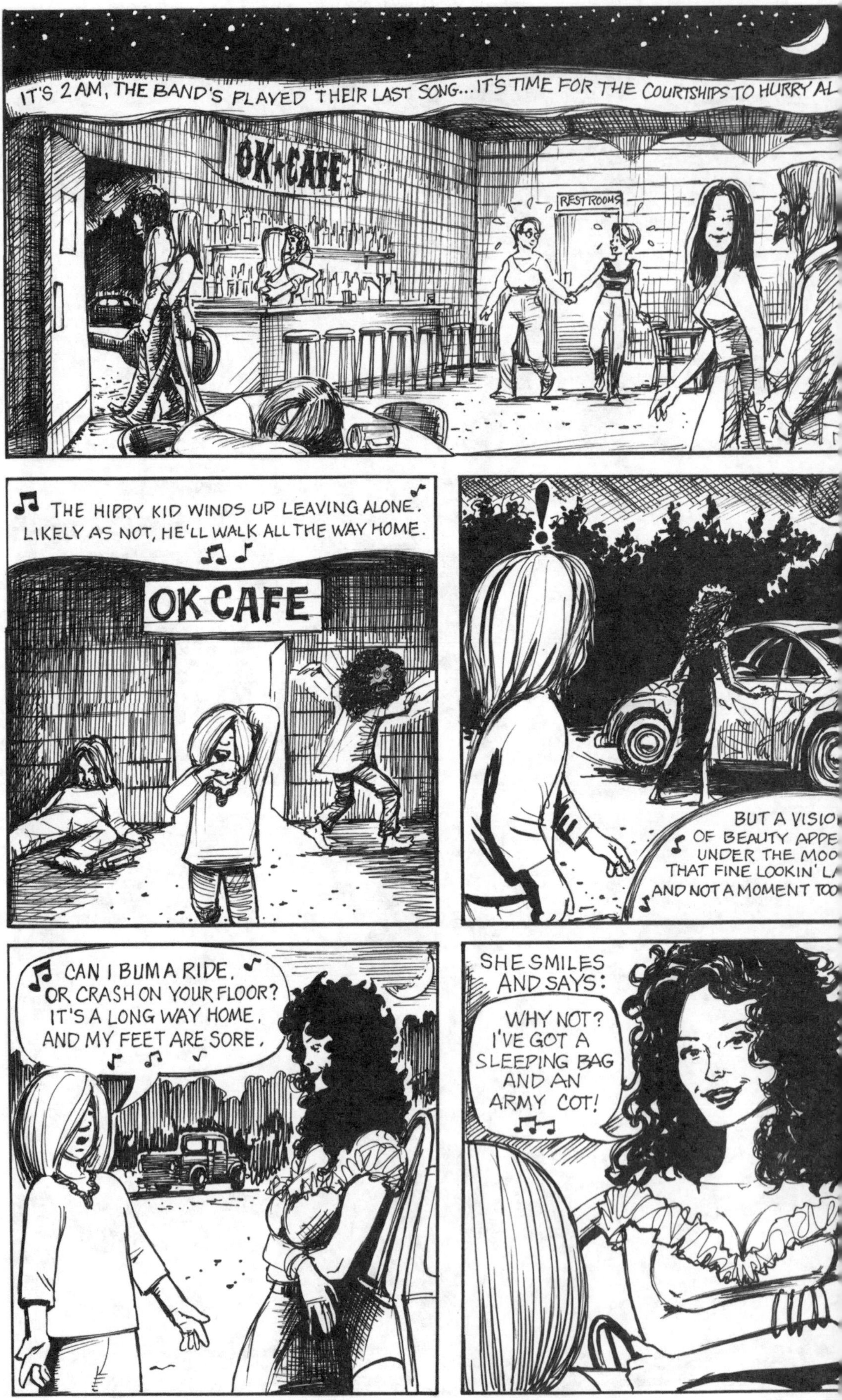
IT'S 2 AM, THE BAND'S PLAYED THEIR LAST SONG... IT'S TIME FOR THE COURTSHIPS TO HURRY AL
OK★CAFE
RESTROOMS
THE HIPPY KID WINDS UP LEAVING ALONE.
LIKELY AS NOT, HE'LL WALK ALL THE WAY HOME.
OK CAFE
!
BUT A VISIO
OF BEAUTY APPE
UNDER THE MOO
THAT FINE LOOKIN' LA
AND NOT A MOMENT TOO
CAN I BUM A RIDE,
OR CRASH ON YOUR FLOOR?
IT'S A LONG WAY HOME,
AND MY FEET ARE SORE,
SHE SMILES AND SAYS:
WHY NOT? I'VE GOT A SLEEPING BAG AND AN ARMY COT!

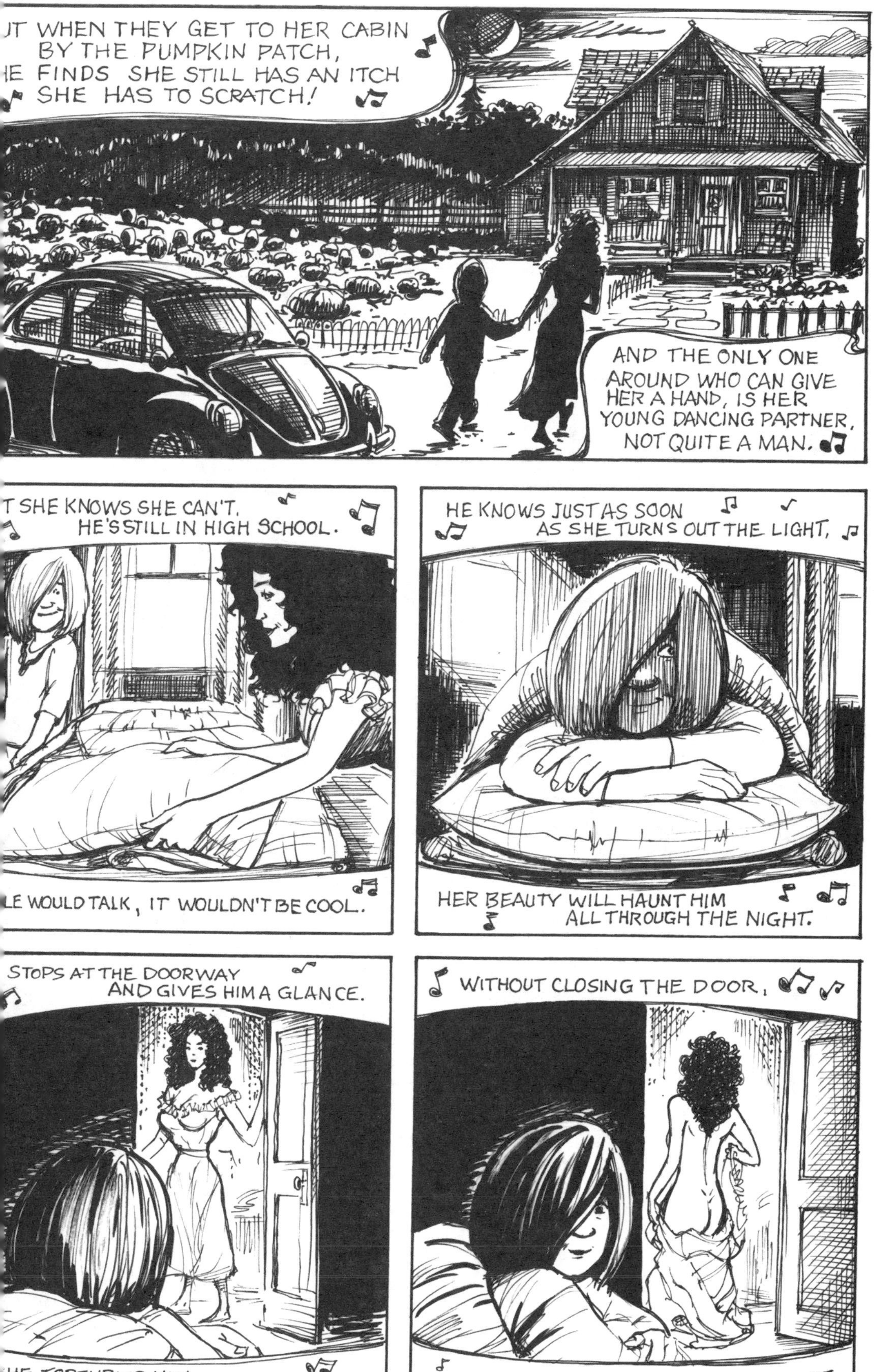
UT WHEN THEY GET TO HER CABIN BY THE PUMPKIN PATCH,
IE FINDS SHE STILL HAS AN ITCH SHE HAS TO SCRATCH!
AND THE ONLY ONE AROUND WHO CAN GIVE HER A HAND, IS HER YOUNG DANCING PARTNER, NOT QUITE A MAN.
T SHE KNOWS SHE CAN'T. HE'S STILL IN HIGH SCHOOL.
LE WOULD TALK, IT WOULDN'T BE COOL.
HE KNOWS JUST AS SOON AS SHE TURNS OUT THE LIGHT,
HER BEAUTY WILL HAUNT HIM ALL THROUGH THE NIGHT.
STOPS AT THE DOORWAY AND GIVES HIM A GLANCE.
HE TORTURING HIM, OR DOES HE STILL HAVE A CHANCE?
WITHOUT CLOSING THE DOOR,
SHE SLIPS OUT OF HER GOWN...

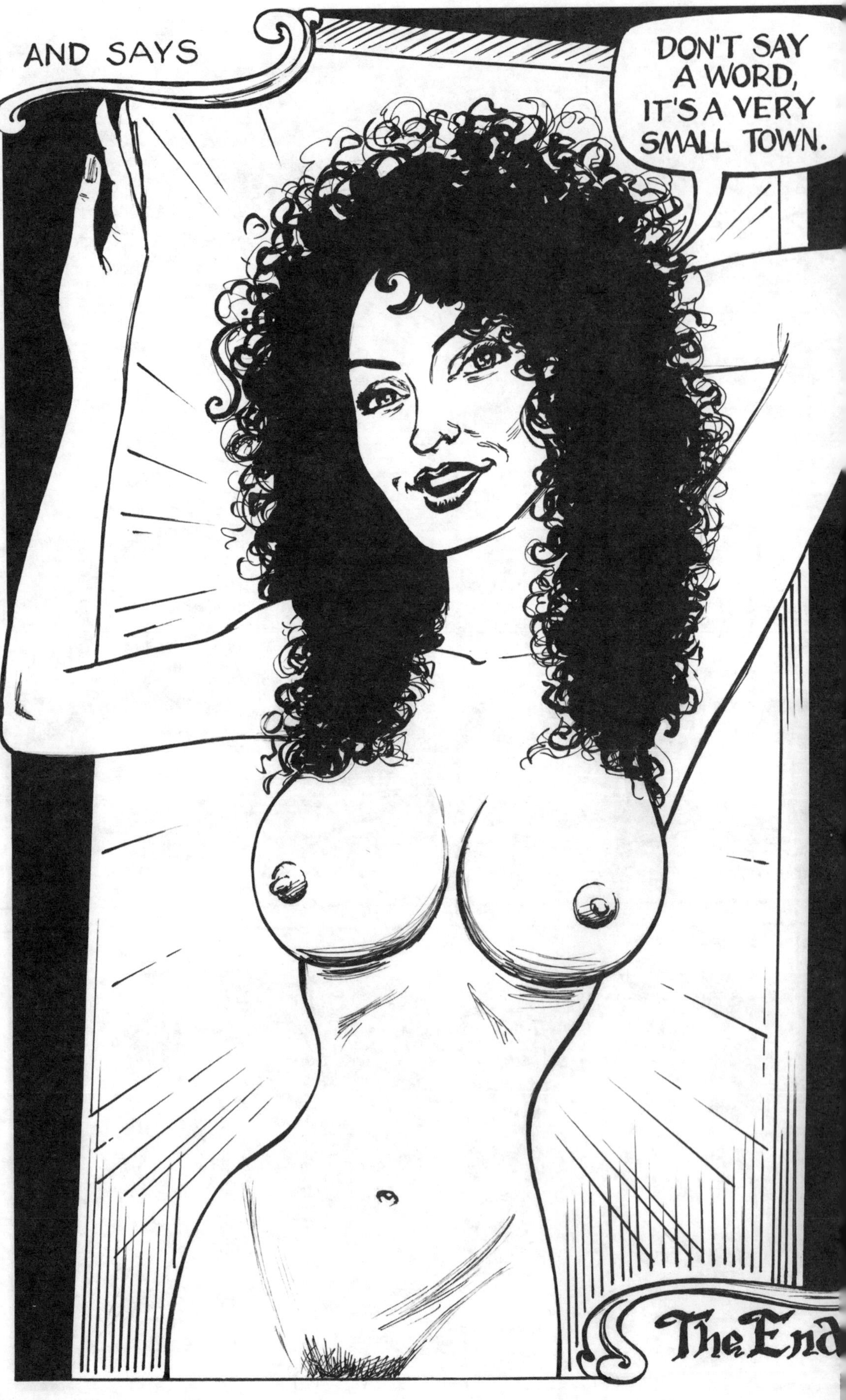
AND SAYS
DON'T SAY A WORD, IT'S A VERY SMALL TOWN.
The End

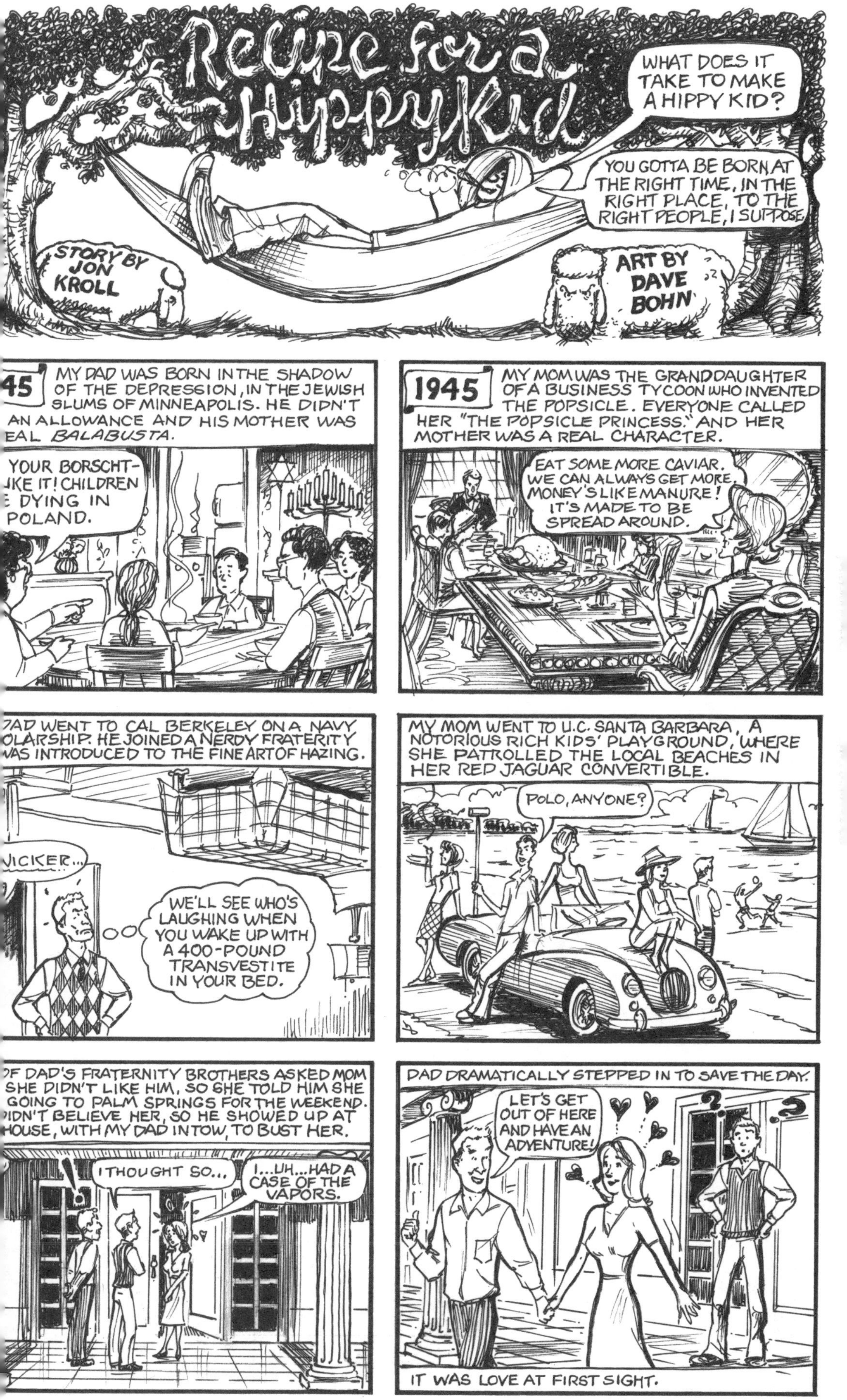
Recipe for a Hippy Kid
WHAT DOES IT TAKE TO MAKE A HIPPY KID?
YOU GOTTA BE BORN AT THE RIGHT TIME, IN THE RIGHT PLACE, TO THE RIGHT PEOPLE, I SUPPOSE.
STORY BY JON KROLL
ART BY DAVE BOHN
45
MY DAD WAS BORN IN THE SHADOW OF THE DEPRESSION, IN THE JEWISH SLUMS OF MINNEAPOLIS. HE DIDN'T AN ALLOWANCE AND HIS MOTHER WAS EAL BALABUSTA.
YOUR BORSCHT- IKE IT! CHILDREN DYING IN POLAND.
1945
MY MOM WAS THE GRANDDAUGHTER OF A BUSINESS TYCOON WHO INVENTED THE POPSICLE. EVERYONE CALLED HER "THE POPSICLE PRINCESS." AND HER MOTHER WAS A REAL CHARACTER.
EAT SOME MORE CAVIAR. WE CAN ALWAYS GET MORE. MONEY'S LIKE MANURE! IT'S MADE TO BE SPREAD AROUND.
DAD WENT TO CAL BERKELEY ON A NAVY OLARSHIP. HE JOINED A NERDY FRATERITY WAS INTRODUCED TO THE FINE ART OF HAZING.
ICKER...
WE'LL SEE WHO'S LAUGHING WHEN YOU WAKE UP WITH A 400-POUND TRANSVESTITE IN YOUR BED.
MY MOM WENT TO U.C. SANTA BARBARA, A NOTORIOUS RICH KIDS' PLAYGROUND, WHERE SHE PATROLLED THE LOCAL BEACHES IN HER RED JAGUAR CONVERTIBLE.
POLO, ANYONE?
OF DAD'S FRATERNITY BROTHERS ASKED MOM SHE DIDN'T LIKE HIM, SO SHE TOLD HIM SHE GOING TO PALM SPRINGS FOR THE WEEKEND. IDN'T BELIEVE HER, SO HE SHOWED UP AT HOUSE, WITH MY DAD IN TOW, TO BUST HER.
I THOUGHT SO...
I...UH...HAD A CASE OF THE VAPORS.
DAD DRAMATICALLY STEPPED IN TO SAVE THE DAY.
LET'S GET OUT OF HERE AND HAVE AN ADVENTURE!
IT WAS LOVE AT FIRST SIGHT.

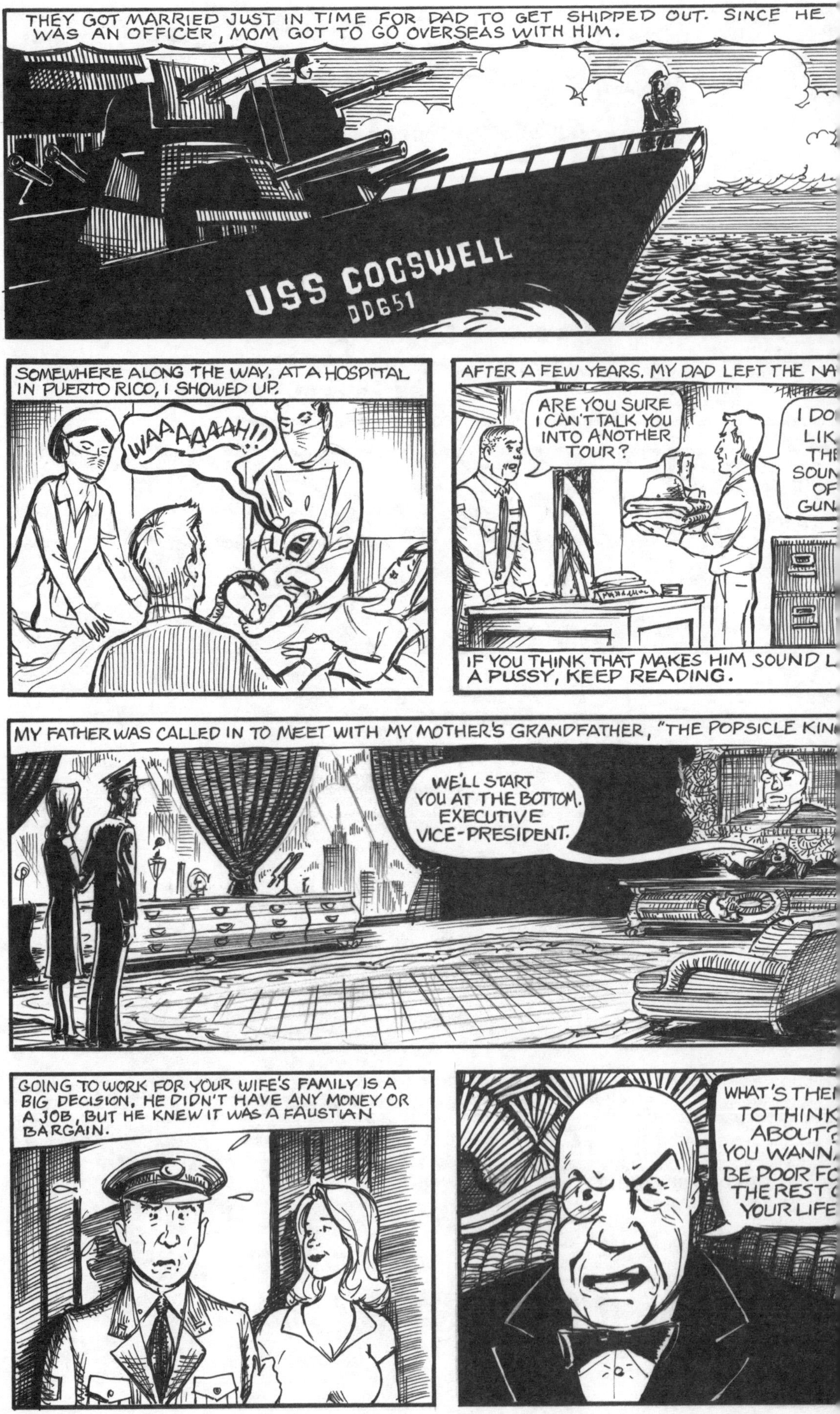
THEY GOT MARRIED JUST IN TIME FOR DAD TO GET SHIPPED OUT. SINCE HE WAS AN OFFICER, MOM GOT TO GO OVERSEAS WITH HIM.
USS COGSWELL
DD651
SOMEWHERE ALONG THE WAY, AT A HOSPITAL IN PUERTO RICO, I SHOWED UP.
WAAAAAAH!!
AFTER A FEW YEARS, MY DAD LEFT THE NA
ARE YOU SURE I CAN'T TALK YOU INTO ANOTHER TOUR?
I DO LIK THE SOUN OF GUN
IF YOU THINK THAT MAKES HIM SOUND L A PUSSY, KEEP READING.
MY FATHER WAS CALLED IN TO MEET WITH MY MOTHER'S GRANDFATHER, "THE POPSICLE KIN
WE'LL START YOU AT THE BOTTOM. EXECUTIVE VICE-PRESIDENT.
GOING TO WORK FOR YOUR WIFE'S FAMILY IS A BIG DECISION. HE DIDN'T HAVE ANY MONEY OR A JOB, BUT HE KNEW IT WAS A FAUSTIAN BARGAIN.
WHAT'S THE TO THINK ABOUT? YOU WANNA BE POOR FO THE REST YOUR LIFE

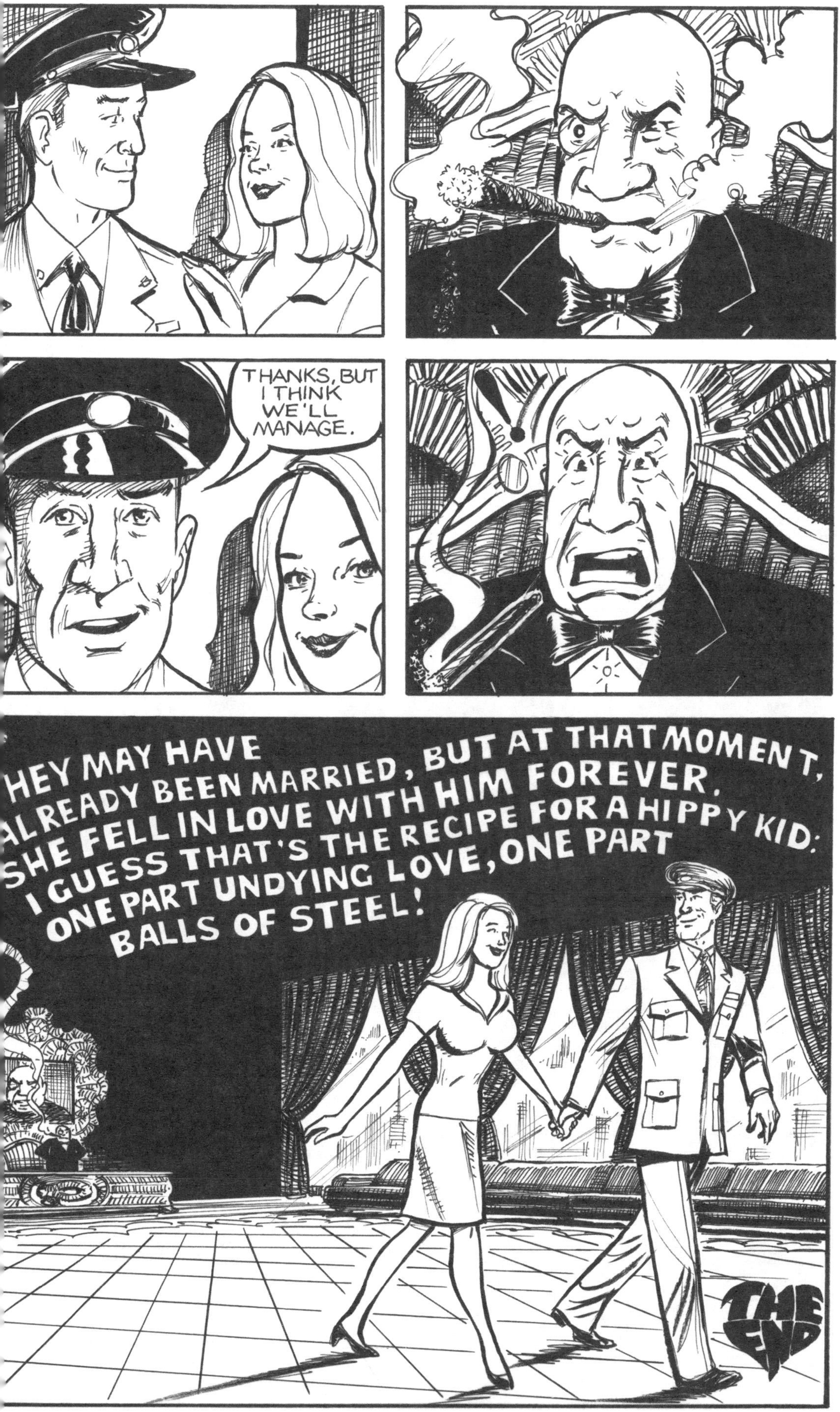
THANKS, BUT I THINK WE'LL MANAGE.
HEY MAY HAVE
ALREADY BEEN MARRIED, BUT AT THAT MOMENT,
SHE FELL IN LOVE WITH HIM FOREVER.
I GUESS THAT'S THE RECIPE FOR A HIPPY KID:
ONE PART UNDYING LOVE, ONE PART
BALLS OF STEEL!
THE END

THE SEVENTIES SPORTING SCENE

STORY: JON H
ART: DAVE B

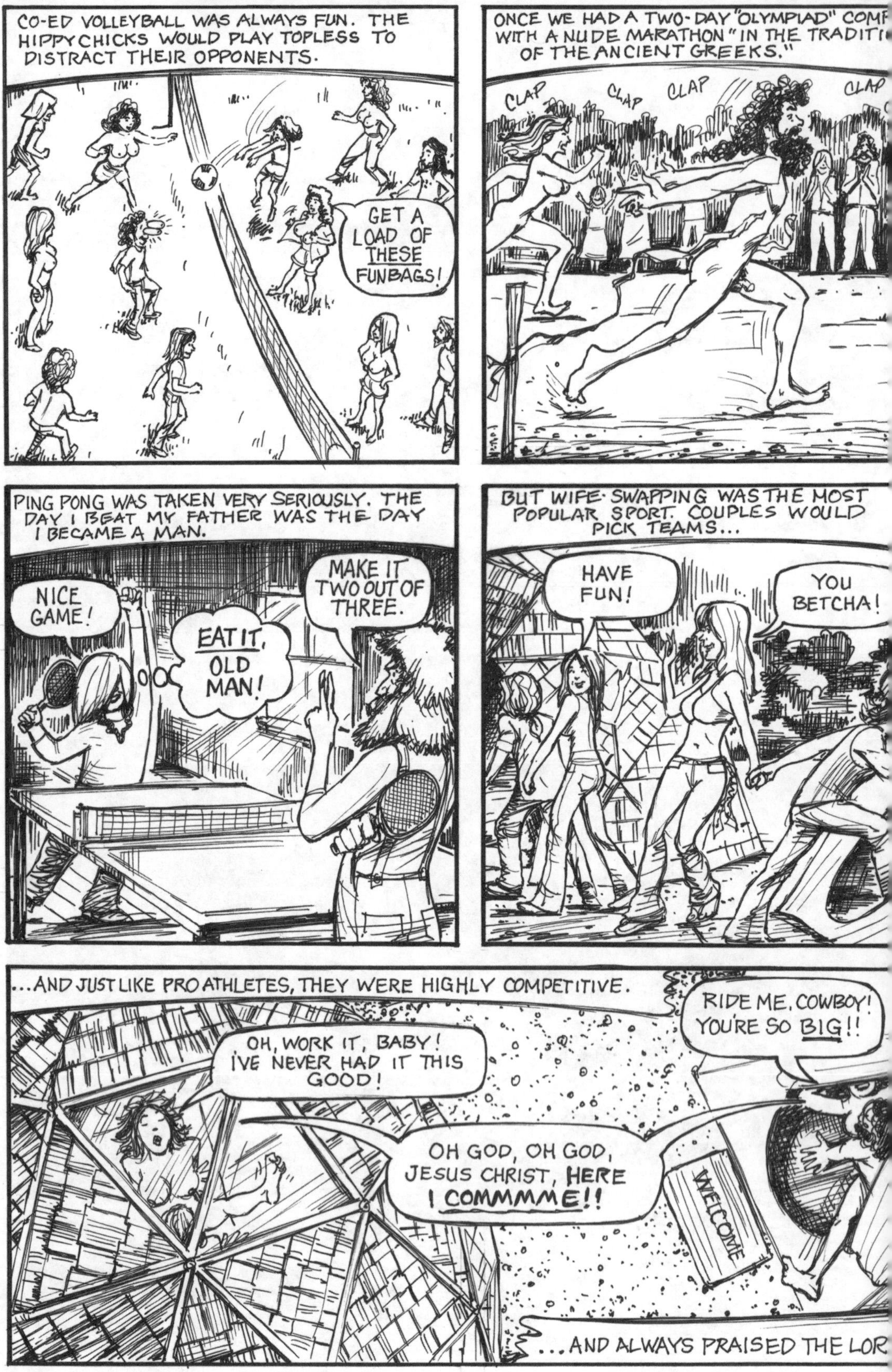
CO-ED VOLLEYBALL WAS ALWAYS FUN. THE HIPPY CHICKS WOULD PLAY TOPLESS TO DISTRACT THEIR OPPONENTS.
GET A LOAD OF THESE FUNBAGS!
ONCE WE HAD A TWO-DAY "OLYMPIAD" COMP WITH A NUDE MARATHON "IN THE TRADITI OF THE ANCIENT GREEKS."
CLAP
CLAP
CLAP
CLAP
PING PONG WAS TAKEN VERY SERIOUSLY. THE DAY I BEAT MY FATHER WAS THE DAY I BECAME A MAN.
NICE GAME!
EAT IT, OLD MAN!
MAKE IT TWO OUT OF THREE.
BUT WIFE-SWAPPING WAS THE MOST POPULAR SPORT. COUPLES WOULD PICK TEAMS...
HAVE FUN!
YOU BETCHA!
...AND JUST LIKE PRO ATHLETES, THEY WERE HIGHLY COMPETITIVE.
OH, WORK IT, BABY! I'VE NEVER HAD IT THIS GOOD!
RIDE ME, COWBOY! YOU'RE SO BIG!!
OH GOD, OH GOD, JESUS CHRIST, HERE I COMMMME!!
WELCOME
...AND ALWAYS PRAISED THE LOR

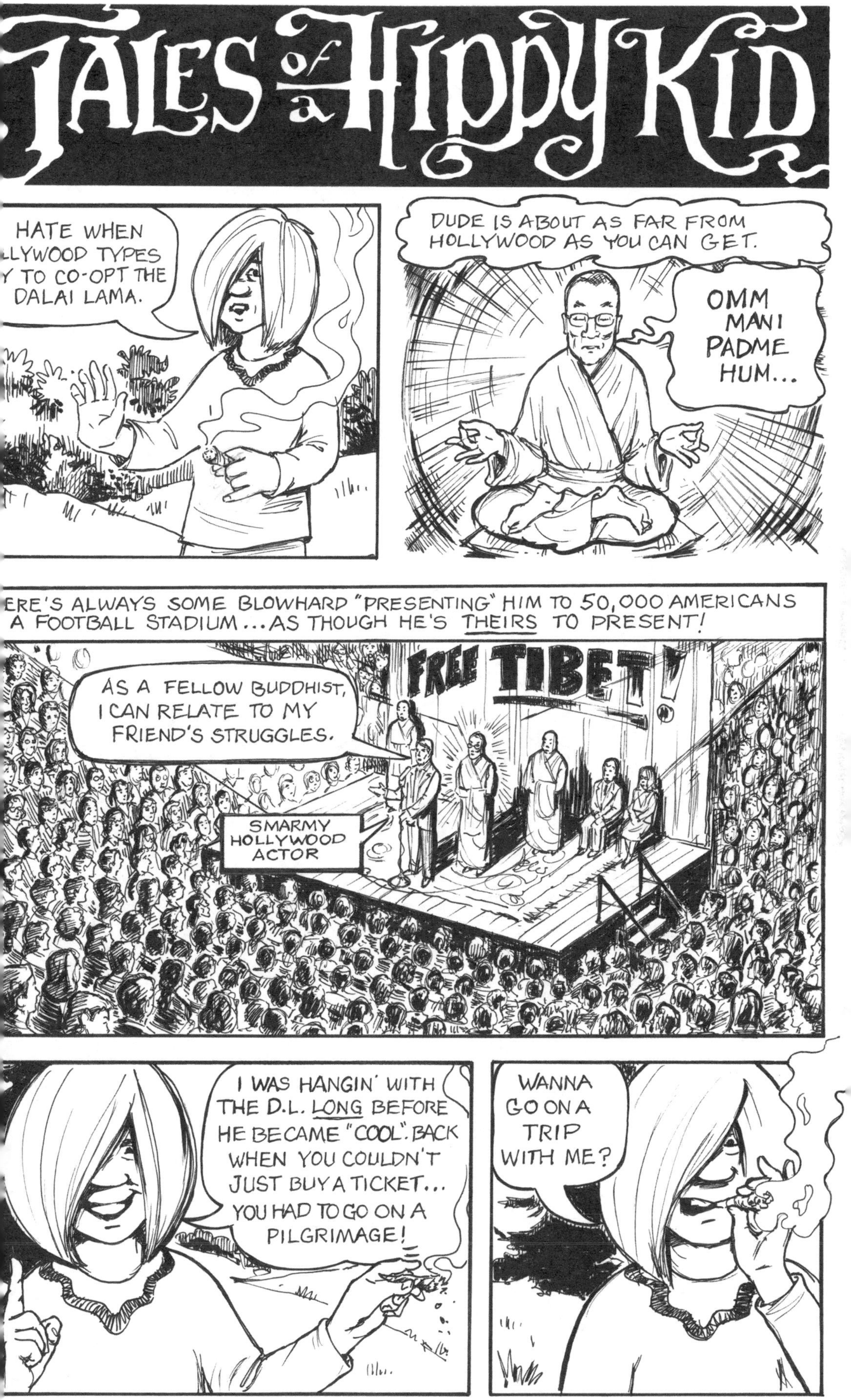
TALES of a HIPPY KID
HATE WHEN
LLYWOOD TYPES
Y TO CO-OPT THE
DALAI LAMA.
DUDE IS ABOUT AS FAR FROM HOLLYWOOD AS YOU CAN GET.
OMM MANI PADME HUM...
ERE'S ALWAYS SOME BLOWHARD "PRESENTING" HIM TO 50,000 AMERICANS A FOOTBALL STADIUM... AS THOUGH HE'S THEIRS TO PRESENT!
FREE TIBET!
AS A FELLOW BUDDHIST, I CAN RELATE TO MY FRIEND'S STRUGGLES.
SMARMY HOLLYWOOD ACTOR
I WAS HANGIN' WITH THE D.L. LONG BEFORE HE BECAME "COOL". BACK WHEN YOU COULDN'T JUST BUY A TICKET... YOU HAD TO GO ON A PILGRIMAGE!
WANNA GO ON A TRIP WITH ME?

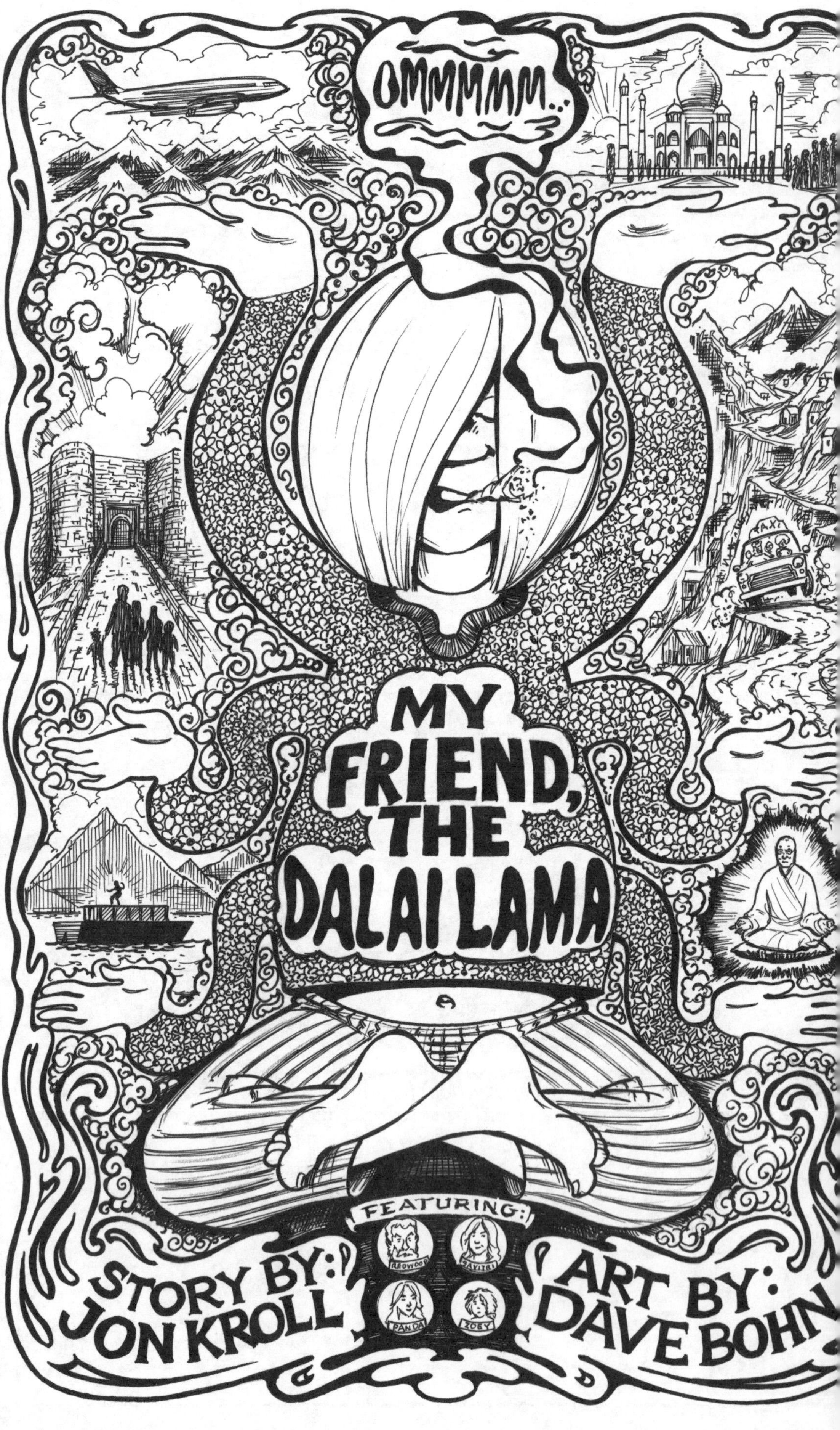
OMMMMM...
MY FRIEND, THE DALAI LAMA
TAXI
FEATURING:
REDWOOD
SAVITRI
PANDA
ZOEY
STORY BY: JON KROLL
ART BY: DAVE BOHN

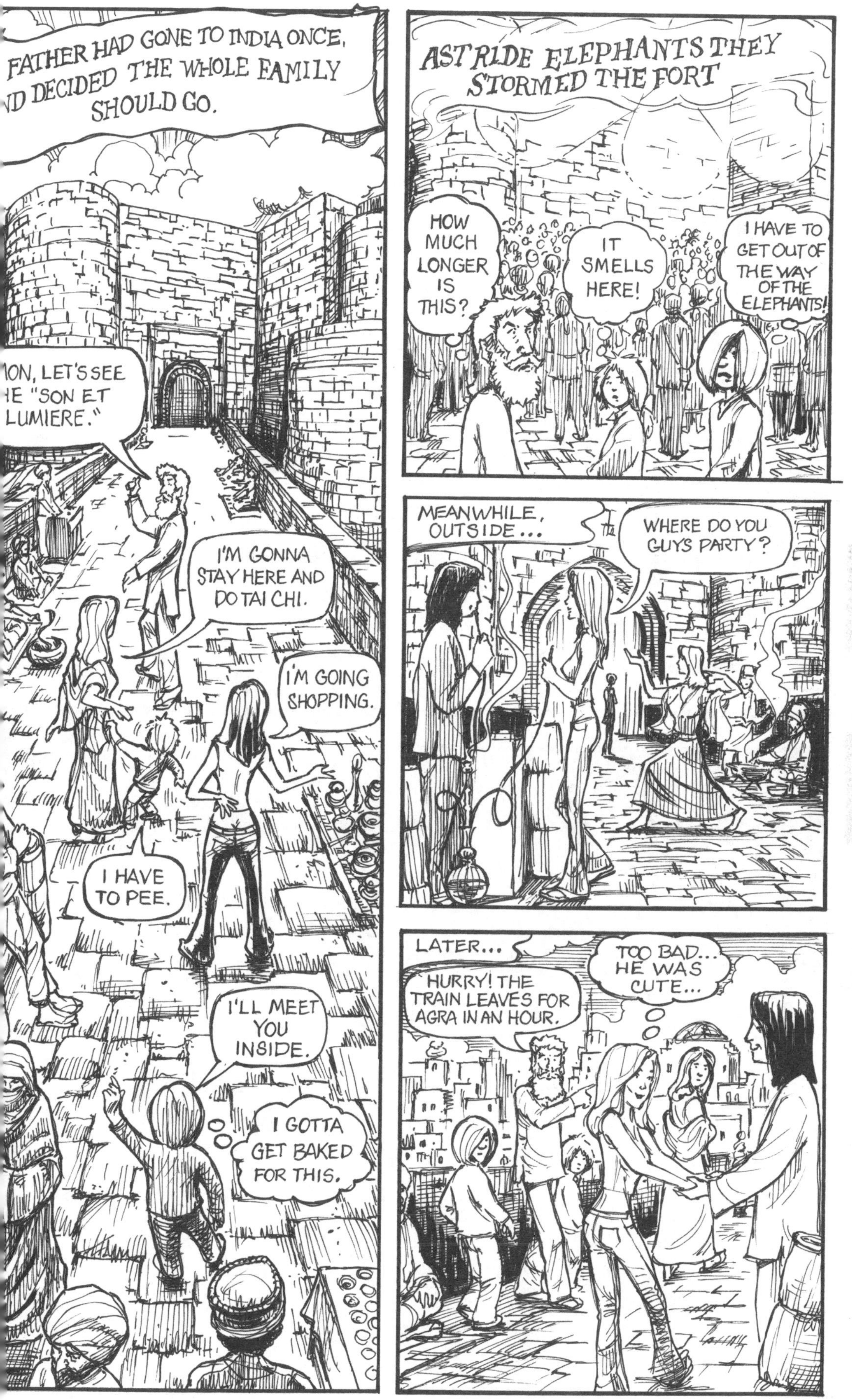

FATHER HAD GONE TO INDIA ONCE, ND DECIDED THE WHOLE FAMILY SHOULD GO.
ON, LET'S SEE HE "SON ET LUMIERE."
I'M GONNA STAY HERE AND DO TAI CHI.
I'M GOING SHOPPING.
I HAVE TO PEE.
I'LL MEET YOU INSIDE.
I GOTTA GET BAKED FOR THIS.
ASTRIDE ELEPHANTS THEY STORMED THE FORT
HOW MUCH LONGER IS THIS?
IT SMELLS HERE!
I HAVE TO GET OUT OF THE WAY OF THE ELEPHANTS!
MEANWHILE, OUTSIDE...
WHERE DO YOU GUYS PARTY?
LATER...
HURRY! THE TRAIN LEAVES FOR AGRA IN AN HOUR.
TOO BAD... HE WAS CUTE...

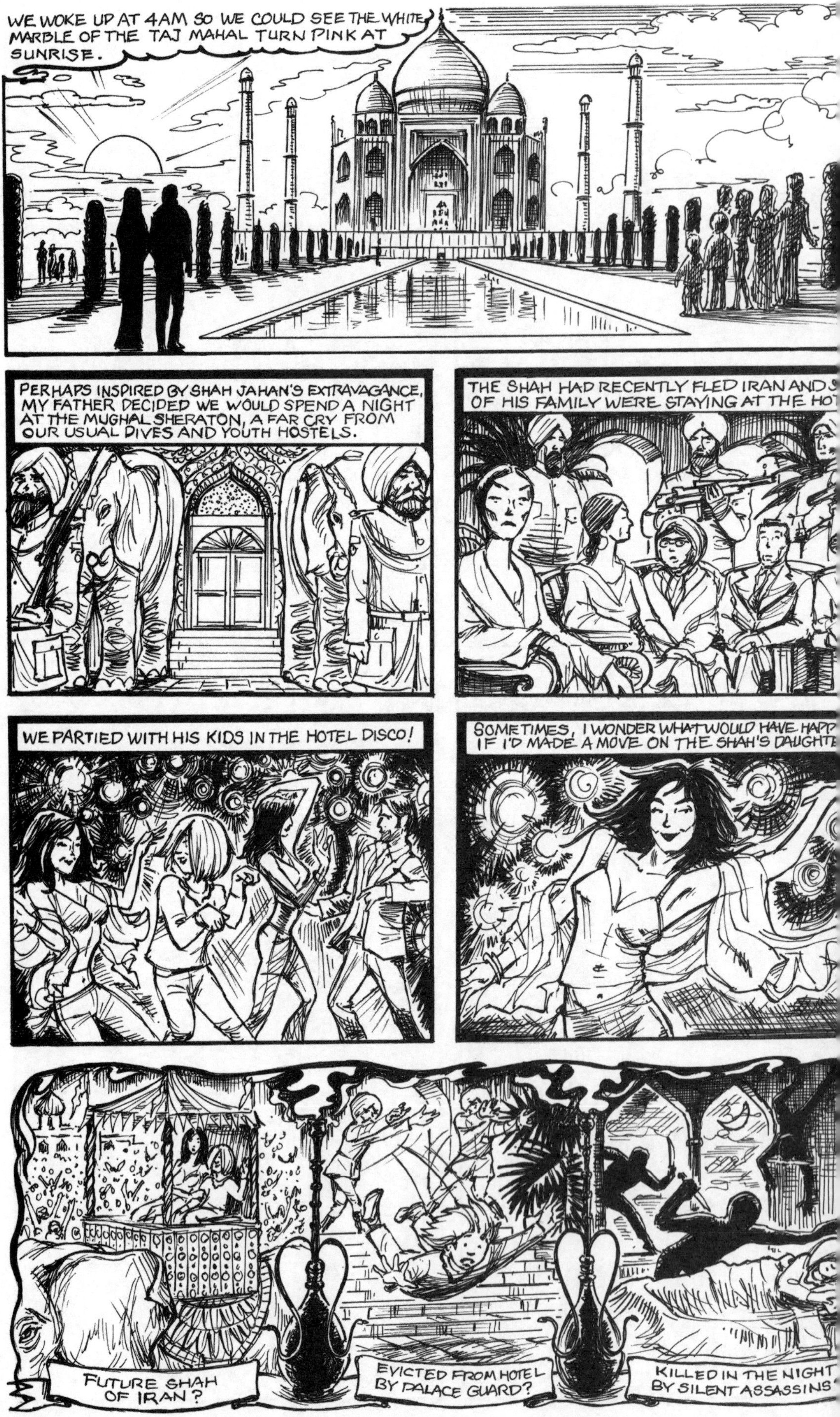

WE WOKE UP AT 4AM SO WE COULD SEE THE WHITE MARBLE OF THE TAJ MAHAL TURN PINK AT SUNRISE.
PERHAPS INSPIRED BY SHAH JAHAN'S EXTRAVAGANCE, MY FATHER DECIDED WE WOULD SPEND A NIGHT AT THE MUGHAL SHERATON, A FAR CRY FROM OUR USUAL DIVES AND YOUTH HOSTELS.
THE SHAH HAD RECENTLY FLED IRAN AND S
OF HIS FAMILY WERE STAYING AT THE HO
WE PARTIED WITH HIS KIDS IN THE HOTEL DISCO!
SOMETIMES, I WONDER WHAT WOULD HAVE HAPP
IF I'D MADE A MOVE ON THE SHAH'S DAUGHTE
FUTURE SHAH OF IRAN?
EVICTED FROM HOTEL BY PALACE GUARD?
KILLED IN THE NIGHT BY SILENT ASSASSINS

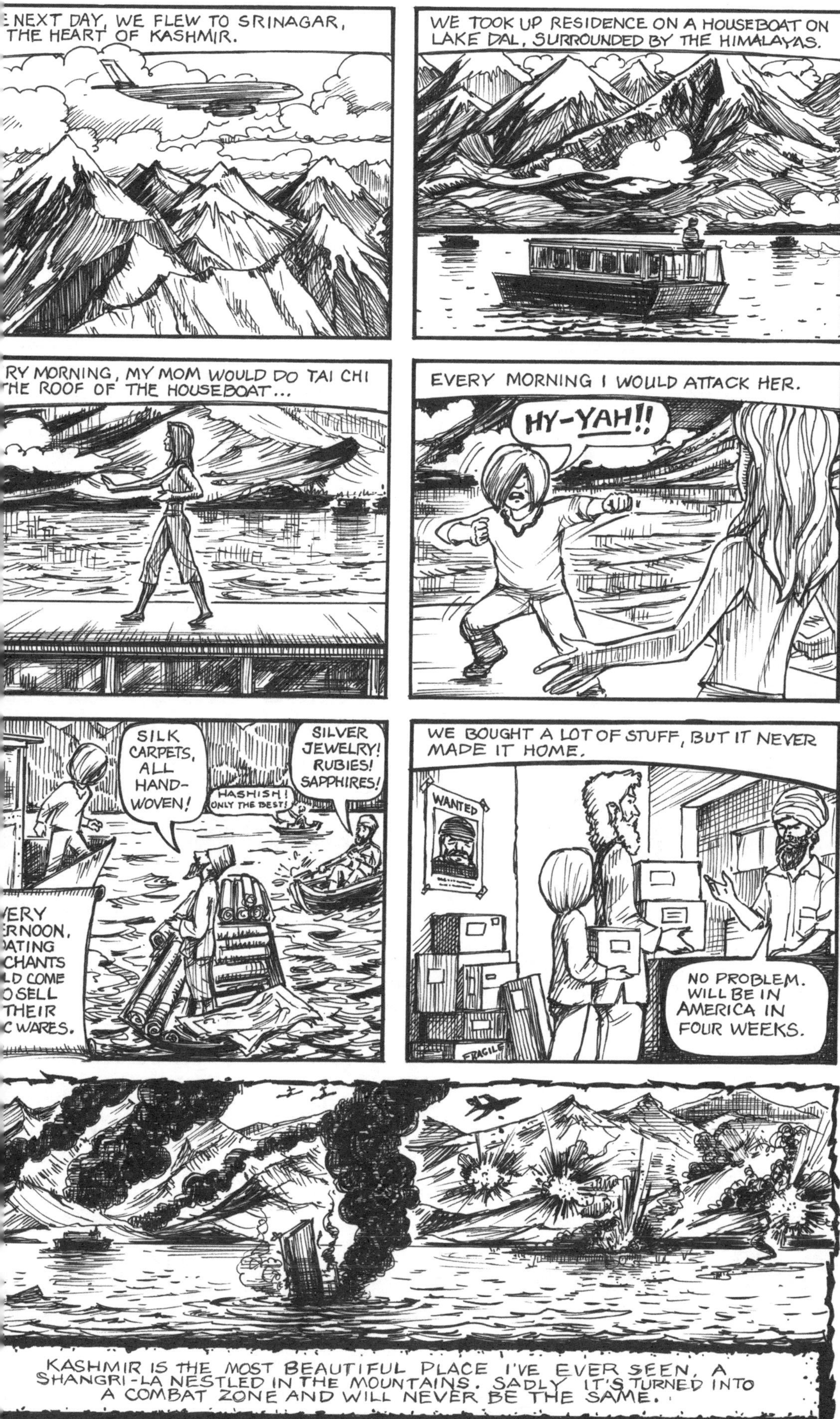

E NEXT DAY, WE FLEW TO SRINAGAR, THE HEART OF KASHMIR.
WE TOOK UP RESIDENCE ON A HOUSEBOAT ON LAKE DAL, SURROUNDED BY THE HIMALAYAS.
RY MORNING, MY MOM WOULD DO TAI CHI HE ROOF OF THE HOUSEBOAT...
EVERY MORNING I WOULD ATTACK HER.
HY-YAH!!
ERY ERNOON, ATING CHANTS LD COME O SELL THEIR C WARES.
SILK CARPETS, ALL HAND-WOVEN!
HASHISH! ONLY THE BEST!
SILVER JEWELRY! RUBIES! SAPPHIRES!
WE BOUGHT A LOT OF STUFF, BUT IT NEVER MADE IT HOME.
WANTED
FRAGILE
NO PROBLEM. WILL BE IN AMERICA IN FOUR WEEKS.
KASHMIR IS THE MOST BEAUTIFUL PLACE I'VE EVER SEEN, A SHANGRI-LA NESTLED IN THE MOUNTAINS. SADLY, IT'S TURNED INTO A COMBAT ZONE AND WILL NEVER BE THE SAME.

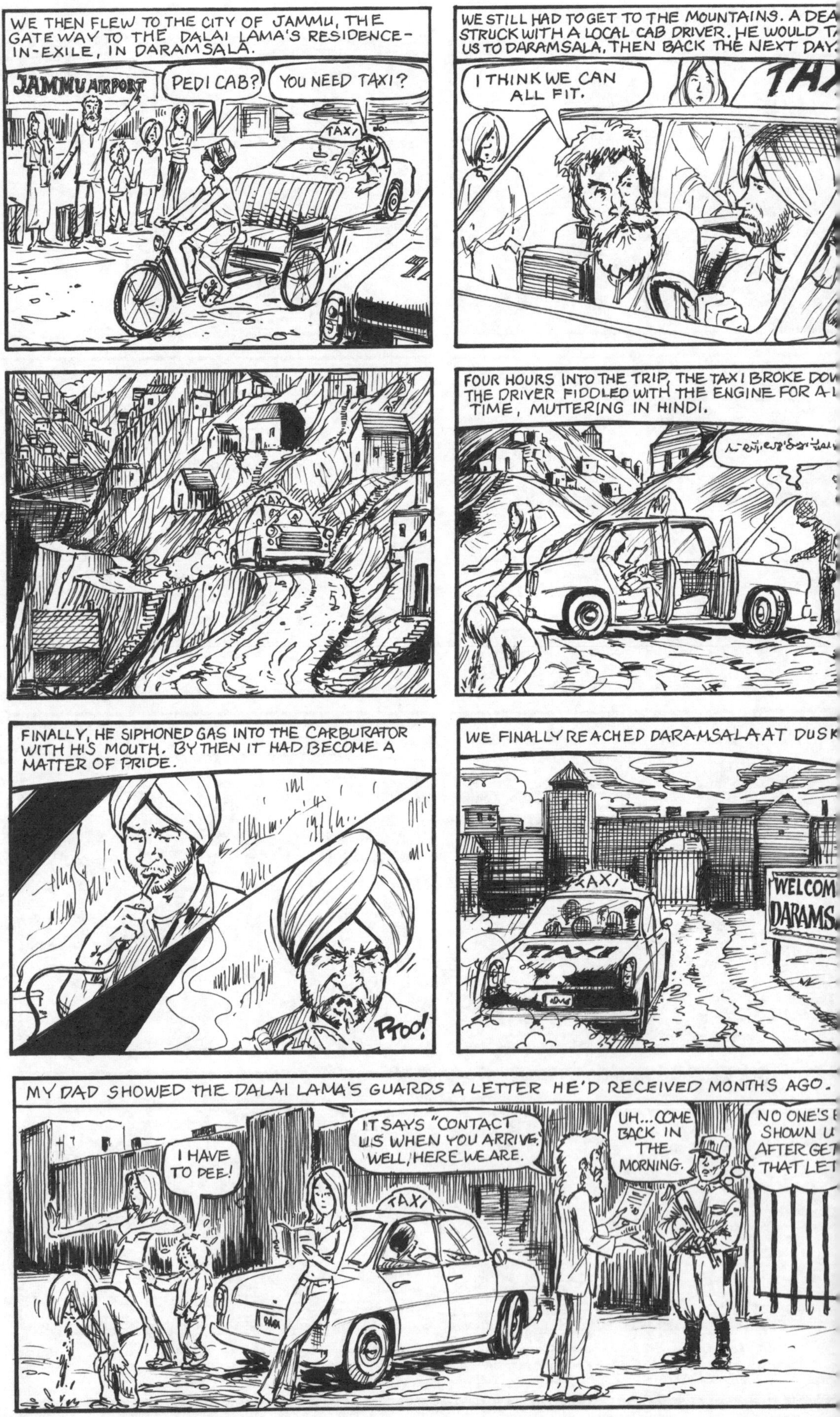
WE THEN FLEW TO THE CITY OF JAMMU, THE GATEWAY TO THE DALAI LAMA'S RESIDENCE-IN-EXILE, IN DARAMSALA.
JAMMU AIRPORT
PEDI CAB?
YOU NEED TAXI?
TAXI
WE STILL HAD TO GET TO THE MOUNTAINS. A DEA
STRUCK WITH A LOCAL CAB DRIVER. HE WOULD TA
US TO DARAMSALA, THEN BACK THE NEXT DAY.
I THINK WE CAN ALL FIT.
TAXI
FOUR HOURS INTO THE TRIP, THE TAXI BROKE DOW
THE DRIVER FIDDLED WITH THE ENGINE FOR A L
TIME, MUTTERING IN HINDI.
FINALLY, HE SIPHONED GAS INTO THE CARBURATOR WITH HIS MOUTH. BY THEN IT HAD BECOME A MATTER OF PRIDE.
PTOO!
WE FINALLY REACHED DARAMSALA AT DUSK
TAXI
TAXI
WELCOM
DARAMS
MY DAD SHOWED THE DALAI LAMA'S GUARDS A LETTER HE'D RECEIVED MONTHS AGO.
I HAVE TO PEE!
IT SAYS "CONTACT US WHEN YOU ARRIVE." WELL, HERE WE ARE.
TAXI
UH...COME BACK IN THE MORNING.
NO ONE'S
SHOWN U
AFTER GET
THAT LET

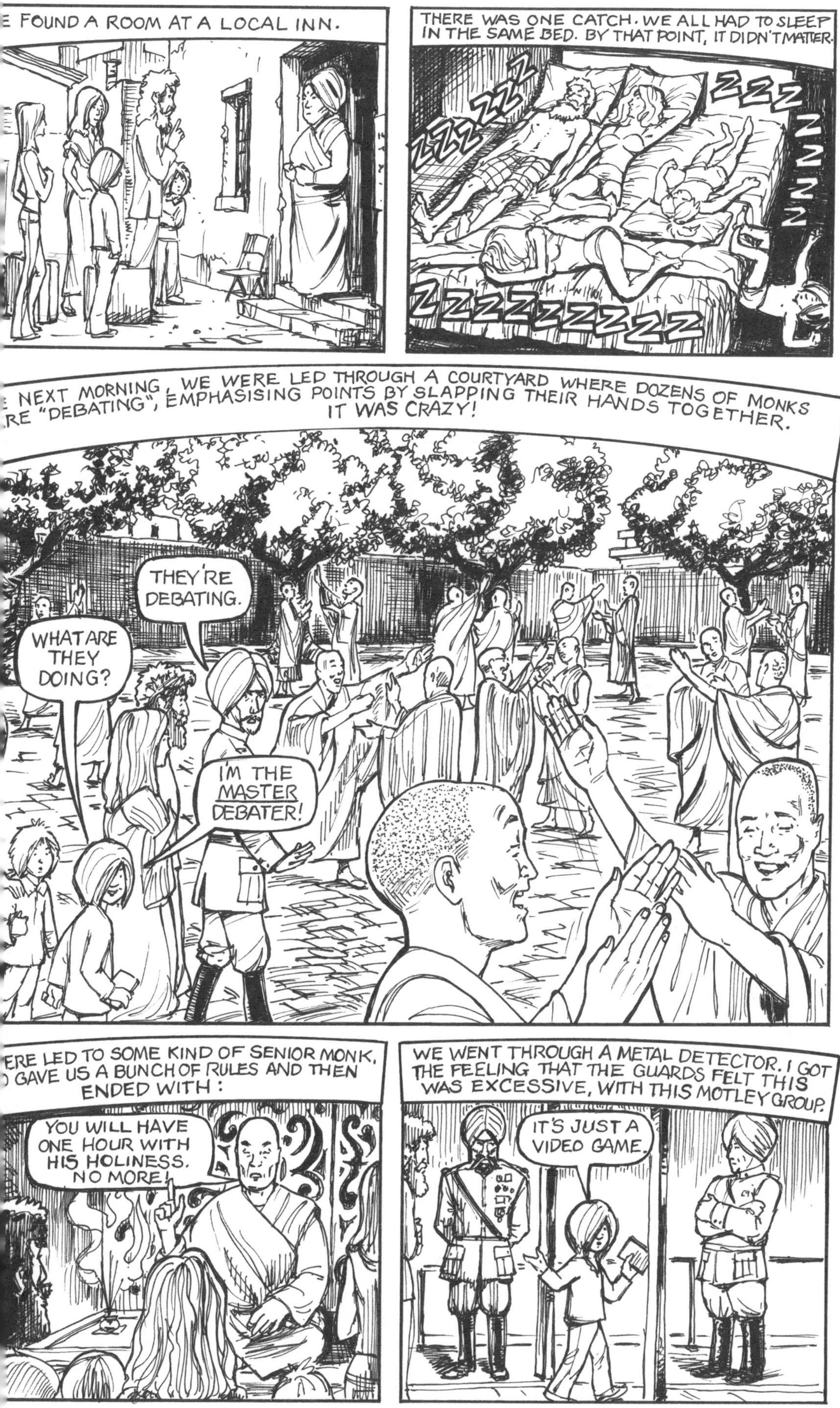
E FOUND A ROOM AT A LOCAL INN.
THERE WAS ONE CATCH. WE ALL HAD TO SLEEP IN THE SAME BED. BY THAT POINT, IT DIDN'T MATTER.
ZZZZZZZ
ZZZ
ZZZ
ZZZZZZZZZZZ
E NEXT MORNING, WE WERE LED THROUGH A COURTYARD WHERE DOZENS OF MONKS
RE "DEBATING", EMPHASISING POINTS BY SLAPPING THEIR HANDS TOGETHER.
IT WAS CRAZY!
WHAT ARE THEY DOING?
THEY'RE DEBATING.
I'M THE MASTER DEBATER!
ERE LED TO SOME KIND OF SENIOR MONK,
GAVE US A BUNCH OF RULES AND THEN ENDED WITH:
YOU WILL HAVE ONE HOUR WITH HIS HOLINESS. NO MORE!
WE WENT THROUGH A METAL DETECTOR. I GOT THE FEELING THAT THE GUARDS FELT THIS WAS EXCESSIVE, WITH THIS MOTLEY GROUP.
IT'S JUST A VIDEO GAME.

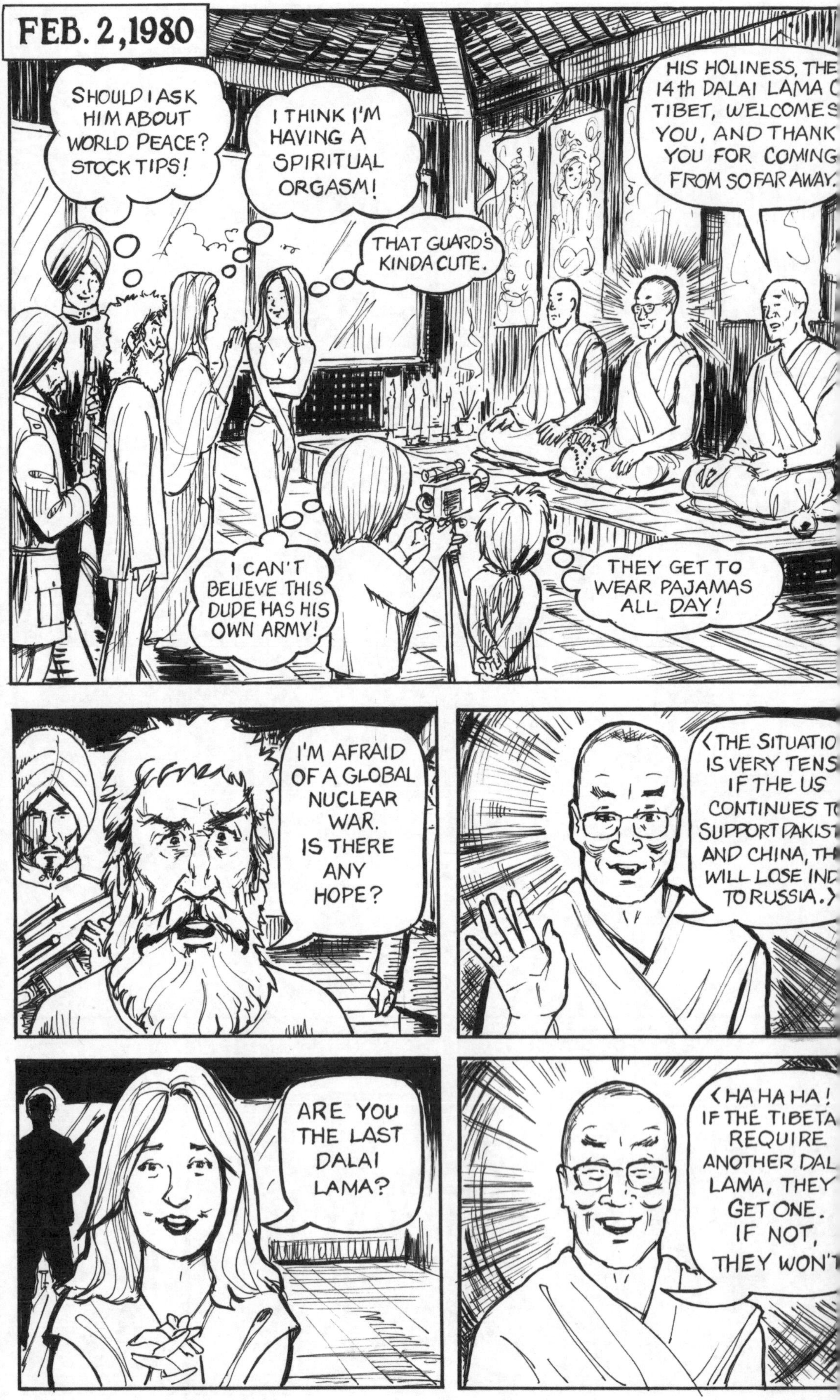
FEB. 2,1980
SHOULD I ASK HIM ABOUT WORLD PEACE? STOCK TIPS!
I THINK I'M HAVING A SPIRITUAL ORGASM!
THAT GUARD'S KINDA CUTE.
HIS HOLINESS, THE 14th DALAI LAMA O TIBET, WELCOMES YOU, AND THANK YOU FOR COMING FROM SO FAR AWAY.
I CAN'T BELIEVE THIS DUDE HAS HIS OWN ARMY!
THEY GET TO WEAR PAJAMAS ALL DAY!
I'M AFRAID OF A GLOBAL NUCLEAR WAR. IS THERE ANY HOPE?
<THE SITUATIO IS VERY TENS IF THE US CONTINUES TO SUPPORT PAKIST AND CHINA, TH WILL LOSE IND TO RUSSIA.>
ARE YOU THE LAST DALAI LAMA?
<HA HA HA! IF THE TIBETA REQUIRE ANOTHER DAL LAMA, THEY GET ONE. IF NOT, THEY WON'T

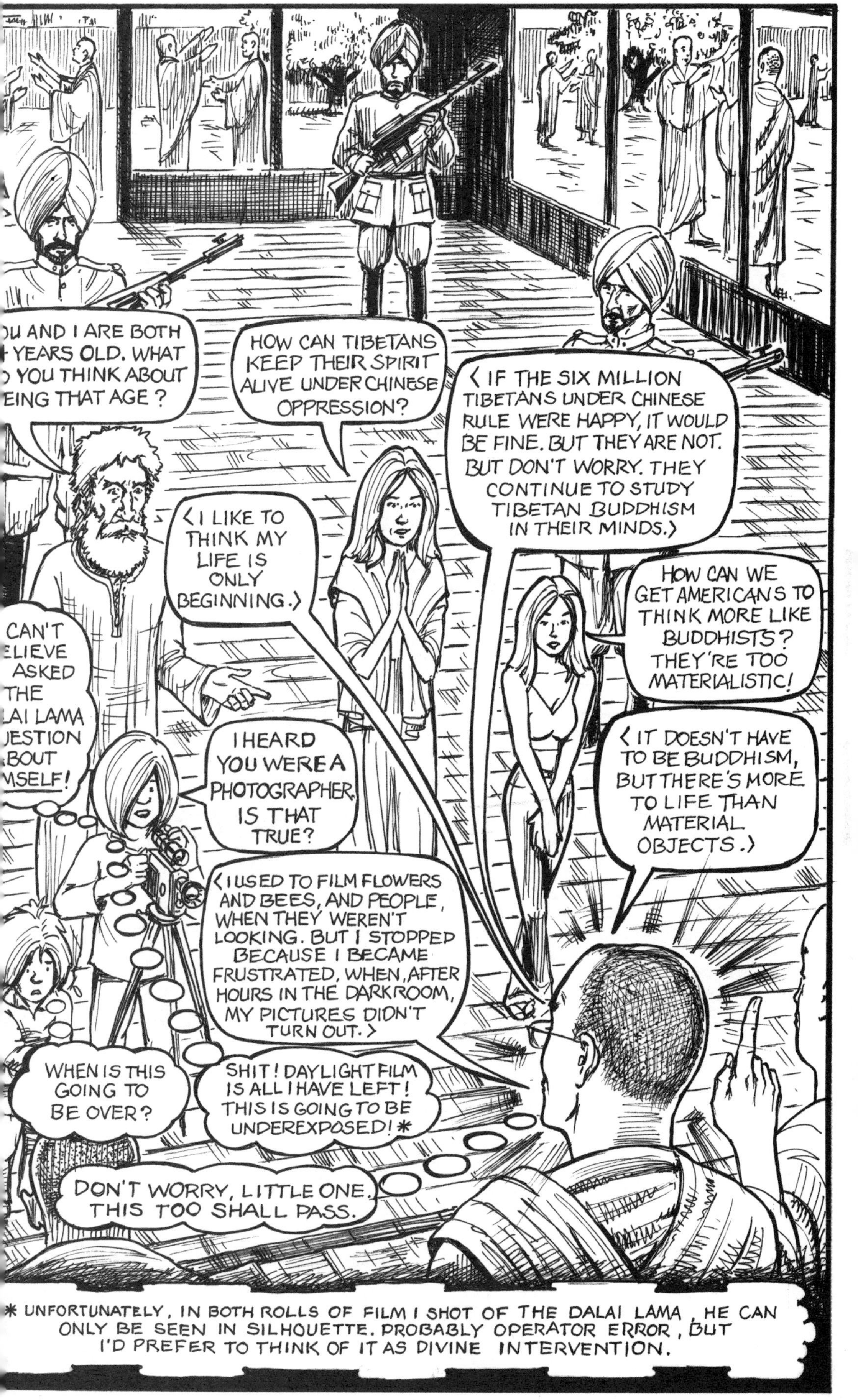

OU AND I ARE BOTH
YEARS OLD. WHAT
O YOU THINK ABOUT
EING THAT AGE?
HOW CAN TIBETANS KEEP THEIR SPIRIT ALIVE UNDER CHINESE OPPRESSION?
‹IF THE SIX MILLION TIBETANS UNDER CHINESE RULE WERE HAPPY, IT WOULD BE FINE. BUT THEY ARE NOT. BUT DON'T WORRY. THEY CONTINUE TO STUDY TIBETAN BUDDHISM IN THEIR MINDS.›
‹I LIKE TO THINK MY LIFE IS ONLY BEGINNING.›
HOW CAN WE GET AMERICANS TO THINK MORE LIKE BUDDHISTS? THEY'RE TOO MATERIALISTIC!
CAN'T
ELIEVE
ASKED
THE
LAI LAMA
UESTION
BOUT
MSELF!
‹IT DOESN'T HAVE TO BE BUDDHISM, BUT THERE'S MORE TO LIFE THAN MATERIAL OBJECTS.›
I HEARD YOU WERE A PHOTOGRAPHER. IS THAT TRUE?
‹I USED TO FILM FLOWERS AND BEES, AND PEOPLE, WHEN THEY WEREN'T LOOKING. BUT I STOPPED BECAUSE I BECAME FRUSTRATED, WHEN, AFTER HOURS IN THE DARKROOM, MY PICTURES DIDN'T TURN OUT.›
WHEN IS THIS GOING TO BE OVER?
SHIT! DAYLIGHT FILM IS ALL I HAVE LEFT! THIS IS GOING TO BE UNDEREXPOSED! *
DON'T WORRY, LITTLE ONE. THIS TOO SHALL PASS.
* UNFORTUNATELY, IN BOTH ROLLS OF FILM I SHOT OF THE DALAI LAMA, HE CAN ONLY BE SEEN IN SILHOUETTE. PROBABLY OPERATOR ERROR, BUT I'D PREFER TO THINK OF IT AS DIVINE INTERVENTION.

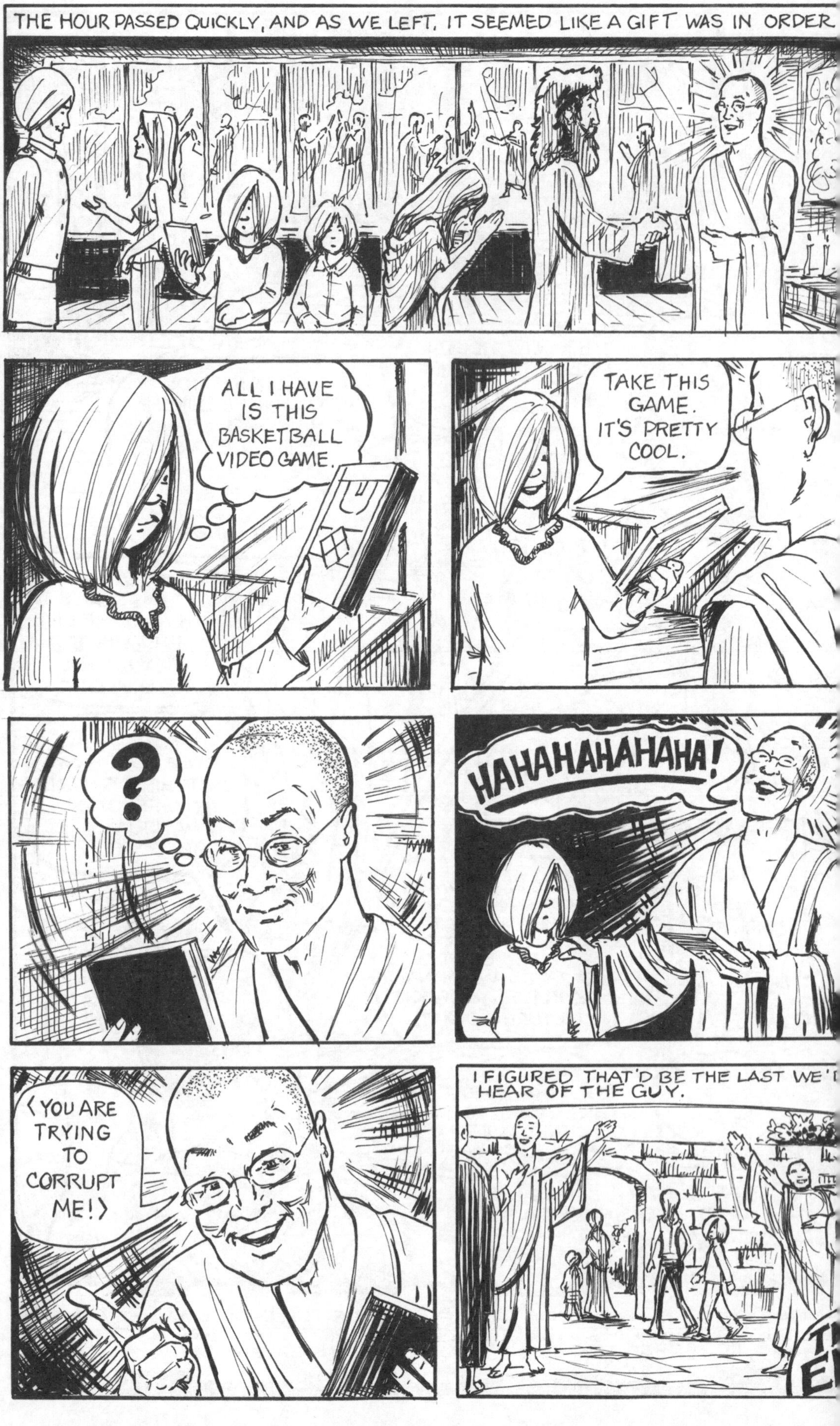

THE HOUR PASSED QUICKLY, AND AS WE LEFT, IT SEEMED LIKE A GIFT WAS IN ORDER
ALL I HAVE IS THIS BASKETBALL VIDEO GAME.
TAKE THIS GAME. IT'S PRETTY COOL.
?
HAHAHAHAHAHA!
‹YOU ARE TRYING TO CORRUPT ME!›
I FIGURED THAT'D BE THE LAST WE'
HEAR OF THE GUY.

THE HIPPY KID SEZ...

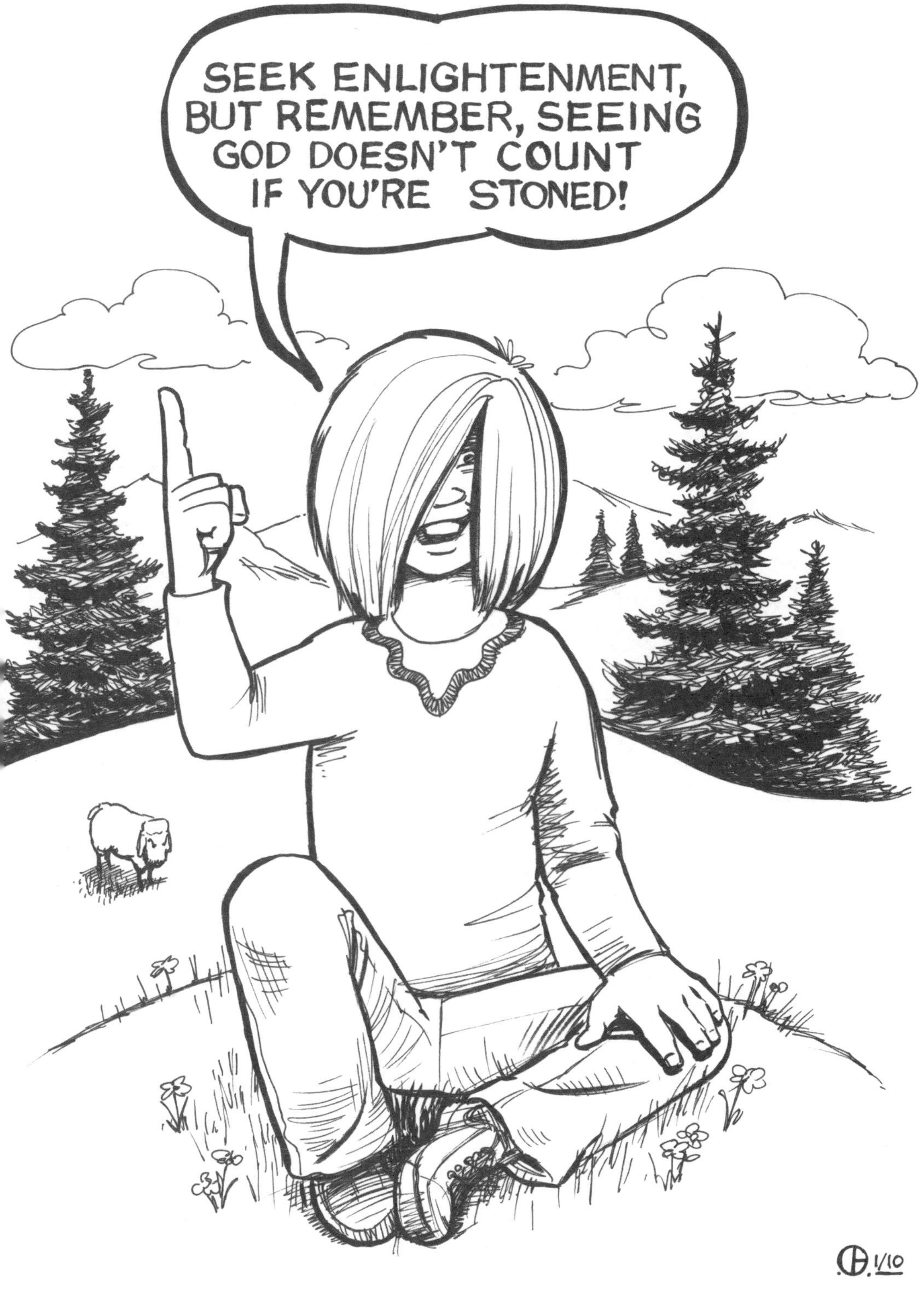
SEEK ENLIGHTENMENT, BUT REMEMBER, SEEING GOD DOESN'T COUNT IF YOU'RE STONED!

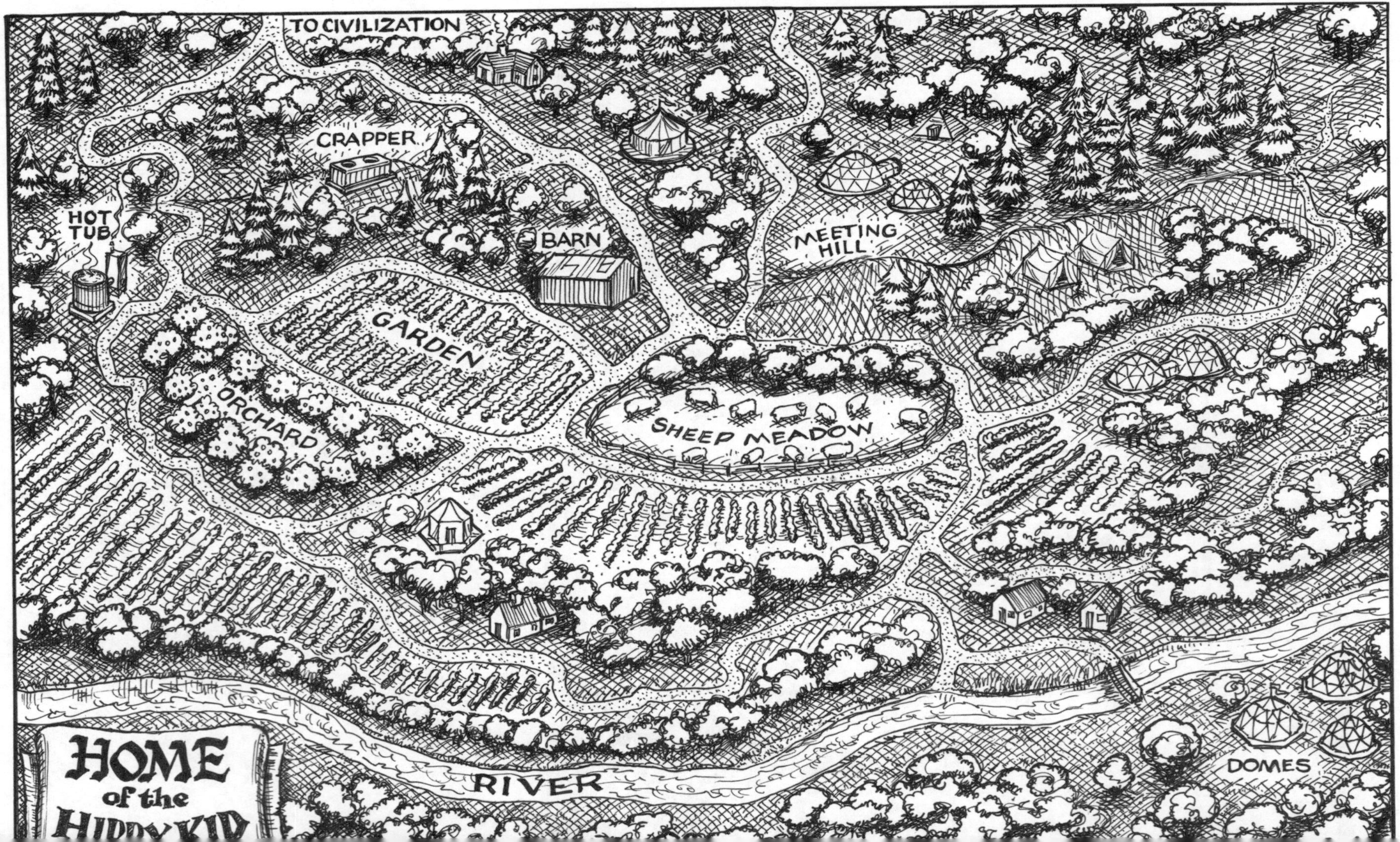
TO CIVILIZATION
CRAPPER
HOT TUB
BARN
MEETING HILL
GARDEN
ORCHARD
SHEEP MEADOW
DOMES
RIVER
HOME
of the

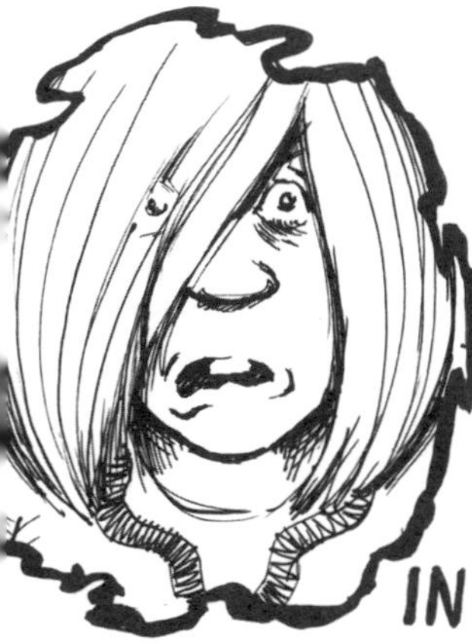

JON KROLL IS KNOWN FOR HIS TELEVISION ENDEAVORS, WHICH INCLUDE FILMING VAMPIRES ON THE STREETS OF VANCOUVER FOR "**BLADE - THE SERIES**", AMISH PEOPLE ON THE STREETS OF LOS ANGELES FOR "**AMISH IN THE CITY**" AND CRAZY PEOPLE ALL OVER THE WORLD FOR "**THE AMAZING RACE**."

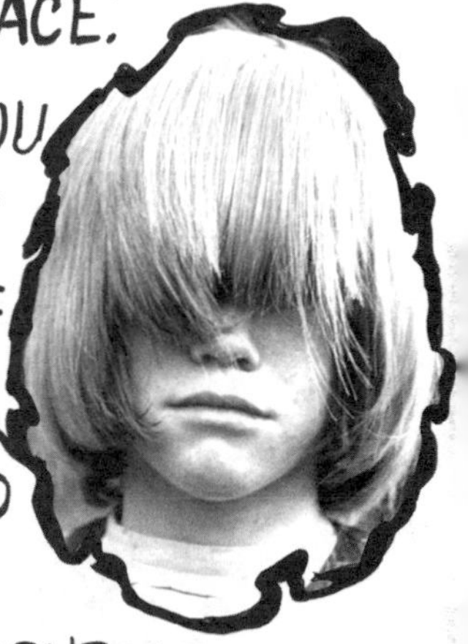

IE'S ALSO DONE A BUNCH OF OTHER STUFF YOU AN READ ABOUT AT **WWW.JONKROLL.COM**. HE SISTS THAT NEARLY EVERYTHING IN "**TALES OF HIPPY KID**" MORE OR LESS HAPPENED, BUT THAT MANY OF THE NAMES HAVE BEEN CHANGED TO DIFFERENT NOUNS.

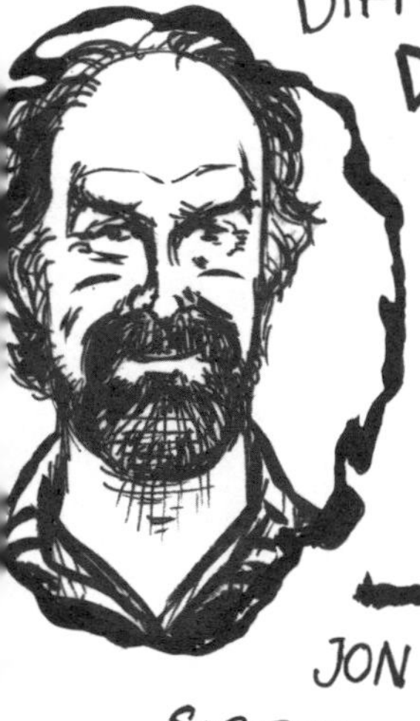

DAVE BOHN HAS BEEN A STORYBOARD ARTIST FOR MANY YEARS. HE'S LOVED COMICS SINCE HE WAS A KID, SO WHEN HIS LONGTIME FRIEND, JON KROLL, ASKED HIM TO DRAW **HIPPY KID**, HE JUMPED AT THE CHANCE. HE'S EXPECTED TO FULLY RECOVER FROM THE EXPERIENCE.

JON OWES A GREAT DEBT TO HIS PARENTS AND SISTERS WHO CHRONICLED THIS ERA WITH JOURNALS, PHOTOGRAPHS AND, OF COURSE, COMICS. THEIR REWARD IS TO SEE VENTS OF THE PAST THAT THEY'D JUST AS SOON FORGET ABOUT BE MORTALIZED FOR WORLD TO SEE.

ART GALLERY

ORIGINAL HIPPY KID CONCEPT SKETCH

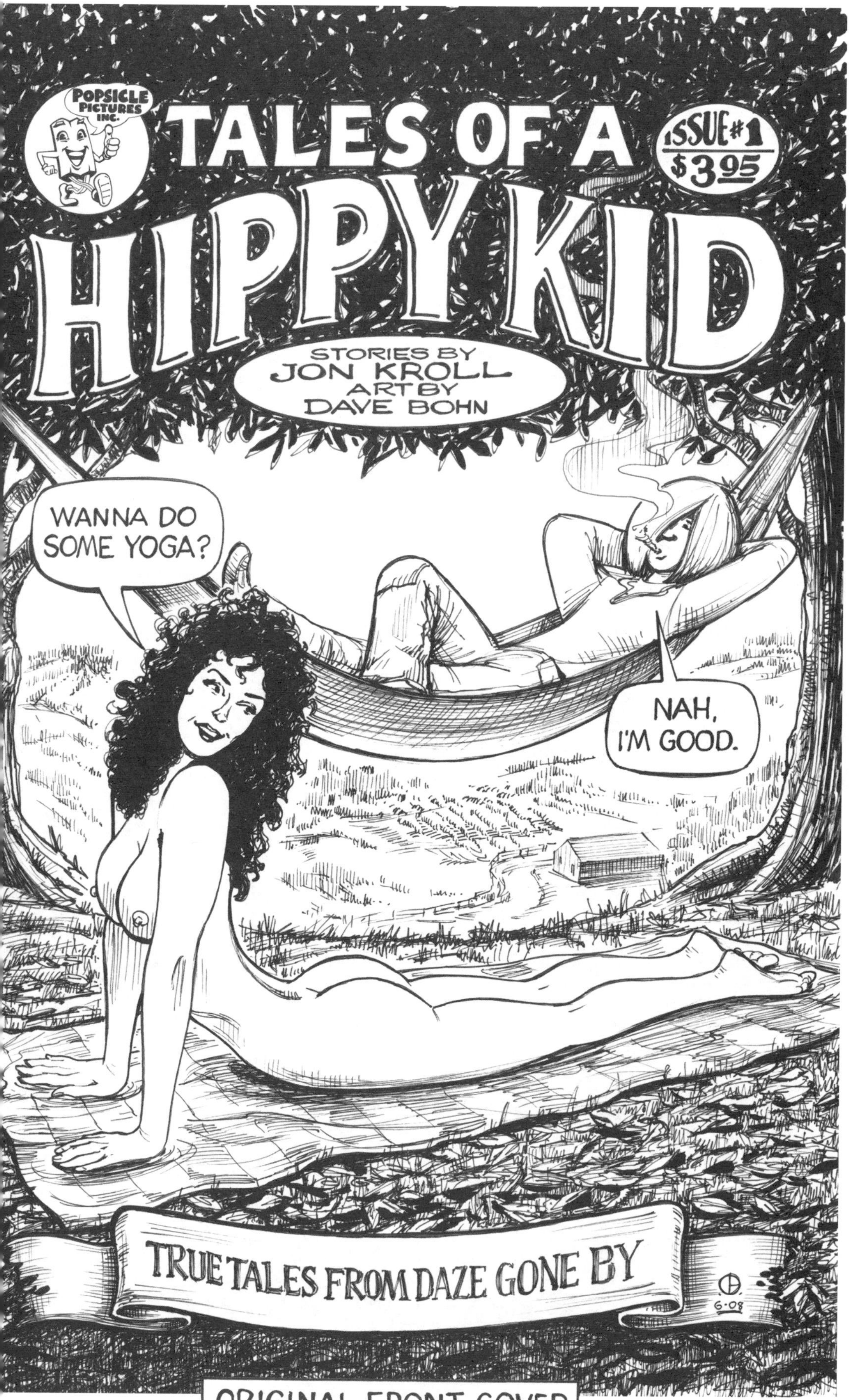
POPSICLE PICTURES INC.
TALES OF A
HIPPY KID
ISSUE #1
$3.95
STORIES BY
JON KROLL
ART BY
DAVE BOHN
WANNA DO SOME YOGA?
NAH, I'M GOOD.
TRUE TALES FROM DAZE GONE BY
6·08

ORIGINAL FRONT COVER

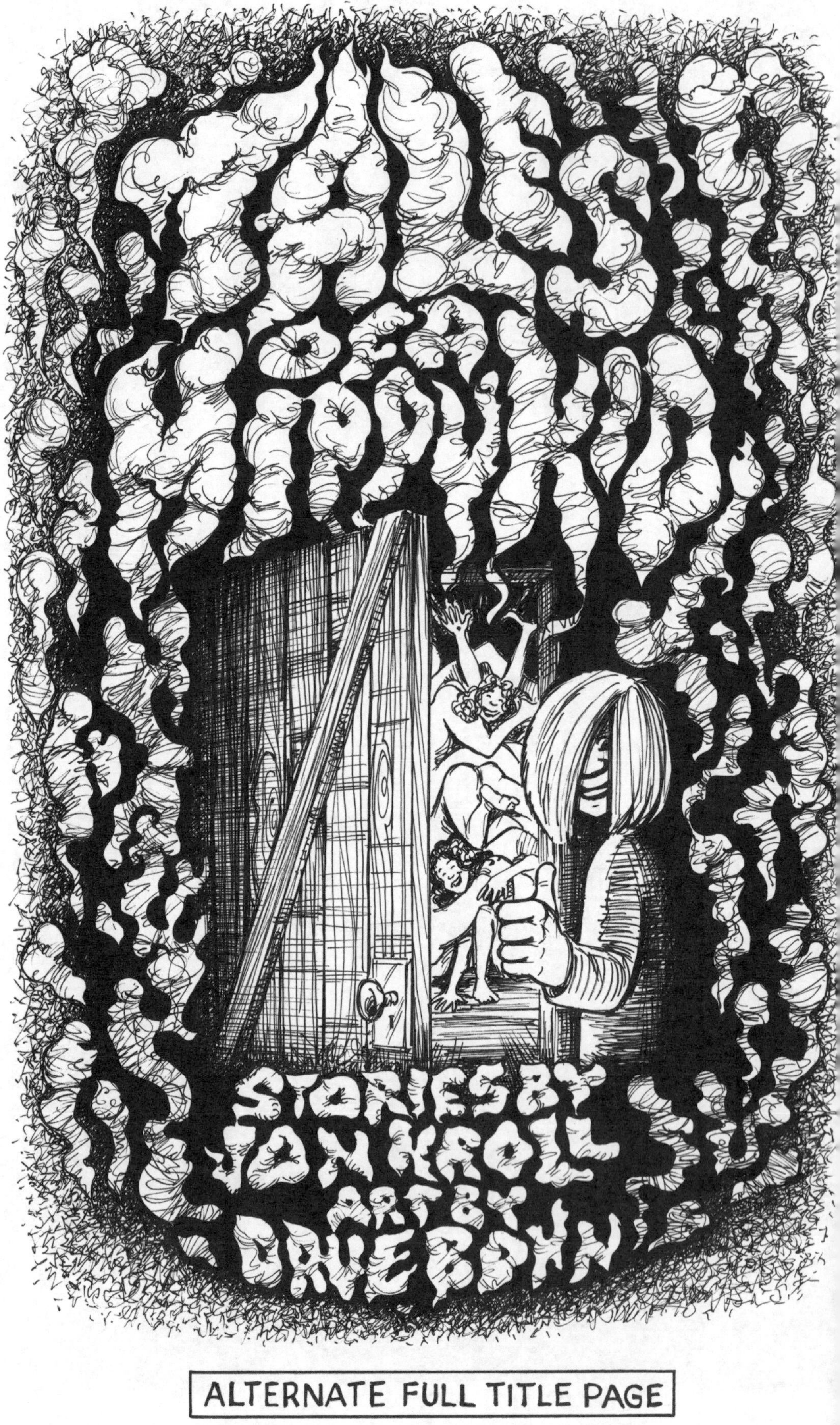
STORIES BY
JON KROLL
ART BY
DAVE BOHN

ALTERNATE FULL TITLE PAGE

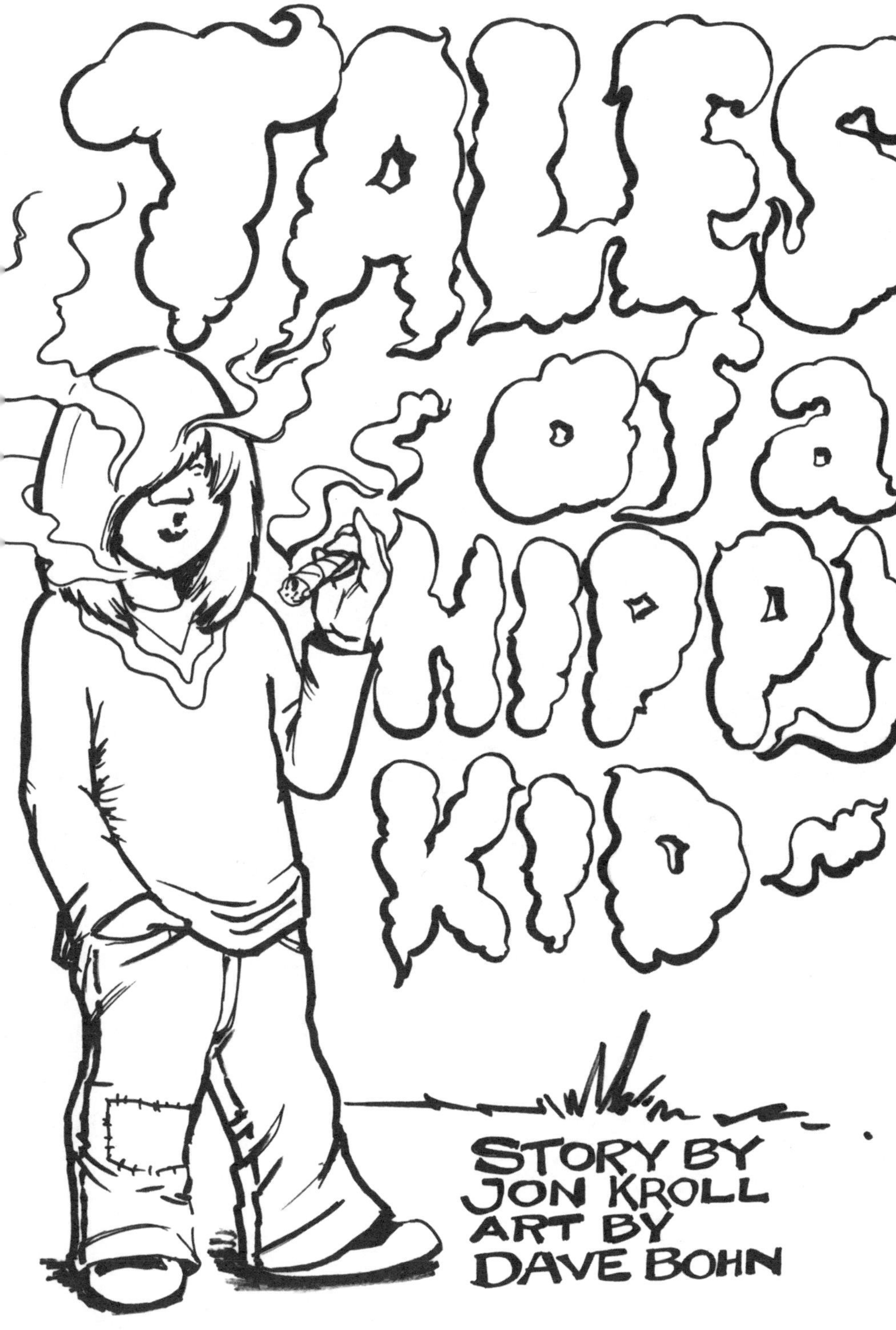

TALES
OF A
HIPPY
KID
STORY BY
JON KROLL
ART BY
DAVE BOHN

ORIGINAL BACK COVER IMAGE

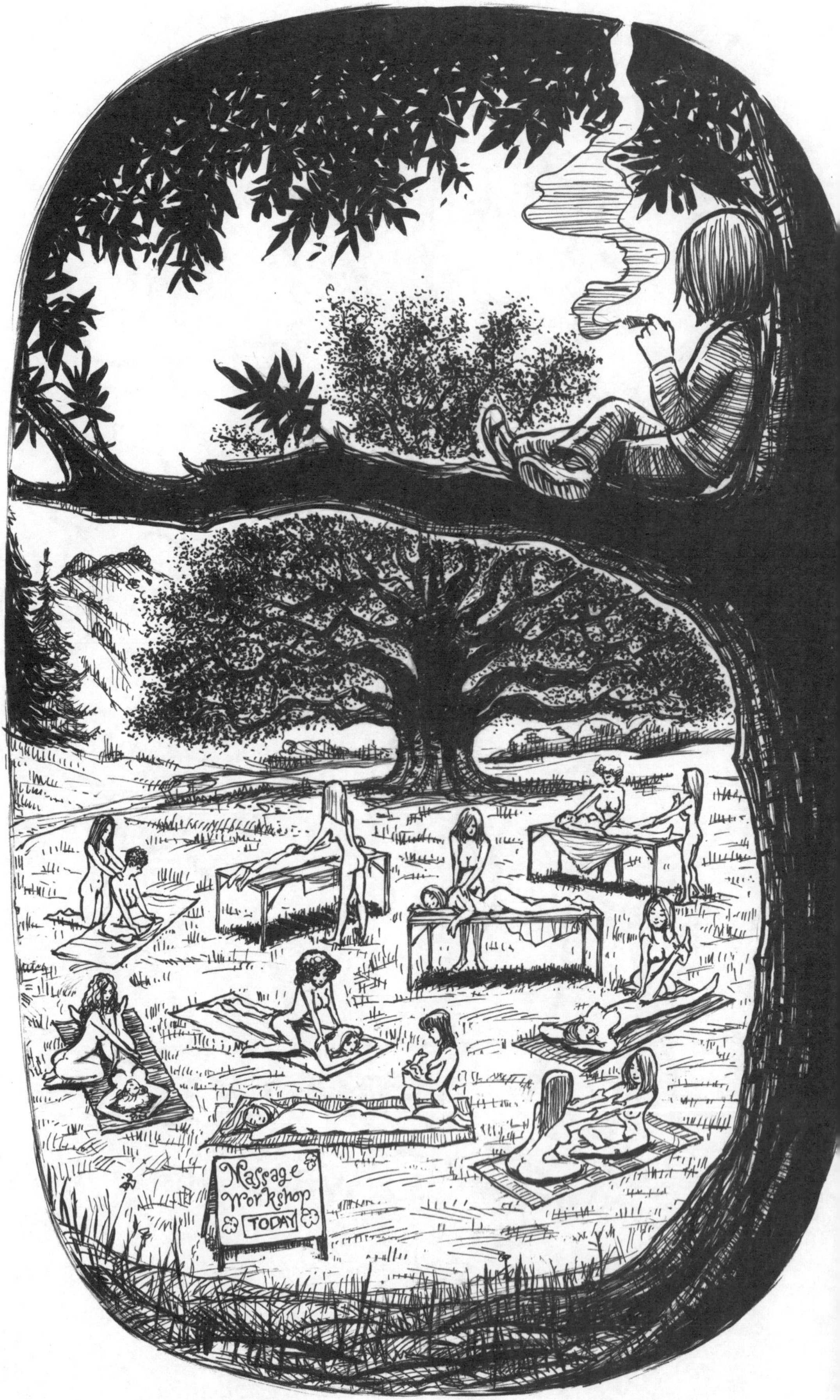
Massage Workshop
TODAY